I0121402

Anonymus

Proceedings of the Grand Commandery of Knights Templar of the State of North Carolina for the years 1897, 1898, and 1899

Anonymus

Proceedings of the Grand Commandery of Knights Templar of the State of North Carolina for the years 1897, 1898, and 1899

ISBN/EAN: 9783741177736

Manufactured in Europe, USA, Canada, Australia, Japa

Cover: Foto ©Thomas Meinert / pixelio.de

Manufactured and distributed by brebook publishing software (www.brebook.com)

Anonymus

Proceedings of the Grand Commandery of Knights Templar of the State of North Carolina for the years 1897, 1898, and 1899

PROCEEDINGS

—OF THE—

Grand Commandery

—OF—

KNIGHTS TEMPLAR

—OF THE—

STATE OF NORTH CAROLINA,

—AT ITS—

SEVENTEENTH ANNUAL CONCLAVE

—HELD AT—

WILMINGTON,

MAY 11TH AND 12TH, A. D. 1897, A. O., 779.

WILMINGTON, N. C. :
JACKSON & BELL CO., PRINTERS AND BINDERS.
1897.

Yours sincerely

W. G. Smith

Proceedings.

----•----

The Grand Commandery of Knights Templar of the State of North Carolina, convened in its Seventeenth Annual Conclave, at the Asylum of Plantagenet Commandery, in the City of Wilmington, on Wednesday, May 12th, 1897, at 8:00 o'clock p. m., and was opened in ample and Knightly form, the acting Grand Prelate leading the devotions.

GRAND OFFICERS PRESENT:

Wm. A. Withers ....Right E. Grand Commander.
Jos. H. Hackburn................V. E. Deputy Grand Commander.
Mumford D. Bailey.............E. Grand Generalissimo.
Walter E. Storm... ....E. Grand Captain General.
Rev. Stewart McQueen....as E. Grand Prelate.
Wm. F. Randolph..............E. Grand Senior Warden.
Jas. D. Bullock.................E. Grand Junior Warden.
Wm. Simpson....................E. Grand Treasurer.
Horace H. Munson.............E. Grand Recorder.
David G Maxwell...............E. Grand Standard Bearer.
J. J. Whitaker.................as E. Grand Sword Bearer.
Edward P. Bailey...............E. Grand Warder.
Robert H. Bradley ....E. Grand Sentinel.

COMMITTEE ON CREDENTIALS.

The Grand Commander appointed Sir Knights E. P. Bailey, Bullock and Randolph, a Committee on Credentials.

ADDRESS OF R. E. GRAND COMMANDER.

The Grand Commander read his annual address, which was on motion referred to a committee of three, announced by the

Deputy Grand Commander, J. H. Hackburn as follows: Sir Knights P. G. C. Liddell, Thompson and Wills.

To the Grand Commandery, Knights Templar:

In accordance with law and custom I have the honor of submitting herewith the report of my official acts for the past year:

NECROLOGY.

It gives me great pleasure to report that during the past year no member of this Grand Commandery was called from us by the Angel of Death. We should be duly grateful for this kind dispensation of Providence. The Committee on Necrology will report the dead in this and sister jurisdictions.

VISITATIONS.

The following assignments of Commanderies were made for visitations by Grand Officers: Plantagenet No. 1, Durham No 3, and Raleigh No. 4, to V. E. Sir J. H. Hackburn, Deputy Grand Commander; Charlotte No. 2, Demolai No. 11, and St. Aldemar No. 12, to E. Sir M. D. Bailey, Grand Generalissimo; Mt. Lebanon No. 7, St. George No. 9, St. John's No. 10, to E. Sir W. E. Storm, Grand Captain General; Cyrene No. 5, Piedmont No. 6 and Ivanhoe No. 8, to the Grand Commander.

On August 27th I had the honor of visiting Cyrene Commandery, and the occasion was a most delightful one. This Commandery had a large attendance, the Sir Knights present were in uniform, and the Order of the Temple was conferred in excellent form. After the close an elegant banquet was served at the Hotel Berkeley. Every possible consideration was shown for me in my official capacity and personally and I feel that I cannot speak in too high praise of this Commandery.

On November 25th I visited Ivanhoe Commandery but it was not possible to get a quorum. By special invitation I made a second visitation to this Commandery on May 7th and conferred the orders upon four candidates. This Commandery has good material but seems to lack enthusiasm. The new Eminent Commander has seemed to inspire them somewhat and I trust that with the assistance of the new material which has been admitted, this Commandery may take the place it should in the fraternity.

On account of the destruction by fire of the Asylum of Piedmont Commandery, it was not convenient for the Sir Knights there to receive me, and consequently this visitation was omitted. If we are to judge by the representatives that this Commandery sends to the Grand Commandery, an official visitor would find much to commend and little to condemn.

The other Grand Officers will report the results of their visitations.

I consider the custom of visitation as of great benefit not only to the Commandery itself, but to the Grand Officer, in giving him a better acquaintance with Templarism in the State.

DISPENSATIONS.

The following dispensations were granted:

To receive and ballot on petitions without the lapse of the usual time, to: Mount Lebanon No. 7, Sept. 4; Charlotte No. 2, Oct. 7; Charlotte No. 2, Dec. 10; Charlotte No. 2, March 25; Cyrene No. 5, April 14; Raleigh No. 4, April 20; Mount Lebanon No. 7, April 22; St. Aldemar No. 12, May 3; Ivanhoe No. 8, May 7.

To assist in the rendition of the Story of the Reformation for the benefit of religious and charitable organizations, to: Piedmont No. 6, Jan. 18; Raleigh No. 4, Jan. 19; St. John's No. 10, Jan. 30.

To attend Easter service in uniform, to: Raleigh No. 4, April 15; Cyrene No. 5, April 16.

To elect and install officers after the time fixed in the by-laws, to: Piedmont No. 6, Dec. 26; Mt. Lebanon No. 7, Jan 22; Ivanhoe No. 8, Mch 20.

To fill vacancies and install officers to Raleigh No. 4, Feb. 4.

To transact business at a special Conclave called to take the place of a regular Conclave to Cyrene No. 5, Feb. 27, a condition being that due notice be given of the same.

Where dispensations were given to ballot without the lapse of the usual time, a condition was always made that due notice be given, so that any Sir Knight who had objections to the petitioner could make them known in the proper way.

NEW GRAND COMMANDERIES.

On Feb. 10th, 1896, the Grand Commandery of Oklahoma was duly constituted under authority of a warrant from M. E. Sir W. LaRue Thomas, Grand Master. I have asked the Recorder to present the congratulations of the Grand Commandery of North Carolina and to ask an exchange of Grand Representatives.

On May 14th, 1888, the Grand Commandery of Montana was duly constituted, and on Nov. 10th, 1893, the Grand Commandery of Arizona was duly constituted, but in some way it seems that their recognition in the way of exchanging Representatives was overlooked by this Grand Commandery. I have asked the Grand Recorder to express to them the regrets for the oversight and to request an exchange of Grand Representatives

GRAND REPRESENTATIVES.

The commissions issued during the year, and those received will be shown in the report of the Grand Recorder. Nominations were made to the Grand Commanders of other jurisdictions in the cases of new Grand Commanderies, and where vacancies existed by reason of death or expiration of term of office. In all cases I nominated those Sir Knights who have shown their interest in Templarism by their attendance at the Grand Conclaves and otherwise. These commissions from our own Grand Commandery and nearly all others expire with each Triennial Conclave of the Grand Encampment. In case a Representative is not present at a Grand Conclave during his three years term of office as such, and does not send in an excuse for his absence, I think he should not be recommended for reappointment. Several Grand Representatives of this body wrote me in advance of the Conclaves of their own Grand Commanderies asking for instructions as to any matter to be brought before them by us. It seems to me this should be done by every Representative. It would bring about a pleasant exchange of courtesies and aid in the accomplishing of the work for which their appointment was made.

RITUALS.

In the distribution of the Rituals a few years ago the Grand Generalissimo and Grand Captain General were overlooked. Application was made for them and after some delay the rituals were issued.

RECOMMENDATIONS.

1. I would recommend the continuation of the committee on the Triennial Conclave of the Grand Encampment at Pittsburg in 1898. Our attendance at Boston was good, and we should endeavor to have a good attendance at Pittsburg. I would recommend in this connection that the Grand Treasurer be authorized and instructed to pay the necessary expenses of the Grand Commander or acting Grand Commander out of moneys not otherwise appropriated.

2. I would recommend that the Grand Commandery be allowed to change if necessary the time and place of its Grand Conclave. This will require an amendment to the Constitution

CONCLUSION.

In concluding this address I wish to congratulate the Order on the peace and harmony which has prevailed during the past year. Our relations with sister Grand Commanderies have been the most cordial and no reports of internal strife have reached my ears May it ever be so.

I wish also to congratulate the Grand Commandery on the selection of its place of meeting, and to remind the Sir Knights that we are on historic ground. When our fathers left their homes in the Old World to find liberty and freedom to worship their God as their own consciences should dictate, faithful hearts brought with them the secrets and principles of freemasonry The Order has always flourished where freedom abounds and soon its altars were erected here. In this beautiful city by the sea was established the oldest lodge in this grand commonwealth. Saint John's No. 1 has existed for more than a century and her lessons have been impressed upon four generations. Some of her sons are with us to-day in the strength of manhood, ready to do battle for the cause; some are with us who most tenderly bind us to the past, while some have gone to their long home. Forty-nine years ago the Grand Chapter of Royal Arch Masons was established here, and here sixteen years and one day ago for the first time the banner of this Grand Commandery was thrown to the breeze. Our first Grand Commander is our Grand Recorder now. This distinguished Sir Knight has truly grown young in the cause, and his pen like his sword has done valiant work for the advancement of Templarism in North Carolina. Between the first and the present Grand Commander the names of those who have been called to fill this high position are three times three. Of these only one—Donald W. Bain, of sainted memory—has been called to his reward.

When we leave this spot so full of glorious and happy memories we should carry with us fresh inspirations for our work.

Before closing, I must return my hearty thanks for the great honor which you did me a year ago in calling me to preside over the deliberations of this Grand Commandery. I wish also to thank the officers and Sir Knights for the courtesies shown me on all occasions. I return to you the symbals of authority you have entrusted to me. I have endeavored to do my duty as best I could. No one is more conscious of his own shortcomings than your Grand Commander, and he begs your leniency and forbearance. May God bless you and the Order most richly and abundantly.

Yours courteously,

W. A. WITHERS,
Grand Commander.

The Deputy Grand Commander J. H. Hackburn and Grand Generalissimo Mumford D. Bailey submitted their reports, which was referred to the Committee on Grand Commanders address.

The Grand Captain General, W. E. Storm submitted a verbal report.

REPORT OF DEPUTY GRAND COMMANDER.

To the Grand Commandery of North Carolina:

Under instructions from R. E. Grand Commander Withers, I made the following official visitations: I visited April 14th, Plantagenet Commandery No. 1, at its stated Conclave, and, as was to be expected from a Commandery, embracing in its membership, so many present and past Grand Officers and Commanders, found nothing to criticise and much to commend Em. Sir E. P. Bailey and his staff were thorougly versed in the Ritual and the Commandery was opened in due form. Each Sir Knight was in full well kept uniform and showed by his movements that the Conclaves of this Commandery were regular and the instructions thorough.

There is no need of speaking of the courtesies received at the hands of these beloved Fraters—no door was closed, no latch-string in sight—simply a taking to their bosoms on my arrival, and released only when the last " God speed thee " was said.

I proceeded April 22nd to Durham to inspect, in Special Conclave, Durham Commandery No. 3. On alighting from the train the massive Southgate was across my path—but there was no need of an alarm—no pass was demanded—his arms were ajar and the strong grip he gave me assured me that the Representative of the Grand Commandery of North Carolina was on loyal ground and in the midst of friends. The Conclave, opened in due form, was well attended, every Sir Knight being in full knightly array. I was struck with the personnel of this Commandery, and confidently hope and expect that these Sir Knights, appreciating the devotion and untiring efforts of R. E. Sir Southgate will throw off the lethargy now clogging its progress, and resume the position. it so long held, as one of the most active Commanderies in North Carolina. Durham No. 3 has the assurance of my deep appreciation of the courtesies shown me and the deference paid to every suggestion made.

Having named April 23rd, for my visit to Raleigh Commandery No. 4, I had barely passed the confines of that city, when I was taken in charge by one Em. Grand Sword Bearer Sir John C. Drewry, who held me under strict surveillance during a most delightful drive and even assisted in protecting me, from my voracious appetite while I was enjoying the privilege of an hour at the hospitable board of our Grand Commander. Raleigh No. 4 opened in due form, each Sir Knight fully equipped. This Commandery has in its membership some of the brightest minds in this Grand Jurisdiction and ought to be, and is, thoroughly up in the Ritual, It was my good fortune to witness the conferring of the "Order of the Temple" by R. E. Sir Withers, ably assisted by the officers and equipments of this progressive Commandery. Many of you have seen the work of R. E. Sir Withers, and this Commandery and I will only say that it was a perfect rendition of what I consider, the peerless degree in masonry.

These annual visitations—these sojournings with the brethren—receiving such marks of consideration, esteem and regard are greatly appreciated by me and will remain green as long as memory lasts. I will only add the words of a distinguished Frater—"There is a measureless blessing in the fellowship of loving kindness ; it makes the world wider and warmer and gives a better zest to human life."

Courteously submitted,

J. H. HACKBURN,
Deputy Grand Commander.

REPORT OF GRAND GENERALISSIMO.

To the Grand Commandery of North Carolina :

The R. E. Grand Commander assigned me to make official visitations to Charlotte Commandery No. 2, Demolai No. 11, and St. Aldemar No. 12. I wrote all these Commanderies, receiving no reply from St. Aldemar No. 12. I did not visit it. The E. C. of Demolai No 11 wrote me that he could not get a quorum, so I did not visit Demolai. On the 29th of March I visited Charlotte Commandery No. 2, on the occasion of a special Conclave for the purpose of conferring the order of the Red Cross and Temple on three companions. I was very courteously received by the Officers and Sir Knights, •and they did the work very well. Charlotte Commandery "is in sound financial condition and well uniformed. It is composed of big men in every sense of the word—except big-headedness. They are big-bodied, big-hearted, whole souled, generous fellows, and after they have become familiar with the work, and proficient in drill, they may be the model Commandery of the State."

Courteously submitted,

M. D. BAILEY,

Grand Generalissimo.

STANDING COMMITTEES.

The Grand Commander announced the following Standing Committees :

On Credentials and Returns : Sir Knights E. P. Bailey, Bullock and Randolph.

On Address of R. E. Grand Commander : Sir Knights W. S. Liddell, Thompson and Wills.

On Warrants and Dispensation : Sir Knights Wilson, Whitaker and Applewhite.

On Finance : Sir Knights Moye, Jacobs and Maxwell.

On Appeals and Grievances : Sir Knights F. G. Schaum, Lat. Williams and J. B. Clark.

On Next Place of Annual Conclave : Sir Knights M. D. Bailey, Storm and Norfleet.

On Templar Jurisprudence : Sir Knights Southgate, Martin and Kitchen.

On Fraternal Correspondence : Sir Knight John C. Chase.

On Necrology : Sir Knights McQueen, Dinwiddie and Toomer.

The Grand Treasurer and Grand Recorder submitted their reports which were referred to the Committee on Finance.

REPORT OF THE GRAND RECORDER.

To the Grand Commandery:

I submit my report of the doings of my office during the current Masonic year.

As soon as possible after the close of the Grand Commandery I sent the usual notice of elective and appointive Grand Officers to other Grand Jurisdictions.

June 27. Distributed proceedings of our Grand Annual Conclave
          Drew draft on Treasurer to pay dues to Grand Encampment.
Mch. 3. Sent blank returns to Recorders.
     13. Issued order of Grand Commander assigning visitations of Grand Officers.
          Distributed notice of Annual Conclave.
          I acknowledge gratefully an invitation extended by Washington Commandery No. 1, Hartford, Conn., to attend their centennial celebration July 14, '96, also a similar one from the Grand Commandery of Ohio.

GRAND REPRESENTATIVES.

The following commissions have been issued by order of the Grand Commander:

1896.
Sept. 4. Wm. H. Reynolds, Orlando, Grand Rep., Florida.
1897.
Feb.   4. Nathan L. Agnew, Valparaiso, Grand Rep., Indiana.
      25. Albert M. Spear, Gardiner, Grand Rep., Maine.
      27. Geo. C. Teall, Eauclaire, Grand Rep., Wisconsin.
Mch. 12. Wm T. Bredwell, Canon City, Grand Rep., Colorado.
           W. H. Vinton, Battleboro, Grand Rep., Vermont.
      19. Ebenezer Thompson, Biloxi, Grand Rep, Mississippi.
           Jas. P. DeMattos, New Whatcover, Grand Rep., Washington.
      22. E. C. Walthall, Richmond, Grand Rep., Virginia.

COMMISSIONS RECEIVED.

1896.
May   23. B. R. Lacy, Raleigh, Grand Rep., Georgia.
      25. Wm. Simpson, Raleigh, Grand Rep., Kansas.
July 17. M. Bowes, Raleigh, Grand Rep., Texas.
      29. W. S. Liddell, Charlotte, Grand Rep., Oregon.
Sept. 4. Geo. Howard, Tarboro, Grand Rep., Florida.

1897.
Feb. 4. James Southgate, Durham, Grand Rep., Indiana.
      25. Rev. Stewart McQueen, Goldsboro, Grand Rep., Kentucky.
           J. D. Bullock, Wilson, Grand Rep., Wisconsin.
Mch. 4. F. Ulrick, Newbern, Grand Rep., New Jersey.
      6. Jno. W. Cotten, Tarboro, Grand Rep., Tennessee.
           A. H. Alderman, Greensboro, Grand Rep., Arkansas.
      12. J. D. Glenn, Greensboro, Grand Rep., Colorado.
      12. Walter E. Storm, Wilmington, Grand Rep., Vermont.
      15. M. S. Willard, Wilmington, Grand Rep., Mississippi.
      18. J. C. Chase, Wilmington, Grand Rep., Washington.
      22. A. H. Stubbs, Asheville, Grand Rep., Virginia.
April 12. P. A. Wilson, Winston, Grand Rep., Missouri.

DEATH.

Death has been busy in our own jurisdiction as well as among our fraters of other States. Among the latter is the name of one whom it was not our privilege to know personally, but whose name coming as it has often done under our especial notice, claims some recognition at our hands. Robert Brewster, Grand Recorder of the Grand Commandery of Texas, departed this life July 25th, 1896, in the eighty-fourth year of his age. For more than thirty years he filled the position of Grand Recorder, and at last fell at his post. "Faithful unto death he has, I trust, received the crown of life."

I report one volume of our proceedings embracing the years 1892 and 1893, bound since our last Grand Conclave.

The following Commanderies have paid dues :
1897.
Mch. 31. St. John's No. 10, Newbern ....$ 25 00
          St. Aldemar No. 12, Enfield.. 14 00
April 5. Cyrene No. 5, Asheville........... .... 41 00
       6. Plantagenet No. 1, Wilmington................... .... 50 00
       9. Durham No. 3, Durham.. 21 00
      12. Raleigh No. 4, Raleigh.. 36 00
      19. Charlotte No. 2, Charlotte.. 54 00
      24. Mt. Lebanon No. 7, Wilson... 22 00
      30. Ivanhoe No. 8, Greensboro... 32 00
                                                                                      $295 00
Which has been paid the Grand Treasurer and his receipt taken therefor.

Charlotte No. 2 is the banner Commandery.
           Durham   No. 3 has lost one by death.
           Raleigh   " 4 "   " two "   "
           St. George " 9 "   " two "   "
           Piedmont " 6 "   " one "   "

The following shows loss and gain during the Templar year:

Plantagenet	No. 1		has gained	2
Charlotte	" 2	"	"	6
Durham	" 3	"	lost	2
Cyrene	" 5	"	"	8
Mt. Lebanon	" 7	"	gained	2
St. George	" 9	"	lost	1
St. John's	" 10	"	gained	3

Net gain............ 2

You readily see by this report that there has been no advancement in Templarism—so far as numbers are concerned. It is to be hoped, however, that there has been great progress in its underlying principles and that we are very properly making haste slowly. I trust your presence with us in our "city by the sea" will redound in full measure to your happiness, as I am sure it is very gratifying to us.

PROCEEDINGS OF FRATERNAL BODIES.

The following proceedings have been received at this office and distributed as usual.

Alabama,	Kentucky,	Nebraska,
Arkansas,	Louisiana and '97,	Ohio,
Arizona,	Michigan,	Oregon.
California,	Maine,	Oklahoma,
Colorado,	Missouri,	Pennsylvania,
Connecticut and '97,	Minnesota,	South Dakota,
Canada,	Maryland,	Tennessee,
District Columbia,	Mississippi,	Texas,
England and Wales,	Montana,	Vermont,
Florida,	Massachusetts and	Virginia,
Georgia,	Rhode Island,	Wyoming,
Indiana,	New Hampshire,	West Virginia,
Iowa,	New Jersey,	Washington,
Illinois,	New York,	Wisconsin.
Kansas,	North Dakota,	

I regret to report that to all appearance Demolai Commandery No. 11, of Oxford, has ceased to exist. Also that St. George No 9, Tarboro, has not paid dues for two years I should regret exceedingly to loose from our fold these two Commanderies, in whose ranks are some of our best and most worthy Sir Knights.

PRINTING.

The Grand Recorder has hithertoo acted unrestrained in the matter of printing the proceedings of this Grand Body. It might be well for the Grand Commandery to appoint a committee to act with a similar commit-

tee from the Grand Chapter or independently of that body in this matter.
The Orphan Asylum is being fitted, I understand, for this work and is de-
sirous of testing its ability in this direction.

Courteously submitted,

H. H MUNSON,
Grand Recorder.

GRAND TREASURER'S REPORT.

WILLIAM SIMPSON, *Grand Treasurer,*

In account with THE GRAND COMMANDERY OF NORTH CAROLINA.

1896.   DR.

June 1.	To balance on hand....................................	$177 43	
1897.			
April 3.	" Cash from H. H. Munson, Grand Recorder	25 00	
3.	" " " " " " "	14 00	
6.	" " " " " " "	41 00	
7.	" " " " " " "	50 00	
10.	" " " " " " "	21 00	
17.	" " " " " " "	36 00	
20.	" " " " " " "	54 00	
29.	" " " " " " "	22 00	
May 1.	" " " " " " "	32 00	
15.	" " " " " " "	45 00— $517 43	

1896.   CR.

June 3.	By cash paid Smith, Faison & Co................. $	5 00	
29.	" " " Grand Encampment Dues	17 35	
30.	" " " Educator Co.............................	125 00	
July 1.	" " " Postage, Pringing, Etc.............	21 85	
Sept. 5.	" " " W. A. Withers, G. Commander.	8 95	
1897.			
April 1.	" " " Postage, Printing, Etc..............	15 85	
6.	" " " H. H. Munson, Gr. Recorder....	50 00	
May 1	" " " W. A. Withers, G. Commander,	11 45	
1.	" " " J. H. Hackburn, D. G. C.........	24 05	
15.	" " ' Oxford Orphan Asylum..........	50 00	
15.	" " " R. H, Bradley, Gr. Sentinel......	12 50	
12.	" " " Wm. Simpson, Gr. Treasurer ...	7 00	
18.	" " " M. B. Bailey, Gr. Generalissimo	7 92	
18.	" " " W. A. Withers, G. Commander,	7 60	
19.	" " " W. A. Withers, G. Commander,	10 95	
19.	" " " Educator Company................	61 20	
19.	" Cash on hand...	80 76— $517 43	

Courteously submitted,

WILLIAM SIMPSON,
Grand Treasurer.

P Deputy Grand Commander E. S. Martin presented a partial History of Masonry in ye oldentime. Whereupon Sir Knight Simpson submitted the following, which was adopted unanimously :

Resolved, That the Grand Commandery has listened with great interest to the remarks of Sir Knight E. S. Martin on the History of Masonry in connection with the City of Wilmington, and that he be requested to furnish a copy of the same for publication in the proceedings of the Grand Commandery.

The following Grand Representatives present were received in the usual *solemn* manner :

M. D. Bailey	Connecticut.
J. Southgate	Indianna.
E. S. Martin	Iowa.
Wm. Simpson	Kansas.
W. F. Randolph	Maryland.
F. M. Moye	Minnesota.
J. C. Munds	New Hampshire.
H. H. Munson	New York.
J. H. Hackburn	North Dakota.
W. E. Storm	Vermont.
W. A. Withers	Wyoming.
J. S. Bullock	Wisconsin.
Rev. Stewart McQueen	Kentucky.
M. S. Willard	Mississippi.
P. A. Wilson	Missouri.

Sir Knight W. F. Randolph from the Committee on Credentials reported as follows, which was received and the Committee continued.

REPORT ON CREDENTIALS.

To the Grand Commandery of the State of North Carolina :

Your Committee on Credentials beg leave to report that they find the following named Commanderies to be properly represented by their proper officers, as named below.

We also find in attendance, and entitled to seats in this Grand Commandery, the officers present and past, as mentioned below :

> E. P. BAILEY,
> J. D. BULLOCK,
> W. F. RANDOLPH,
> *Committee.*

GRAND OFFICERS PRESENT:

W. A. Withers...R. E. Grand Commander.
J H. Hackburn.............................V. E. Deputy Gr. Commander.
M. D. Bailey..E. Grand Generalissimo.
W. E. Storm.......................................E. Grand Captain General.
Rev. S. McQueen.........................as E. Grand Prelate.
W. F. Randolph................................E. Grand Senior Warden.
J. D. Bullock ....E. Grand Junior Warden.
William Simpson.............................E. Grand Treasurer.
H. H. Munson...................................E. Grand Recorder.
D. G. Maxwell..............................as E. Grand Standard Bearer.
J. J. Whitaker...............................as E. Grand Sword Bearer.
E. P Bailey.....................................E. Grand Warder.
R. H. Bradley...................................E. Grand Sentinel.

PAST GRAND OFFICERS PRESENT:

James Southgate, P. G. C.,   H. H. Munson, P. G. C.
F. M. Moye, P. G. C.,   W. S. Liddell, P. G. C,
E. S. Martin, P. Dep. G. C ,   P A. Wilson, P. G. Gen.
D. G. Maxwell, P. G. C. G.

PLANTAGENET COMMANDERY, No. 1.—WILMINGTON.

E. P. Bailey.....................................Eminent Commander.
W. P. Toomer.................................Generalissimo.

CHARLOTTE COMMANDERY, No. 2.—CHARLOTTE.

D. G Maxwell....................................Proxy for Officers.

DURHAM COMMANDERY, No. 3.—DURHAM.

James Southgate.......................Proxy for Eminent Commander.
Rev. S. McQueen......................Proxy for Generalissimo.
James Southgate ....Proxy for Captain General.

RALEIGH COMMANDERY, No. 4.—RALEIGH.

John W. Thompson................Proxy for Eminent Commander.
James Dinwiddie ....Generalissimo.
John W. Thompson..................Proxy for Captain General.

CYRENE COMMANDERY, No. 5.—ASHEVILLE.

A. J. Wills................Em. Com. and Proxy for General'o. and Capt. Gen.

PIEDMONT COMMANDERY, No. 8.—WINSTON.

F. G. Schaum................................Proxy for Eminent Commander.
W. C. Brown...................................Proxy for Generalissimo.
J. K. Norfleet.................................Captain General.

MT. LEBANON COMMANDERY. No. 7.—WILSON.

F. M. Moye......................................Proxy for Eminent Commander.
Lat. Williams......................................Proxy for Generalissimo.

ST. JOHN'S COMMANDERY. No. 11.—NEW BERNE.

J. B. Clark......................................Proxy for Officers

ST. ALDEMAR COMMANDERY. No. 12.—ENFIELD.

J. J. Whittaker......................................Proxy for Officers.

Sir Knight Wills, from the committee on Grand Commander's address, submitted the following, which on motion of Sir Knight E. S Martin, was received and the recommendations therein contained carried out :

To the Grand Commandery of North Carolina :

Your committee to whom was referred the address of the Grand Commander, beg leave to report as follows:

That so much as refers to dispensations be referred to the Committee on Jurisprudence.

That so much as refers to new Grand Commanderies be referred to a special committee of three.

That we are glad the system of Grand Visitations has been continued by' the R. E. Grand Commander and his council, believing that the best interests of the cause of Templarism are promoted thereby, but would suggest that the Commanderies from whom no answers are received to communications sent them regarding official visits are the Commanderies that need to be visited.

We concur heartily in the Grand Commander's suggestions regarding Grand Representatives and hope that all future Grand Commanders will be governed thereby.

We recommend that the recommendation of the Grand Commander regarding the power to change time and place of meeting in emergency be referred to the Committee on Jurisprudence.

We regret that we cannot approve the recommendation of the R. E. Grand Commander relative to paying the expenses of one Representative to the Grand Encampment, feeling as they do that it is the duty of all Grand and Past Grand Officers of the Grand Commandery to be present either in person or by proxy and would suggest that the Committee on Triennial Conclave be requested to formulate some plan by which subordinate Commanderies may assist in defraying the expenses of the Representatives. At the last Grand Encampment we had six Representatives, all paying their own expenses, and the interests of the Grand Commandery was better served than would be the case at Pittsburg should we pay the expenses of one Representative, thereby causing other members of this Grand Commandery entitled to a vote in the Grand Encampment, who would otherwise attend, to remain at home.

Your committee appreciate the earnest interest and zeal displayed by the R. E. Grand Commander during his term of office and congratulate the Grand Commandery upon the success achieved under his administration.

The feelings of every Sir Knight present must have been deeply moved by his closing remarks, calling up, as they do, memories of some we have loved and lost and whose noble and chivalric example remain to us as a precious legacy; and in conclusion we quote from his address and say, "That when we leave this spot so full of glorious and happy memories we should carry with us fresh inspiration for our work."

W. S. LIDDELL,
ARTHUR J. WILLS,
J. W. THOMPSON.
Committee.

The Grand Commander appointed the following special committee on new Grand Commanderies: P. G. C. W. S. Liddell, P. G. C. J. Southgate and Sir Knight E. P. Bailey.

The Grand Commandery adjourned till to-morrow morning, 9:30 o'clock.

THURSDAY MORNING, MAY 13, 9:30 O'CLOCK.

The Grand Commandery met according to adjournment. Grand Officers in their stations. The minutes of last night's session were read and approved. The following telegram was read:

H. H. Munson, Grand Recorder, Wilmington, N. C.:

I regret exceedingly my inability to be present during the Grand Conclave. My best wishes for a harmonious session. Courteously,

JOHN C. CHASE.

The Report of Sir Knight Chase, Ch'mn Fraternal Correspondence, was presented, received and ordered printed with the proceedings.

Letters of regret from E. Grand Prelate Rev. C. L. Hoffman and Grand Sword Bearer John C. Drewry were read—accepted.

On motion of Deputy Grand Commander J. H. Hackburn, all Sir Knights in this city in good standing were invited to the sessions of this Grand Body. Adopted.

Sir Knight E. S. Martin, from Committee on Jurisprudence, submitted the following report which was adopted :

To the Grand Commandery of North Carolina :

The Committee on Jurisprudence, to whom was referred the following portions of the address of the Grand Commander, having carefully considered the same, now report:

DISPENSATIONS.

The Committee are of opinion that the several dispensations granted by the Grand Commander reported in his address are correct and authorized by law except in the following: Dispensations to certain Commanderies to appear in Templar uniform "to assist in the rendition of the Story of the Reformation for the benefit of religious and charitable organizations." The Committee are of opinion that the purpose for which these dispensations were granted was not "Masonic" and therefore said dispensations should not have been granted.

RECOMMENDATIONS.

"That the Grand Commandery be allowed to change if necessary the time and place of its Grand Conclave." The Committee construe this to mean that the Grand Commandery shall have power at a special Conclave called for that purpose to change the time and place of the annual Conclave appointed (as the Constitution now requires) by the preceding annual Grand Conclave. The purpose of this recommendation (if such is its purpose) is approved, but with the following modification:

That the Grand Commander, by and with the advice and consent of the Deputy Grand Commander, Grand Generalissimo and Grand Captain General, or any two of them, shall have power to change the time and place of holding the next annual Grand Conclave appointed by the Grand Commandery at its preceding annual Conclave, when in their opinion circumstances demand it.

And as this requires an amendment to the Constitution, the Committee recommend and propose the above as an amendment to the Constitution—Section 5 to be added thereto—preceded by the word "provided."

JAMES SOUTHGATE,
E. S. MARTIN,
Committee.

Past Grand Commander F. M. Moye from the Finance Committee reported as follows, which was adopted :

To the Grand Commandery of North Carolina :

Your Committee on Finance beg leave to courteously report :

We have carefully examined the books and vouchers of the Grand Treasurer and Grand Recorder, find them correct in every particular and kept in an exceedingly nice and business like manner.

We recommend that the printing of the proceedings be left as heretofore with our Eminent Grand Recorder, who has had large experience in the matter and evinces at all times the deepest interest in the welfare of the Grand Commandery.

Courteously,

F. M. MOYE,
D. G. MAXWELL,
FRED. L. JACOBS,
Committee.

Sir Knight M. D. Bailey, from the Committee on Time and Place, reported Raleigh as being the place selected, and Wednesday after the third Tuesday in May, 1898, as the time (being May 18th.)   Adopted.

M. D. BAILEY,
W. E STORM,
J. K. NORFLEET,
Committee.

On motion of F. M. Moye, P. G. C., the Grand Commandery proceeded to the election of Grand Officers for the ensuing Templar year, Sir Knights Dinwiddie and Clark acting tellers, resulting as follows :

JOSEPH H. HACKBURN......Newbern........R. E. Grand Commander.
MUMFORD D. BAILEY........Winston ....V E. Deputy Grand Commander.
WALTER E. STORM...........Wilmington ...E. Grand Generalissimo.
WILLIAM F. RANDOLPH...Asheville.......E. Grand Captain General.
REV. CHAS. L. HOFFMAN...Asheville.......E. Grand Prelate.
JAMES D. BULLOCK...........Wilson ....E. Grand Senior Warden.
DEWITT E. ALLEN...........Charlotte.......E. Grand Junior Warden.
WILLIAM SIMPSON.............Raleigh.........E. Grand Treasurer.
HORACE H. MUNSON.........Wilmington...E. Grand Recorder.

APPOINTED.

JOHN C. DREWRY..............Raleigh.........E. Grand Standard Bearer.
EDWARD P. BAILEY.........Wilmington...E. Grand Sword Bearer.
JOSEPH B. CLARK.............New Bern......E. Grand Warder.
ROBERT H. BRADLEY.......Raleigh.........E. Grand Guard.

REPORT ON NEW COMMANDERIES.

Your committee appointed on so much of the Grand Commander's address as refers to new Commanderies, beg leave to recommend that hearty
welcome be extended to the Grand Commandery of Oklahoma, and that
Grand Representatives be exchanged with that Grand Body, also with the
Grand Commanderies of Arizona and Montana. (Adopted)

W. S. LIDDELL,
JAMES SOUTHGATE,
E. P. BAILEY,
Committee.

Sir Knight Rev. Stewart McQueen, from the Committee on
Necrology, submitted the following, which was adopted by a
rising vote :

To the R. E. Grand Commandery :

As was noted in the Address of the R. E. Grand Commander, there have
been no deaths among the members of this Grand Commandery.

It is proper to record in this connection, the names of Grand Officers who
have died in other Grand Commanderies, as follows :

Alabama—R. E. Sir Daniel Smith, P. Grand Com.
Alabama—E Sir John L. Risou, P. Grand Treas.
Arkansas—E. Sir Frederick Kramer, Grand Treas.
Colorado—R. E. Sir Webster D Anthony, P. Grand Com.
District of Columbia—E. Sir Joseph Brummett, G. S. B.
   "   "   "   —E. Sir Robert E. Constant, G. S. B.
Illinois—Rev. and E Sir James Miller, D. D., Grand Prelate.
   "   —R. E. Sir Vincent L. Hurlburt, P. G. Com.
Indiana—R. E. Sir Erville B. Bishop, P. G. Com.
Iowa—E. Sir Theo. Schreiner, P. G. S.
   " —E. Sir Archibald B. Cor, P. G. Gen'l.
Kansas—R. E. Sir Owen A. Basset, P. G. Com.
Massachusetts—M. E. Sir Benj. Dean, P. G. Com.
Maryland—R. E. Sir C. B. Kleibacker, P. G. Com.
Michigan—R. E. Sir Heman M. Moore, P. G. Com.
   "   —R. E. Sir Hollis F. Knapp, P. G. Com.
   "   —E. Sir Alex. McGregor, P. G. Sent.
Nebraska—R. E. Sir Joseph K. Marlay, P. G. Com.

New Jersey—R. E. Sir Robert Dingwell, P. G. Com.

New York—R. E. Sir Robert Black, P. G. Com.

Ohio—E. Sir Thos. J. Melish, P. G. Prelate.

Pennsylvania—R. E. Sir Edmund H. Turner, P. G. Com.

Tennessee—V. E. Sir Joseph M. Anderson, P. G. Com.

Texas—E. Sir Robert Brewster, P. G. Rec.

The names of Sir Knights who have passed away, being members of the various Commanderies in this Grand Commandery, will be inscribed on a silent page of our proceedings.

It is with feelings of grateful appreciation that we place a tribute of veneration and respect upon their graves. They have fought the Battle of Life; fought it courageously and faithfully, we trust, and fought it as Knights without fear and without reproach.

We may well believe that when each laid down his armor he could make his own that glorious and soul comforting assurance of the Great Apostle to the Gentiles: "I have fought a good fight, I have kept the faith, I have finished my course; henceforth there is laid up for me a crown of righteousness which the Lord, the righteous Judge, will give me in that day."

Let us, Sir Knights, who are still in the land of the living, take courage from their high examples. Let us put on the breast-plate of righteousness, taking the shield of faith, grasping the sword of Truth, our feet shod with the preparation of the Gospel of Peace, more calmly and bravely onwards to do battle for the glorious cause of Right and Justice and Humanity.

As we think of the noble dead, now we trust in the joy and felicity of Paradise, may we take to our own hearts that beautiful warning of the poet:—

"We, too, shall come to the river side,
　　One by one;
We are nearer its waters at eventide,
　　One by one;
We can hear the noise and the dash of the stream,
Now and again this our life's deep dream;
Sometimes the floods o'er the banks o'erflow,
Sometimes in ripples the small waves go,
　　One by one."

STEWART McQUEEN,
JAMES DINWIDDIE.
Committee.

COMMITTEE ON WARRANTS AND DISPENSATIONS.

Your Committee on Warrants and Dispensations beg leave to report that no business has come before them. Accepted.

P. H. WILSON,
W. H. APPLEWHITE,
J. J. WHITAKER,
Committee.

The Grand Commandery adjourned till 3 o'clock this after-noon.

AFTERNOON SESSION.

The Grand Commandery convened, with officers in their sta-tions, pursuant to adjournment.

The minutes of the morning session were read and approved.

The Grand Commandery proceeded to the installation of elective Grand Officers by the retiring Grand Commander, W. A. Withers, P. G. C. W. S. Liddell as Grand Marshal, all of whom were installed except Rev. C. L. Hoffman, E. Grand Pre-late, DeWitt E. Allen, Grand Junior Warden, and John C. Drewry, Grand Standard Bearer, who were not present.

Sir Knight J. Dinwiddie offered the following resolution, which was adopted :

Resolved, That the thanks of this Grand Commandery be extended to St. John's Lodge No. 1, Concord Chapter No. 1, Plantagenet Commandery No. 1, and to citizens generally for courtesies rendered and their most cordial hospitality.

No further business, appear-ing, the minutes having been read and approved, the Grand Commandery closed at 4 15 P. M. in ample form.

✠ JOSEPH H. HACKBURN,

Grand Commander.

Attest :

✠ HORACE H. MUNSON,

Grand Recorder.

RETURNS

OF

Subordinate Commanderies,

———◆———

PLANTAGENET COMMANDERY No. 1, WILMINGTON.

Time of stated Conclave: Second Wednesday in each month, 8 P. M.

OFFICERS.

E. P. Bailey	Eminent Commander.
W. P. Toomer	Generalissimo.
J. W. Monroe	Captain General.
G. Z. French	Prelate.
James C. Munds	Treasurer.
H. G. Smallbones	Recorder.
A. S. Heide	Senior Warden.
J. W. Jackson	Junior Warden.
S. G. Hall	Standard Bearer.
F. H. Stedman	Sword Bearer.
J. F. Post, Jr.	Warder.
T. H. Johnson	Sentinel.

SIR KNIGHTS.

Allen, W. W., P. G. C.	Harriss, Geo.	Mann, J. C., P. C.
Boatwright, E. P.	Horn, J. M.	Noble, M. C. S.
Burbank, T. S.	Jones, W. C.	Price, R. W.
Chadbourn, W. H., P. C.	Kenan, W. R., P. C.	Pond, E. W.
Chase, J. C., P. C.	Knowles, F. M.	Robinson, U. M.
Comfort, C. I.	Loder, J. C.	Smith, W. J.
Chadbourn, J. H., Jr.	Latimer, E. S.	Storm, W. E., P. C.
Cantwell, J. L.	Lawrence, J. R.	Scott, A. L.
Evans, DeL.	Munson, H. H., P. G. C.	Williams, W. A., P. C.
Emerson, T. M.	Martin, E. S., P. C.	Willard, M. S.
Forshee, J. M.	McEachern, D.	Williams, D. M.
French, J. McD.	McKeithan, D. F.	Baltzer, E. V.
Grant, R. H.	Morton, G. L.	

CHARLOTTE COMMANDERY No. 2, CHARLOTTE.

Time of stated Conclave: Second Tuesday of each month.

OFFICERS.

Thomas S Franklin...Eminent Commander.
Robert Walter Smith..Generalissimo.
Samuel Harrison Hilton ....Captain General.
Chas. L. Hoffman...Prelate.
Geo. H. King..Treasurer.
George A. Page..Recorder.
William Benjamin Somersett ....Senior Warden.
Harvey McLelland Day...Junior Warden.
Silas W. Neece...Standard Bearer.
John F. Orr...Sword Bearer.
David Guy Maxwell..Warder.
Edgar M. Purefoy...Sentinel.

SIR KNIGHTS.

Anderson, William	Farrior, John	Misenheimer, J. F.,
Allen, Dewit Edward	Hopkins, C. L.,	Morse, J. H.,
Belk, John Montgomery	Helms, J. D.,	Owens, W. W.,
Belk, William Henry	Hunt, F. D.,	Parks. S. L ,
Bridgers, Whitney L.,	Hotchkiss,	Quinn, M. C.,
Carpenter, Jonathan B.,	Hennessee, J. E.,	Robertson, James F.,
Curtis, F. O. S.,	Herring, H. C.,	Reinhardt, R. S.,
Creasy, Walter S.,	Lipscomb, C. F.,	Robertson, T. R.,
Campbell, George	Lawton, Charles L.,	Springs, H. G.,
Clarkson, Heriot	Liddell, Walter S.,	Smith, W. M.,
Davis, B. S.,	McDonald, Robert E.,	Worrell, William W.,
Dixon, Henry McK.	McFarland, J. T.,	Woodrum, W. J.,
Eccles, Henry Easton	McAden, John Henry	Williams, W. H ,
Fitzgerald, W. H.	Meredith, George W.,	Young, Earnest F.,

DURHAM COMMANDERY No. 3, DURHAM.

Time of stated Conclave: First Tuesday in each month.

OFFICERS.

James Southgate...Eminent Commander.
James Gattis..Generalissimo.
William A. Slater...Captain General.
Herbert J. Bass...Prelate.
Thomas E. Cheek...Treasurer.

Charles C. Taylor ....Recorder.
William L. Wall...Senior Warden.
John L. Markham..Junior Warden.
Norman M. Johnson...Standard Bearer.
James W. Blackwell...Sword Bearer.
Merritt H. Jones ....Warder.
Wyatt P. Rollins ....Sentinel.

SIR KNIGHTS.

Adkisson, L. A.	Carr, J. S.	McQueen, S.
Bishop, F. A.	Lee, J. W.	Parrish, E. J.
Blackwell, W. T.	Markham, F. D.	Wilbon, John D.

RALEIGH COMMANDERY No. 4, RALEIGH.

Time of stated Conclave: First Thursday in each month.

OFFICERS.

Z. P. Smith, P. C.. Eminent Commander.
D. S. Hamilton..Generalissimo.
A. L. Baker ....Captain General.
B. R. Lacy ....Prelate.
William Simpson, P. C..Treasurer.
W. A. Withers, P. G. C...Recorder.
M. Bowes, P. C..Senior Warden.
H. B. Greason...Junior Warden.
Chas. Wallin...Standard Bearer.
J. Ueltscht, Jr...Sword Bearer.
T. W. Blake..Warder.
R. H. Bradley...Sentinel.

SIR KNIGHTS.

Adams, D. L.	Eberhardt, T. L.	Sexton, J. A.
Andrews, A. B.	Edwards, C. B.	Thompson, J. W.
Bain, W. H.	Harrell, E. G.	Uzzell, E. M.
Blake, W. R.	Heartt, L. D.	Wait, S. D.
Busbee, F. H.	Irby, Benj.	Walters, G. N.
Clarke, A. M.	Jones, W. E.	Watson, F. A.
Dobson, J. F.	Massey, C. F.	Wetherell, W. P.
Drewry, John C., P. C.	Potter, E. C.	Woodruff, C. A., P. G. C.

CYRENE COMMANDERY No. 5, Asheville.

Time of stated Conclave: Fourth Thursday in each month.

OFFICERS.

Arthur J. Wills..Eminent Commander.
John A. Wagner...Generalissimo. ·
Claude H. Miller..Captain General.
A. H. Stubbs ....Prelate.
Henry C. Fagg..Treasurer
Marcus W. Robertson...Recorder.
John H. Woody...Senior Warden.
John A. Nichols, P. C..Junior Warden.
John W. Schurtle..Standard Bearer.
Charles R. Whittaker..Sword Bearer.
Rufus J. Sherrell..Warder.
F. T. Merriweather..Sentinel.

SIR KNIGHTS.

Brookshire, Jas. M.	Fullbright, Cassius S.	Rathbone, Rev. Scott B.
Brookshire, John A.	Gudger, Hezekiah A.	Shope, William L.
Brevard, John D.	Gudger, William J.	Sprinkle, Wm. C.
Burroughs, Jas. A.	Herndon, David F.	Smith, Van
Bell, George H.	Jacobs, Fred L., P. C.	Tweed, Chapel W.
Cobb, A. H., P. G. C.	Lawson, Thomas	Toms, Chas. F.
Collins, David K.	Moore, Charles A.	Vance, Robert B.
Carter, John H.	Moore, Walter E.	Weeks, Francis M.
Dickerson, Jos. E.	Porter, Jas. A., P. G. C.	Williams, John Key
Fletcher, Robert L.	Reed, Thomas J.	

PIEDMONT COMMANDERY No. 6, Winston.

Time of stated Conclave: Fourth Monday in each month.

OFFICERS.

Robert E. Dalton..Eminent Commander.
Robert H. Jones...Generalissimo.
Jas. K. Norfleet...Captain General.
Robert E. Caldwell..Prelate.
Fred. G. Schaum..Treasurer.
Sam'l H. Smith..Recorder.
Rufus W. Nading..Senior Warden.
John H. Foote ....Junior Warden.

Wm. F. Franklin...Standard Bearer.
Albert J. Hauser... Sword Bearer.
Wm. C. Brown...Warder.
Peter W. Dalton..Sentinel.

SIR KNIGHTS.

Allen, S. E.	Farrow, T. L.	Rich, E. D.
Alspaugh, J. W.	Griffith, J. W.	Ruffin, J. R.
Bahnson, H. T., P. C.	Hunter, J. W., P. E. C.	Spach, E.
Bahnson, W. S.	Hawes, P. H.	Summerell, W. H.
Baily, M. D., P. C.	Jones, E. L.	Trauson, R. E.
Bessent, J. C.	Johnston, R. D.	Thomas, DeLos
Brown, W. T.	Long, V. W.	White, J. A.
DeVane, D. L.	Mast, D. P., P. E. C.	Wilson, N. T.
Dalton, R. I.	McArthur, R. M.	Wilson, P. A., P. C.
Dalton, W. E. L.	Norfleet, R. C.	Whitaker, C L.
Ebent, E. A.	Quincey, G. R.	Yerex, J. W.

MT. LEBANON COMMANDERY No. 7, WILSON.

Time of stated Conclave: Fourth Monday of each month.

OFFICERS.

R. S. Barnes...Eminent Commander.
David Woodard...Generalissimo.
Jas Lipscomb...Captain General.
S. C. Wells, P. C..Prelate.
B. F. Briggs, P. C...Treasurer.
W. J. Boykin, P. C..Recorder.
W. J. Harriss..Senior Warden.
J. D. Bullock, P. C... Junior Warden.
T. B. Sugg..Standard Bearer.
E. C. Exum..Sword Bearer.
R. G. Briggs..Warder.
W. P. Snakenberg...Sentinel.

SIR KNIGHTS.

W. H. Applewite, P. C.	Farmer, Wiley	Richardson, W. W.
Cobb, Jas. T.	Moye, F. M. P. G. C.	Ward, W. M.
Daniel, Willie	Peacock, J. H.	Ward, J. M.
Hays, Jas. W.		

IVANHOE COMMANDERY No. 8, GREENSBORO.

Time of stated Conclave : First Thursday in each month.

OFFICERS.

James D. Glenn... Eminent Commander.
Henry C. Berger..Generalissimo.
C. C. Johnson...Captain General.
O. W. Corr...Prelate.
Chas. H. Ireland..... ....Treasurer.
Geo. W. Whitsett...... ....Recorder.
Samuel Brown...Senior Warden.
J. H. Holt...Junior Warden.
C. M. Vanstory..Standard Bearer.
Geo. Woodroffe..Sword Bearer.
A. H. Alderman...Warder.
John J. Thornton...Sentinel.

SIR KNIGHTS.

Alderman, S. L., P. c.	Holt, Edwin C.	Marsh, Myron
Cortland, H. H.	Hackett, C. M.	Newell, Dwight W.
Dodson, S. C.	Hill, W. B.	Richardson, W. R.
Eckle, Eugene	Hale, W. B.	Stevens, Jesse H.
French, W. C.	Jones, B. E.	Short, J. F.
Groom, P. L.	Kautner, J. E.	Williams, J. M.
Hall, N. L., P. c.	Lindley, J. Van	

ST. GEORGE COMMANDERY No. 9, TARBORO.

Time of stated Conclave: First Friday night in each month.

OFFICERS.

J. R. Pender..Eminent Commander.
J. R. Gaskill..Generalissimo.
D. Williams...Captain General.
H. I. Clarke...Prelate.
John W. Cotten...Treasurer.
C. J. Austin...Recorder.
A. M. Farley..Senior Warden.
J. M. Baker..Junior Warden.
E. B. Harlin...Standard Bearer.
Geo. Studdard..Sword Bearer.
O. Williams, Jr...Warder.
Geo. Howard, Jr...Sentinel.

ST. JOHN'S COMMANDERY No. 10, NEWBERN.

Time of stated Conclave: First and Third Fridays in each month.

OFFICERS.

H. I. Lovick..Eminent Commander.
J. B. Clark..Generalissimo.
S. R. Street..Captain General.
T. W. Dewey...Prelate.
T. A. Green..Treasurer.
C. D. Bradham ....Recorder.
Jas. Redmond...Senior Warden.
J. C. Green..Junior Warden.
L. J. Taylor ....Standard Bearer.
E. F. Rowe..Sword Bearer.
W. A. McIntosh..Warder.
W. R. Waters...Sentinel.

SIR KNIGHTS.

Hackburn, J. H.	Abbott, D. H.	Neal, B. B.
Ulrich, F.	McCarthy, T. F.	Hyman, T. G.
Daniels, Thos.	Basnight, J. S.	Warren, J. E.
Hackburn, E. B.	Guion, O. H.	Henderson, Geo.
Bryan, H. R., Jr.		

ST. ALDEMAR COMMANDERY No. 12, ENFIELD.

Time of stated Conclave: Third Friday in each month.

OFFICERS.

David Bell...Eminent Commander.
J. J. Whitaker..Generalissimo.
W. F. Parker..Captain General.
F. L. Pippen..Prelate.
J. H. Parker..Treasurer.
John A. Collins ....Recorder.
W. D. Pittman..Senior Warden.
C. E. McGwigan..Junior Warden.
H. S. Harrison..Standard Bearer.
F. W. Gregory..Sword Bearer.
M. J. Carr..Warder.
C. A. Williams..Sentinel.

SIR KNIGHTS.

Atkinson, H. C.	Taylor, T. H.

Abstract Returns of Subordinate Commanderies

COMMANDERIES.	NUMBERS.	LOCATION.	MEMBERS 1896.	KNIGHTED.	ADMITTED.	DEMITTED.	SUSPENDED.	DIED.	MEMBERS 1897.
Plantagenet	1	Wilmington	48	2	...	...	...	...	50
Charlotte	2	Charlotte	48	7	1	2	...	...	54
Durham	3	Durham	23	1	...	...	2	1	21
Raleigh	4	Raleigh	36	2	1	1	...	2	36
Cyrene	5	Asheville	49	1	1	5	5	...	41
Piedmont	6	Winston	45	2	...	1	...	1	45
Mt. Lebanon.	7	Wilson	20	1	...	...	...	...	21
Ivanhoe	8	Greensboro	30	3	...	1	...	...	32
St. George	9	Tarboro	12	...	...	...	...	2	10
St. John	10	Newbern	22	3	...	...	...	...	25
St. Aldemar	12	Enfield	14	...	...	...	...	...	14
....		....	347	22	3	10	7	6	349

Grand Officers of the Grand Commandery of North Carolina
From 1881 to 1897, Inclusive.

Year	Grand Commanders.	Deputy Grand Commanders.	Grand Generalissimos.	Grand Captain General.	Grand Treasurer.	Grand Recorders.
1881	Horace H. Munson....	Lee W. Battle........	George H. King......	*Samuel S. Everitt....	William Simpson......	James C. Munds......
1882	Horace H. Munson....	Lee W. Battle........	George H. King......	Julian S. Carr........	William Simpson......	James C. Munds......
1883	†Eugene Grissom....	George H. King......	*Andrew J. Blair....	William R. Cox.......	William Simpson......	James C. Munds......
1884	†Eugene Grissom....	*Andrew J. Blair.....	*George W. Blount....	David G. Maxwell.....	William Simpson......	James C. Munds......
1885	*Donald W. Bain....	George H. King......	John A. Porter......	William W. Allen.....	William Simpson......	James C. Munds......
1886	*Donald W. Bain....	John A. Porter......	William W. Allen.....	Carl A. Woodruff.....	William Simpson......	Horace H. Munson.....
1887	Carl A. Woodruff....	William W. Allen.....	*Francis H. Glover...	*Edward M. Nadal.....	William Simpson......	Horace H. Munson.....
1888	John A. Porter	*Edward M. Nadal....	*Francis H. Glover...	Alfred H. Stubbs......	William Simpson......	Horace H. Munson.....
1889	John A. Porter	William W. Allen.....	James Southgate......	Eugene S. Martin.....	William Simpson......	Horace H. Munson.....
1890	William W. Allen....	James Southgate......	Eugene S. Martin.....	Francis M. Moye......	William Simpson......	Horace H. Munson.....
1891	William W. Allen....	James Southgate......	Eugene S. Martin.....	Francis M. Moye......	William Simpson......	Horace H. Munson.....
1892	James Southgate.....	Eugene S. Martin.....	Francis M. Moye......	Peter A. Wilson, Jr....	William Simpson......	Horace H. Munson.....
1893	Francis M. Moye.....	Alphonso H. Cobb....	Peter A. Wilson......	John C. Chase........	William Simpson......	Horace H. Munson.....
1894	Alphonso H. Cobb....	John C. Chase........	Walter S. Liddell.....	Wm. A. Withers.......	William Simpson......	Horace H. Munson.....
1895	Walter S. Liddell....	Wm. A. Withers......	Joseph H. Hackburn...	James D. Glenn.......	William Simpson......	Horace H. Munson.....
1896	Wm. A. Withers.....	Joseph H. Hackburn...	Munford D. Bailey...	Walter E. Storm......	William Simpson......	Horace H. Munson.....
1897	Joseph H. Hackburn	Mumford D. Bailey...	Walter E. Storm......	William F. Randolph.	William Simpson......	Horace H. Munson.....

*Deceased. †Removed from Jurisdiction.

EMINENT COMMANDERS.

William H. Chadbourn...Plantagenet No. 1.
William R. Kenan...Plantagenet No 1.
E. P. Bailey .... Plantagenet No. 1.
A. G Breuizer..Charlotte No. 2.
John H McAden..Charlotte No. 2.
William Anderson..Charlotte No. 2.
T. R. Robertson ....Charlotte No. 2.
Thos. S. Franklin...Charlotte No 2.
William L. Wall...Durham No. 3.
John C. Drewry...Raleigh No. 4.
Michael Bowes...Raleigh No. 4.
William Simpson...Raleigh No. 4.
Z. P. Smith..Raleigh No. 4.
John A. Nichols ....Cyrene No. 5.
F. L. Jacobs...Cyrene No. 5.
William F. Randolph ....Cyrene No. 5.
Arthur J. Wills...Cyrene No. 5.
Henry T. Bahnson...Piedmont No. 6.
Daniel P. Mast...Piedmont No. 6.
Samuel H. Smith...Piedmont No. 6.
Robert E. Dalton..Piedmont No. 6.
Stephen C. Wells..Mt. Lebanon No. 7.
James D. Bullock..Mt. Lebanon No. 7.
Benjamin F. Briggs..Mt. Lebanon No. 7.
W. H. Applewhite..Mt. Lebanon No. 7.
John J. Thornton...Ivanhoe No. 8.
Charles H. Ireland...Ivanhoe No. 8.
Nathaniel N. S. Hall..Ivanhoe No. 8.
Sidney L. Alderman..Ivanhoe No. 8.
Albert H. Alderman..Ivanhoe No. 8.
James D. Glenn..Ivanhoe No. 8.
John W. Cotten...St. George No. 9.
George Howard, Jr...St. George No. 9.
J. R. Pender...St. George No. 9.
H. J. Lovick...St. John No. 10.
F. Ulrich ....St. John No. 10.
William J. Boykin..DeMolai No. 11.
Simeon H. Smith...DeMolai No. 11.
B. S. Royster...DeMolai No. 11.
David Bell...St. Aldemar No. 12.

Subordinate Commanderies Working Under the Jurisdiction of the Grand Commandery of North Carolina.

CHAPTERS.	NO.	LOCATION.	COUNTY.	DATE OF CHARTERS.	RECORDERS.
Plantagenet	1	Wilmington	New Hanover	May 11, 1881	H. G. Smallbones
Charlotte	2	Charlotte	Mecklenburg	May 11, 1881	Geo. A. Page
Durham	3	Durham	Durham	May 11, 1881	Chas C. Taylor
Raleigh	4	Raleigh	Wake	Oct 11, 1882	Wm A. Withers
Cyrene	5	Asheville	Buncombe	Oct 11, 1882	M. W. Robertson
Piedmont	6	Winston	Forsyth	Oct 15, 1881	Samuel H. Smith
Mt. Lebanon	7	Wilson	Wilson	Oct 15, 1884	W. J. Boykin
Ivanhoe	8	Greensboro	Guilford	Aug 2, 1887	G. W. Whitsett
St. George	9	Tarboro	Edgecombe	June —, 1892	C. J. Austin
St. John	10	Newbern	Craven	Feb'y 15, 1893	C. D. Bradham
St. Aldemar	12	Enfield	Halifax	May 9, 1894	John A. Collins

Grand Representatives Commissioned by the Grand Commandery of North Carolina.

GRAND COMMANDERIES.	FROM NORTH CAROLINA.	
	GRAND REPRESENTATIVE.	POSTOFFICE.
Alabama	John B. Porterfield	Tuscumbia.
Arkansas	John I. Sumpter	Hot Springs.
California	Reuben H. Lloyd	San Francisco.
Colorado	William T. Bridwell	Canon City.
Connecticut	James H. Welsh	Danbury.
District of Columbia	John H. Olcott	Washington.
Florida	Wm. H. Reynolds	Orlando.
Georgia	James L. Fleming	Augusta.
Illinois	Gilbert W. Barnard	Chicago.
Indiana	Nathan L. Agnew	Valpariso.
Indian Territory	James A. Scott	Muscogee.
Iowa	Alfred Wingate	Des Moines.
Kansas	Edward P. Allen	Independence.
Kentucky	Henry T. Jefferson	Louisville
Louisiana	William H. Chaffe	New Orleans.
Maine	Albish M. Spead	Gardnier.
Maryland	Joseph F. Hindes	Baltimore.
Massachusetts and R. I.	Edward L. Freeman	Central Falls.
Minnesota	John C. Munro	St. Cloud.
Mississippi	Ebenezer Thompson	Biloxi.
Missouri	F. J. Tygard	Butler.
Nebraska	W. K. Williams	York.
New Hampshire	Don. H. Woodward	Keene.
New Jersey	Joseph D. Congdon	Paterson.
New York	William Brandreth	Sing Sing.
North Dakota	John D. Black	Valley City.
Ohio	William T. McLean	Sidney.
Oregon	William Preston	Eugene City.
Pennsylvania	William H. Dickson	Philadelphia.
South Dakota	Martin G Carlisle	DeSmith.
Tennessee	W. C. Smith	Nashville.
Texas	Daniel S. Malvin	Austin.
Vermont	William H. Vinton	Battleboro.
Virginia	Elbert C. Walthall	Richmond.
West Virginia	S. B. Crandall	Huntington.
Wisconsin	George C. Teall	Eau Clare.
Washington	James P. DeMattos	New Whatcom
Wyoming	Perry L. Smith	Rawlins.

Grand Representatives Commissioned to the Grand Commandery of North Carolina.

TO NORTH CAROLINA.

GRAND COMMANDERIES.	GRAND REPRESENTATIVE.	POSTOFFICE.
Alabama	Rev. Geo. H. Bell	Bell.
Arkansas	A. H. Alderman	Greensboro
California	Samuel H. Smith	Winston.
Colorado	James D. Glenn	Greensboro.
Connecticut	M. D. Bailey	Winston.
District of Columbia	Thomas R. Robertson	Charlotte.
Florida	Geo. Howard	Tarboro.
Georgia	B. R. Lacy	Raleigh.
Illinois	Julian S. Carr	Durham.
Indiana	James Southgate	Durham.
Indian Territory	John C. Drewry	Raleigh.
Iowa	Eugene S. Martin	Wilmington.
Kansas	William Simpson	Raleigh.
Kentucky	Rev. Stewart McQueen	Goldsboro.
Louisiana	Jacob E. Kantner	Greensboro.
Maine	John A. Porter	Asheville.
Maryland	William F. Randolph	Asheville.
Massachusetts and R. I.	George H. King	Charlotte.
Minnesota	Francis M Moye	Wilson.
Mississippi	Martin S. Willard	Wilmington.
Missouri	P. A. Wilson	Winston.
Nebraska	Alphonso H. Cobb	Asheville.
New Hampshire	James C. Munds	Wilmington.
New Jersey	F. Ulrich	Newbern
New York	Horace H. Munson	Wilmington.
North Dakota	Joseph H. Hackburn	Newbern.
Ohio	John J. Thornton	Greensboro.
Oregon	Walter S. Liddell	Charlotte.
Pennsylvania	E. J. Parrish	Durham.
South Dakota	Charles J. Austin	Tarboro.
Tennessee	John W. Cotten	Tarboro.
Texas	Michael Bowes	Raleigh.
Vermont	Walter E. Storm	Wilmington.
Virginia	Alfred H. Stubbs	Asheville.
West Virginia	Rev. Walter S. Creasy	Winston.
Wisconsin	J. D. Bullock	Wilson.
Washington	John C. Chase	Wilmington.
Wyoming	William A. Withers	Raleigh.

ADDRESS OF GRAND RECORDERS.

Arizona....................Geo. J. Roskruge................Tucson.
Alabama..........................H Clay Armstrong.............Montgomery.
Arkansas....................James A. Henry..................Little Rock.
Australia...................Charles Chapman................271 Collins St. Victoria.
California...................Thomas H. Caswell..............San Francisco.
Colorado................. Edward C. Parmelee............Masonic Temp .Denver.
Connecticut...............Eli C Birdsey ....Meridian.   [Ontario
Canada......................Daniel Spry. Gr. Chancellor,288 Princess St, London,
District of Columbia..I. L. Johuson........................Washington.
England and Wales...C. F. Matier......................Mark Masous' Hall.
Florida......................N. A. McLean...................Jacksonville.
Georgia...... ....Samuel P Hamiltou............Savannah.
Grand Encampment..William H. Mayo.. ....Security Bld'g,St L.,Mo
Illinois.............. ......Gilbert W. Barnard.............19t0 Mas. Tem., Chicago
Indiana....................William H. Smythe.............Indianapolis.
Indian Territory........Leo E. Bennett..... ....Muskogee
Iowa........................Alfred Wingate...................Des Moines.
Ireland..... ....John A. Baker...................Dublin.
Kansas ....Andrew M. Callaham............211 E. Ave., Topeka.
Kentucky ....Lorenzo D. Croninger..........Covington.
Louisiana .... .Richard Lambert................New Orleans.
Maine........ ....Albert M. Spear.................Gardener.
Maryland.................John H Miller..................Baltimore, Brown's whf.
Massachusetts & R. I.,Benjamin W. Rowell........... Lynn
Michigan...................John A. Gerow...................Detroit.
Minnesota ....Thomas Montgomery..........St. Paul.
Mississippi..............John L. Power...................Jackson.
Missouri ....William H. Mayo...............Security Bld'g, St. Louis
Montana ....Edward D. Neil................Helena.
Nebraska..................William R. Bowen.............Omaha
New Hampshire........George P. Cleaves.... ....Concord.
New Jersey..............Charles Bechtel....................Trenton.
New York................John F. Shafer...................Albany.
North Carolina..........Horace H Munson.............Wilmington.
North Dakota............Frank J. Thompson............Fargo.
Ohio ....John N. Bell...................Dayton.
Oregon....................James F. Robinson.............Eugene.
Oklahoma................Harper S. Cunningham........Guthrie.
Pennsylvania ....William W. Allen.............Masonic Temp., Phila.
South Dakota............George A. Pettigrew............Flandreau.
Scotland..................Lindsay Mackersey..............Edinburg.
Tennessee.................Wilbur F. Foster................Nashville.
Texas......................J. C. Kidd......................Houston.
Vermont ....Warren G. Reynolds............Burlington.
Virginia....................James B. Banks...... ....Petersburg.
Victoria....................J. C. Kennedy, Gr. Chan......36 Darling St.,So. Yarra.
                                                                       Melbourne.
Washington..............Yancey C. Blalock..... ....Walla Walla.
West Virginia............Robert C. Dunnington........Fairmont.
Wisconsin ....John W. Laflin ....Milwaukee.
Wyoming.................John C. Baird....................Cheyenne.

Distinguished Dead in Other Jurisdictions.

ALABAMA.

DANIEL SMITH, P. G. C.
Died May 25th, 1896.

JOHN L. RISON, Grand Treasurer,
Died June 15th, 1896.

ARKANSAS.

FREDERICK KRAMER, Grand Treasurer,
Died September 8th, 1896.

COLORADO.

WEBSTER D. ANTHONY, P. G. C.,
Died June 22nd, 1896.

ILLINOIS.

Rev. JAMES MILLER, Grand Prelate,
Died November 24th, 1896.

VINCENT L. HURLBRET, P. Gr. Master,
Died July 24th, 1896.

INDIANA.

E. B. BISHOP, P. G. C.,
Died April 19th, 1896.

KANSAS.

OWEN A. BASSETT, P. G. C.,
Died July 19th, 1896.

MASS. AND RHODE ISLAND.

BENJ. DEAN, P. Gr. Master,
Died April 9th, 1897.

MARYLAND.

CHRISTIAN B. KLEIBACKER, P. G. C.

Died January 26th, 1897.

MICHIGAN.

HEMAN N. MOORE,

Died November 3rd, 1896.

GARRA B. NOBLE,

Died February 9th, 1897.

HOLLIS F. KNAPP, P. G. C.,

Died February 4th, 1897.

NEBRASKA.

JOSEPH K. MARLAY, P. G. C.,

Died April 5th, 1897.

NEW JERSEY.

ROBERT DINGWELL, Grand Commander,

Died August 6th, 1896.

NEW YORK.

ROBERT BLOCK, P G. C.,

Died December 12th, 1896.

OHIO.

THOS. J. MELISH, Grand Prelate,

Died November 11th, 1896.

PENNSYLVANIA

EDMUND H. TURNER, Grand Commander.

Died July 12th, 1896.

TENNESSEE.

JOSEPH M. ANDERSON, P. D. G. C.

Died July 14th, 1896.

TEXAS.

ROBERT BREWSTER, Grand Recorder,

Died July 25th, 1896.

We Mourn Our Fraternal Dead.

———◼———

DURHAM COMMANDERY. No. 3.—DURHAM.

W. B. BREWER,

Died September 17th, 1896.

———

RALEIGH COMMANDERY. No. 4.—RALEIGH.

H. M. COWAN,

Died August 29th, 1896.

R. B. DeVAULT,

Died December 27th, 1896.

———

PIEDMONT COMMANDERY. No. 6.—WINSTON.

F. W. MANN,

Died February 28th, 1897.

EDWARD M. NADAL, P. D. G. C.,

Died April 13th, 1896.

———

ST. GEORGE COMMANDERY No. 9.—TARBORO.

D. MELLENS,

GEO. P. HEBBARD.

BIOGRAPHICAL SKETCH
WILLIAM ALPHONSO WITHERS,
PAST GRAND COMMANDER.
—BY—
JOHN C. DREWRY, GRAND STANDARD BEARER.

The subject of this sketch was born May 31st, 1864, on River View Plantation in Mecklenburg county, N. C., and is a member of the family bearing that name and well known in both Virginia and South Carolina.

He is the youngest occupant of the Grand Commander's station in this State. His father had been a successful merchant at Beattie's Ford, but spent the latter years of his life on his plantation.

His mother was a Miss Rutledge, whose ancestors were Scotch-Irish, and pioneer settlers in that portion of the State where she met her husband.

Prof. Withers was prepared for college by Rev. L. K. Glasgow at Bethel Academy. He was a graduate of Davidson College in 1883 and received the degree of Master of Arts from that institution in 1885.

In 1884 he was appointed Assistant Chemist in the North Carolina Experiment Station by the Director, Dr. Charles W. Dabney, Jr., since Assistant Secretary of Agriculture of the United States.

From 1888 to 1890 he was a Post Graduate student in Chemistry at Cornell University, New York; after one year's work there he was elected to a fellowship, the highest honor of the University. While at Cornell he became a member of the Chi Phi. fraternity and of the Sigma Xi Society, whose membership is made up of the leading students in Science and Technology. On the establishment of the North Carolina College of Agriculture and Mechanical Arts he was elected Professor of Chemistry, which position he still holds. In 1895 he was appointed Statistical Agent of the United States Department of Agriculture for North and South Carolina. The first knowledge he had that his name was under consideration being a telegram tendering him the position.

He is a member of the German Chemical Society, and a fellow

of the American Association for the advancement of Science. He is also a member of the American Chemical Society, and on the formation of the North Carolina section he became its first Secretary.

He has been a contributor to the chemical journals, and has been called on in several instances by the counties of the State as a chemical expert

On June 18th, 1887, he was raised a Master Mason in Mecklenburg Lodge No. 176, but he transferred his membership to Wm. G. Hill Lodge No 218, in Raleigh, of which he became Master. He has been High Priest of Raleigh Chapter No. 10, and is now Grand High Priest of Royal Arch Masons

He was Commander of Raleigh Commandery No. 4, Knights Templar, and during the past year was Grand Commander. He is a member of the Council and of the Shrine.

He is a member of the Presbyterian Church, and has served as Deacon for ten years; he was instrumental in organizing the Westminster League of Albemarle Presbytery, and was elected its first President. This is the first Presbyterian League organized in the Presbyterian Church.

On June 11th, 1896, Prof Withers married Miss Elizabeth Witherspoon Daniels, daughter of Dr. Eugene Daniels, and a descendant of John Witherspoon of Princeton, a signer of the Declaration of Independence.

The above simple statement of facts shows the subject of this sketch to be a man possessed of true sterling worth, and of such a nature that his nobility of character impresses itself upon those around him.

He has always filled every position of trust and honor to which he has been called with marked ability and zeal. He is faithful and conscientious in the performance of every duty however small.

He is loyal to his friends, and scrupulously upright in all the walks of life, which demonstrates that his character is wrought of that pure golden texture which stamps him a true man and Mason.

His friends have always delighted to honor him, and he never disappoints them, but shines with brilliancy in every position in which it has pleased them to place him.

REPORT OF THE
Committee on Correspondence.

REPORT OF THE

COMMITTEE ON CORRESPONDENCE.

TO THE GRAND COMMANDERY OF NORTH CAROLINA.

For the fourth time we present the result of our labors as Correspondent. The proceedings reviewed are arranged in the usual alphabetical order. We have been able to muster the whole force with the exception of Indian Territory and that will be found at the foot of the column, should it pass under the wire ahead of the printer.. Any further general remarks are held in reserve for a conclusion, and we take up the line of march by paying our respects to

ALABAMA.

THIRTY-SIXTH ANNUAL CONCLAVE.   Montgomery, May 13th, 1896.

SIR FLETCHER J. COWART, R. E. Grand Commander.

Nine Grand Officers were present and eight Commadneries represented, but no mention is made of the presence of Grand Representatives, although they still have them "on the list," a fresh lot just having been commissioned.

The reports of the Grand Officers, who have officially visited the several Commanderies, are incorporated in the Grand Commander's address, and referring to them he says:

"Judging from the tenor of these reports, the general status of Knight Templary in Alabama, barring an exception or two, does not indicate very much progress. Still it is gratifying to believe that while no very marked advancement is being made a healthy tone prevails in most of the Subordinate Commanderies."

The general mention of banqueting festivities by the visitors would indicate that a "healthy" appetite existed in most of the Commanderies. We are pleased to see that Knightly courtesy flourishes if accessions to the ranks are few in number.

No decisions were called for and but few dispensations were issued, the majority being to permit balloting out of time.

The Alabama Sir Knights were in evidence at the Triennial and their finances were so well managed that they brought back about one-fourth of their appropriation. The Grand Commander congratulates himself on having been present and sums up as follows:

"Although as a pageant the Grand Encampment was without precedent in the annals of Masonry, as a legislative body it accomplished little of general moment. Indeed its action, or rather its lack of action, has called forth caustic criticism from high authorities. There seemed to be an inclination toward recreation rather than business."

The Grand Treasurer reports that his cash balance is $335, a shrinkage of one-sixth during the year.

The business of the Conclave was not extensive, the adoption of a revised Constitution being the *piece de resistance.*

In the evening the usual devotional services were conducted by the Grand Prelate, Rev. Owen P. Fitzsimmons, followed by an instructive oration by Sir and Rev. W. P. Powers. A copy was desired for publication, but on application were informed that it was not in manuscript, nor could it be reproduced. They should look out in season and have a stenographer on hand.

Frater Moore asked for an expression of opinion in regard to his new method of preparing the Report on Correspondence and the Grand Commandery by resolution approved the change and told him to "keep it up," but his priming must have been poor, or he did not keep his powder dry, for ten months after they adjourned the following appeared as a frontispiece to the proceedings:

"Your Committee on Correspondence had prepared a report in topical form, but owing to a press of business and other affairs it has not been put in proper form for publication. The delay in printing the Proceedings has been due to the fact that the Grand Recorder has waited to get the Report.

We shall have our next Report printed and distributed in advance of the next meeting of the Grand Commandery, and will endeavor to include in it all that is of interest in the Proceedings of the various Grand Bodies. The absence of our Report is not an "unmixed evil," as it will "save cost" to the Grand Commandery."

Better have stuck to the old way of Frater Moore, but we desire to say right here that there is no "unmixed evil" about it, your reports are worth all that they will ever cost the Grand Commandery.

A reception at the Beauvoir Club after the church service with the concomitants of ladies and toothsome refreshments appears to have been the "Afterwards" for this Conclave.

The proceedings contain portraits of Past Grand Commanders, William S. Foster and Daniel Smith.

Ten Commanderies, 382 Knights; gain 6.

Sir Robert L. Douglass, Mobile, Grand Commander.

Sir H. Clay Armstrong, Montgomery, Grand Recorder, (re-elected.)

Sir George F. Moore, Montgomery, Committee on Correspondence.

Next Conclave, Birmingham, May 12th, 1897.

ARIZONA.

THIRD ANNUAL CONCLAVE.   Prescott, November 13th, 1895.

SIR ALEXANDER G. OLIVER, R. E. Grand Commander.

Nine Grand Officers responded at roll call and there were also present representatives from their three subordinate Commanderies and seven Grand Jurisdictions. North Carolina does not appear to be on their "exchange list" at the present writing.

The Grand Commander's address is quite brief and contains little of general interest. He and the Grand Captain General appear to have been the only representatives of their jurisdiction at the Triennial and he reports a delightful experience. The sight of the grand parade moves him to recommend the procuring of "an appropriate United States flag and a beauseant to be borne in all processions of this Grand Commandery," which recommendation was adopted. No decisions or dispensations were called for and they appear to have passed through the year without grievance or complaint.

The Grand Treasurer reports $369 in his hands, which is nearly double the amount he had at the beginning of the year.

The business of the Conclave was light and of purely local interest. The Masonic Collectors' Association was endorsed and membership in the same authorized. A banquet was tendered the members of the various Grand Bodies then holding their sessions in the city and the Grand Commandery accepted an invitation to be present.

No report on correspondence appears to have been presented.

Three Commanderies, 114 Knights; gain 11.

Sir Ephraim J. Bennett, Phœnix, Grand Commander.

Sir George J. Roskruge, Tucson, Grand Recorder, (re-elected.)

Sir Archibald J. Sampson, Phœnix, Chairman of Committee on Correspondence.

Next Conclave, Tucson, November 11th, 1896.

ARKANSAS.

THIRTY-FOURTH ANNUAL CONCLAVE.   Little Rock, April 21st, 1896.

SIR GEORGE P. TAYLOR, R. E. Grand Commander.

Officers present with one exception and representatives from eight of the thirteen Commanderies. Sir Knight John J. Sumpter, who holds the commission of North Carolina, made up the unlucky number of thirteen Grand Representatives who honored the occasion by their presence.

The Grand Commander presented a brief address. Fraternal dead are tenderly mentioned. Decisions few and apparently sound. He declares that one of the Commanderies erred in allowing the affiliation of several Sir Knights, members of a Commandery whose charter had been arrested. They should only have been received under a certificate from the Grand Recorder and, without some special action having been taken by the Grand Commander, or Grand Commandery, the Sir Knights became members of their former Commandery when the forfeited charter was restored. Five of the six dispensations permitted premature balloting on petitions, most of them being cases where the candidate desired to get through in time to attend the Triennial. The following expression of opinion is not far out of the way in our estimation:

"While I confess that I do not deem it wise or expedient to grant dispensations unless great emergencies exist, my observation has led me to believe that it is oftener neglect of duty than great emergencies that causes the asking for dispensations for balloting and conferring the orders out of time."

Official visitation was indulged in to a limited extent, under enjoyable conditions, and he reports that the order is at peace within their borders and that nothing calculated to disturb their relations with sister jurisdictions has been reported. The Triennial comes in for enthusiastic mention.

The Grand Treasurer reports $498 to his credit, a slight shrinkage during the year.

The office of Inspector General was abolished and the duties of the office apportioned among the four principal officers of the Grand Commandery.

A portrait of Grand Commander Thornburgh appears in the proceedings.

The Report on Correspondence comes from Sir Knight F. J. H. Rickon and is a general review of the doings of 36 Grand Bodies, filling 80 pages. It is his fourth effort in this line and we regret to see that with it his career as Correspondent draws to a close. He characterizes it as a "labor of love" and we presume that he feels as though he had performed his share. North Carolina for 1895 has kindly notice. He quotes Grand Commander Cobb's decision on the "sojourner" case and says:

"The Decision is perfectly in accord with Templar law, but the writer never remembers hearing of a similar circumstance where a man appeared so absolutely without a home."

We quote from his review of Vermont as follows:

"Though we cannot quite agree with you (the reviewer,) on the 'Masonic occasion' question, we do not know that it cuts any figure one way or the other, for we constantly note Dispensations granted for parades on occasions where it requires some application of the X rays to see the pretext for calling them Masonic occasions."

The following criticism, under Wyoming, is frequently well deserved:

"We see time and again questions sent up to the Grand Commander for decision that surely any Commander ought to be able to answer if he was only ordinarily competent to fill the position. But many Commanders seem to think that it is not a part of their duty to know anything about the Rules and Regulations of the Order, but refer the simplest matters that come up to the Grand Commander."

There is much in this entertaining report that we would like to
quote did space permit and we regretfully part company with the
genial Sir Knight whose term of service began but a short time
before our own. To his successor, the namesake of the redoubt-
able Roundhead captain, Sir Oliver Cromwell Gray, we extend a
hearty welcome.

Thirteen Commanderies, 536 Knights; loss 19.

Sir George Thornburgh, Little Rock, Grand Commander.

Sir James A. Henry, Little Rock, Grand Recorder, (re-elected.)

Sir Oliver C. Gray, Little Rock, Committee on Foreign Correspondence.

Next Conclave, Little Rock, April 20th, 1897.

CANADA.

THIRTEENTH ANNUAL ASSEMBLY.   London, Ont., Sept 26th, 1896.

SIR WILLIAM H. WHYTE, Supreme Grand Master.

A good proportion of the Grand Officers were conspicuous by
their absence, but only seven of the thirty-six Preceptories were
unrepresented.

The Great Priory received a hearty welcome from His Worship
the Mayor of London and the local Preceptory also came to the
front with an address of greeting, to both of which the Grand
Master responded in feeling terms.

The Grand Master's address begins with congratulations on the
steady although slow growth of the Order and counsels the utmost
care to prevent accessions that will not redound to the credit of an
Order with such high ideals. A glowing account is given of his
courteous reception at the Triennial. Official visits at home were
few but enjoyable. Dispensations to form three new Preceptories
were issued, all of which start off in good shape. Referring to a
suspicion that the Orders had been conferred for a less fee than
provided for by the statutes, he says:

"I trust this suspicion is not well founded, for it seems to me that our
fees are certainly low enough and any candidate that is unable to meet our
present fee, is not a desirable addition to our Order. A Preceptory that
would offer such inducements to candidates is placing the Order on a par
with those business firms who offer cut rates in their wares to induce pur-

chasers. Templarism, I trust, will never reach that low ebb when mone-
tary considerations are offered to attract candidates.   This adoption of
commercial tactics is very reprehensible, and is not conducive to the dignity
nor credit of the Order."

We commend the foregoing as good "horse sense."

Our Canadian fratres are apparently not satisfied with the ritual,
which is the text for the following:

"Our present work was adopted after considerable labor, and although it
may not suit the individual ideas of every one, yet I strongly deprecate any
change.   Perfection is not to be found this side of the grave, and an ever-
lasting tinkering with the ritual does not conduce to the efficient working
of the subordinates.   The members become unsettled and do not want to
perfect themselves, once they get imbued with the idea that the Grand Body
is going to change or alter at every meeting."

They are also beginning to have an attack of "fuss and feathers,"
desiring to imitate their fratres across the border, whose uniforms
and drill are prominent features.   He is rather disposed to favor
more attention being paid to uniform and drill, but hopes that when
the present uniform is remodelled, it will be made "distinctively
Canadian."   Well, we are not going to quarrel with him, but we are
disposed to believe in working for uniformity rather than indi-
viduality.

He closes with some sound advice in regard to filling the chairs
with unwilling, or ambitious but incompetent fratres, the recommendation of the last named being that they are "good fellows"
who deserve the title but not the labor and are seldom seen at the
meetings.

The usual reports of the Provincial Priors appear and show faithful work on the part of these officers.   We reckon they got their
full quota of banquets, although rather sparse mention is made of
these festive occasions.

Their treasury has gained about fifty per cent. during the year,
the credit balance now being $2,223.

. One of the Encampments in New Brunswick has signified its intention of joining the Canadian body and there is good reason to
believe that the other independent Encampment will soon follow
suit.

The Committee on Ritual found the work assigned them so arduous that they were obliged to ask for further time, which was
given them.

. A pleasant feature of the Assembly was a visit from Detroit Commandery of Detroit, Mich. They were cordially welcomed and
after a parade and dinner exemplified the Order of the Temple, according to the American Ritual, to the great satisfaction of the
Canadian fratres. The evening was given up to a banquet, which
was apparently all that its name implies. The following day
witnessed a grand parade, which, with various courtesies extended
to the visiting Sir Knights, closed an occasion long to be remembered by all who were fortunate enough to participate.

. Sis Knight Henry Robertson, as chairman, presents the Report
on Correspondence, which fills 82 pages and reviews the doings of
39 Templar Grand Bodies including the Grand Encampment. He
quotes largely and is very sparing in criticism, which may be the
better way, although it does not make such lively reports as emanate
from some of our more disputatious Correspondents. At the outset he notes the principal topics being discussed in the current reviews. We find that he is opposed to enforced membership, holding that the Lodge and Chapter can take care of themselves and
that those whose interest is greater in Knighthood and are not able
to maintain membership in all of the bodies should have the privilege of serving "the cause of Fraternity" in the body where they
can do the most good. On the liquor question he believes that
debarring sellers and dealers from membership is right, "as a
general rule." The doctrine of perpetual jurisdiction is strongly
condemned. He also believes in the commutation of dues if the
proportion is made a proper one. The observance of the Christian
Days is commended if the love of display is not too much encour-
aged.

North Carolina for 1895 has brief notice without comment.

Thirty-five Preceptories, 1,548 Knights ; gain 180.

Sir Will. H. Whyte, Montreal, Supreme Grand Master, (re-
elected.)

Sir Daniel Spry, Barrie, Ont., Grand Chancellor, (re-elected.)

Sir Henry Robertson, Collingwood, Ont., Chairman of Committee on Correspondence.

Next Assembly, Montreal. Date not given.

CALIFORNIA.

THIRTY-EIGHTH ANNUAL CONCLAVE.   San Francisco, April 23rd, 1896.

SIR EDWARD S. LIPPITT, R. E. Grand Commander.

Four Grand Officers failed to appear but every Commandery was represented. Twenty-seven Grand Commanderies were represented by 15 Sir Knights, who, we presume, bore the weight of their official honors with becoming dignity. Our own jurisdiction has the honor of being represented by V. E. Sir Reuben Hedley Lloyd, who was present. We do not understand whether the position of Grand Representative is looked upon as a duty or a privilege in this jurisdiction, but, in either event, believe that no Sir Knight should hold more than one commission, in order to give the "boys a chance," if it is an honor, or require them to assist in bearing the burden, if it is considered as being one.

The Grand Commander's address is a sound and well written document of 17 pages. He notes the decease of R. E. Sir William C. Belcher, Past Grand Commander and E. Sir Stillman H. Fickett, Past Grand Captain General. Reports having constituted Eureka Commandery No. 35 and also issued dispensations to form two new Commanderies. Of his 15 dispensations, 7 permitted public appearance in uniform to escort the Grand Lodge at a corner-stone laying. He declined to permit a Commandery to appear in the parade of a local carnival, not deeming it a "Masonic occasion."

He mildly complains that many of the questions submitted for decision indicate an inexcusable lack of familiarity with the laws of the Grand Bodies. Replying to a query in regard to the secrecy and sanctity of the ballot he makes the following sound and sensible comments, which should be pasted in the chapeau of every Sir Knight.

"There can be no question but that the exercise of this sacred right of a Knight Templar to gratify any prejudice or personal ill-will against the companion whose application is being considered, or the exercise of any spirit of revenge toward the applicant, or any ill-will toward the Commandery itself, or any spirit of hostility to the growth or prosperity of the Commandery, or to be revenged for any supposed or real slight of the Commandery to a Sir Knight would not justify him in casting a black ball against a companion every way worthy, and whose accession to the Commandery would be beneficial."

The action of two Commanderies that had arraigned, tried and expelled a rascally Sir Knight, who had defrauded the widow of a Past Grand Commander of her entire estate, is heartily approved, and we fully agree with him that "if it is Knightly to help destitute widows, it must be most unknightly to render the widow of a Past Grand Commander destitute by a course of procedure condemned by all right-thinking men."

Nearly every Commandery was officially visited and he is gratified at the general improvement and more than ever convinced that great benefit arises from these visitations. We have sometimes thought that such occasions were the only times that some Sir Knights had a chance of indulging in a "square meal ;" any way they are conspicuous by their absence when work is the only thing on the programme.

A glowing description is given of the salient features of the parade at the Triennial and he speaks with no uncertain sound in regard to the lack of value of the Grand Encampment, when considered from any other point of view. He does not consider that it can ever be a success as a legislative body, if the triennial gathering of the Commanderies is held at the same time and place. He favors Washington. D. C. as a permanent meeting place and hopes that Frater Carson may live to see his idea of a magnificent Temple for the order at the nation's capital carried into effect.

The public installation of Commandery officers is commended and the opinion expressed that the annual change in commanding officers in the smaller Commanderies is a mistake. He also strongly condems the "unknightly solicitation of companions to join the Commandery."

A fine portrait of Sir Knight Lippitt appears as a frontispiece.

The several inspecting officers present full reports of their visitations, which indicate a good degree of efficiency and prosperity. Courteous treatment is duly acknowledged, but only one reports that " The fraternal banquet was a prominent feature at each of the Commanderies visited."

The Grand Treasurer's cash on hand amounts to $1,981, a shrinkage of nearly one-third during the year, but then they went to the Triennial.

The two Commanderies that had been working under dispensation were granted charters.

The Committee on Templar Tactics and Monitor reported that their work would be ready for publication in a short time. As the volume will contain some 550 pages it would appear that the California Sir Knights are not going to lack for means of instruction. Their appearance at the Pittsburg Triennial will indicate the zeal with which they make use of the work of the Committee.

Sir William A. Davies presents the Report on Correspondence, which is fully abreast of his former ones in interest and entertainment. It is the third from his pen and fills 120 pages, reviewing the proceedings of 40 Grand Commanderies, the Grand Encampment and the Great Priories of Canada, England and Wales and Victoria.

North Carolina for 1895 receives due and kindly notice. Our Horace's banquet note is quoted and calls forth the following:

"Here is a characteristic note from citizen, who seems to have some knowledge of matters in the old North State and whose conscience is always *full* of his performance of duty to the Craft."

We cannot plead guilty to his statement that we through their Committee on Jurisdiction were *afraid* to tackle a certain question, as we said that they did not " feel able " to do so. It appears that they merely let go for awhile in order to get a better hold.

From his review of Texas we take the following:

"Poor old twenty-sixth Triennial, your sins of omission were numerous, let alone those things you did which you ought not to have done, reflect on those you didn't do which you ought to have done, and sleep if you can. The fratres of Texas will conclude, with the rest of us, that Pittsburgh must close the 'boarding round business.' The interests of Templarism demand that the Grand Encampment should be located somewhere, in the near future, by adopting Carson's proposition, or our codes and statutes will be useless for the purpose for which they were enacted."

In another place he expresses the opinion that the great parades should be relegated to special conclaves, the time and place to be designated by the Grand Encampment, in order that the business sessions may not be interfered with, and he also expresses the hope that "the next Triennial will dispose of the questions of perpetual jurisdiction and non-affiliation."

We fully agree with him in regard to divorcing the parade from the legislative sessions, if the latter are to be made of any great value, but do not believe that the parades would survive the divorce. What effect the ultimate decease of the former would have on the Order we are not able to conjecture.

Thirty-six Commanderies, 2,941 Knights; gain 54.

Sir Trowbridge H. Ward, San Francisco, Grand Commander.

Sir Thomas H. Caswell, San Francisco, Grand Recorder, (re-elected.)

Sir William A. Davies, Sacramento, Chairman of Committee on Correspondence.

Next Conclave, San Francisco, April 22d, 1897.

COLORADO.

TWENTY-FIRST ANNUAL CONCLAVE.   Denver, June 2d, 1896.

SIR WILLIAM W. ROWAN, R. E. Grand Commander.

The Grand Officers were present with two exceptions and all but two of the Commanderies were represented. Eighteen Grand Representatives, including North Carolina's, were present and we note with pleasure that they were cordially welcomed by the Grand Commander. Truly the lot of some of these dignitaries is cast in pleasant places.

The Grand Commander's address is not a lengthy document, but it reports peace and harmony and a fair increase in membership, notwithstanding the hard times. The ranks of the Grand Commandery remain unbroken by death.

Eight dispensations were granted for various purposes, none of which call for adverse comment.

Ten Commanderies attended church on Christmas Day and then participated in the Toast to the Grand Master. Easter was observed by 13 Commanderies and Ascension Day by three. These observances are heartily recommended and the hope expressed that coming years will see a goodly increase in the number participating.

Twelve official visits were made, which resulted in much pleasure and showed that as a whole the Commanderies visited were in a flourishing condition. The excursion to the Triennial has enthusiastic mention.

An "Official Drill Master" is recommended, to have the emolument of $10 per day and necessary expenses, to be paid by the Commandery employing him.

The Grand Treasurer reports a cash balance of $1,654, their funds having shrunk about one-third during the year.

The Committee on Necrology present a fitting report.

The recommendation for an Official Drill Master was adopted, but the proposed compensation was cut in two, $5 per day and expenses being made the compensation. We are curious to see how many Commanderies indulge in the luxury. We notice the appointment of a committee to investigate the failure of a Commandery to discipline one of the Past Commanders, who is said to be serving a term in the penitentiary.

A 60 page Report on Correspondence appears as the sixteenth effort of our Frater Harper M. Orahood. He pays his respects to 42 Grand Jurisdictions, North Carolina for 1895 coming in for a share.

He does not seem to think it an unmixed evil that the Grand Encampment failed to accomplish any more business, saying:

> "As we have said of former Triennials, the social feature is the predominant idea. We seem to get along very well without much legislation, and the statement made that the world is governed too much is, to an extent true, and may be applicable to our order. So we join with the majority and vote this Triennial a grand success socially, and will continue under the statutes and regulations as they stand. They seem to answer the purpose, and if so, it may be well enough to adopt the adage, 'Let well enough alone.' "

A goodly portion of the report is made up of judicious quotations, as he does not consider that the sole function of a report is to voice the writer's opinions. Nevertheless they are not missing when the occasion calls for them.

Twenty-four Commanderies, 1,651 Knights; gain 3.

Sir Eugene P. Shove, Gunnison, Grand Commander.

Sir Ed. C. Parmelee, Denver, Grand Recorder, (re-elected.)

Sir Harper M. Orahood, Denver, Chairman of Committee on Correspondence.

Next Conclave, Denver, June 1st, 1897.

CONNECTICUT.

SIR HUGH STIRLING, R. E. Grand Commander.

All of the Grand Officers were at their posts and every Commandery represented. Among the 21 Grand Representatives present we look in vain for the one holding the "Tar Heel" commission.

The Grand Commander gratefully announces that their ranks have remained unbroken by death during the year. The business of the Triennial is briefly recapitulated. The Connecticut fratres had rather an unpleasant experience, as the proprietor of the hotel they had engaged as headquarters failed to keep his agreement.

The Grand Commandery escorted the Grand Lodge on the occasion of the dedication of the Masonic Home and every Commandery made a liberal donation for the purpose of equipping the dining-room. Anything that relates to eating appeals strongly to the heart of the average Sir Knight.

Only one official visit was made, as the Grand Inspector seemed to have a cinch on that particular pastime, and the Grand Commander did not think it best for both of them "to dazzle the eyes of the beholders" the same night.

Frater Birdsey sent in a communication expressing a belief in his unfitness for the post of Correspondent, and he was relieved from the honor.

The Grand Commander very properly decided that Sir Knights who had become life members under an existing by-law, and before the promulgation of the Grand Encampment law on the matter, could not be deprived of the right they had gained. Dispensation business was good, but the majority were necessitated by their organic law that the Order of the Temple shall be conferred on only one candidate at the same time.

Apparently he is not in favor of coercing members of the Commandery into remaining affiliated in Lodge and Chapter, nor inquiring too closely into the occupation of candidates, as witness the following:

"We believe that membership in a Masonic Body should be voluntary. Measures to compel affiliation are contrary to the spirit as well as the first principle of our Ancient Craft, and the ballot should be sufficient to prevent any undesirable or unworthy person from being received into our Order, no matter what particular business he may be engaged in. The character of the man, rather than his occupation, should concern us most.

"If the question of profession or occupation of a candidate is to be a qualification, it is difficult to say where the line would eventually be drawn."

We have no hesitancy in saying that we should prefer to have the moral eligibility settled on the application instead of leaving it to the caprice of those balloting.

The death, after the address was prepared, of Past Grand Commander William W. Storey, is duly announced in an appendix.

A fine steel engraved portrait of Grand Commander Stirling appears as a frontispiece.

The Grand Treasurer reports having $681 to his credit, a slight shrinkage during the year.

The Grand Inspector visited seven of the eleven Commanderies and reports an improvement in the character of the work done since his last visit.

Long continued official service is evidently highly appreciated, as $300 was appropriated for a testimonial to Past Grand Commander William R. Higby, who has filled the office of Grand Treasurer for more than a quarter of a century. If, as appears by his last report, he has had no salary all of these years, they are commuting at a pretty low figure. The beauty of the whole business is, that the committee are to find out what sort of a testimonial would be most gratifying, so there appears to be no chance of a misfit, as is sometimes the case.

A new Code of Statutes was presented, which will come up for action at the next conclave.

A special conclave was held the day before the regular one convened, for the purpose of dedicating the new Asylum of Hamilton Commandery No. 5, of Bridgeport. The reception and banquet that followed the dedication so affected the participants that "all declared ' Hamilton's ' Grand Commandery evening to be one of the most successful of the many enjoyed since this custom was inaugurated in this jurisdiction." So says Eli.

The Report on Correspondence is from the prentice hand of Sir Knight Albert L. Eugene, who was pressed into service to fill the yawning chasm caused by Frater Birdsey's defection. He fills

CXXXVI pages with a judicious and entertaining review of the proceedings of 37 Grand Commanderies and the Grand Encampment. We regret that North Carolina does not have a seat at the table, but a private note of explanation says that she arrived all right but was missing at meal-time; out prospecting perhaps for those ligneous viands for which the "Nutmeg" State is famous. -

Frater Eugene takes a very optimistic view of affairs in general as witness his conclusion:

"The questions which have chiefly occupied the Templar mind during the year just closed, are: The effect upon Templar standing of non-affiliation in Lodge or Chapter; Perpetual Jurisdiction; Life Membership and the Liquor Question, neither of which is more likely to endanger the foundations of Templarism, than the gentle tossings of a ship would drag its well-imbedded anchor, or the swaying of the branches of a tree would disturb its roots."

We regret that he retires from the corps with his maiden effort and another hand comes to the bat, to whom we extend a Knightly welcome.

Eleven Commanderies, 2,298 Knights; gain 84.

Sir Lyman H. Johnson, New Haven, Grand Commander.

Sir Eli C Birdsey, Meriden, Grand Recorder, (re-elected.)

Sir Hugh Stirling, Bridgeport, Committee on Correspondence.

Next Conclave, New Haven, March 16th, 1897.

DISTRICT OF COLUMBIA.

SECOND ANNUAL CONCLAVE.   Washington, May 11th, 1896.

SIR NOBLE D. LARNER, R. E. Grand Commander.

All of the Grand Officers were at their posts and every Commandery represented. No mention made of Grand Representatives, although numerous commissions as such have been issued.

M. E. Sir Warren L. Thomas, Grand Master of the Grand Encampment being in attendance was received with the honors befitting his high office.

The Grand Commander's address is a well written account of his offical acts; correspondence and general orders being eliminated.

Congratulations are indulged in on the success that has attended the formation of the Grand Commandery and he fully believes that this action will be of great benefit to the Order in the District.

He dwells upon the fact that the future success of Templarism in their jurisdiction is now in their own hands and that prosperity can only be maintained by strict devotion to duty and to proper attention to rules and regulations.

He pays a glowing tribute to the many virtues of E. Sir Abner T. Longley, the first member of their body to be removed by death

Official visitation has received due attention, each Commandery having had two visits, in one of which he was accompained by the M. E. Grand Master.

No decisions or dispensations reported.

The question of a permanent home for the Grand Encampment is duly considered and he makes a good showing for its necessity and, as might be expected, its location in Washington. He does not favor the permanent location of the Triennial Conclave, believing that "the assembling of the Sir Knights in large numbers every three years in different cities of our Union is of great advantage to our Order, and the proposition to abolish these assemblages I would not for a moment think of advocating."

A general inspection and review was held and appears to have been highly satisfactory. He regrets to announce that it revealed the fact that many of the Sir Knights are without uniforms and calls upon them to make good their deficiencies.

The Grand Commandery funds amount to $718.

Business light. A ritual and tactics were adopted and a committee appointed to revise the Grand Commandery Constitution.

Three special conclaves were held since our last report, but nothing of general interest appears.

No report on correspondence.

After the Grand Commandery adjourned its officers and members were regaled with a collation given them by Esther Chapter No. 5, Order of the Eastern Star. Androgynal Masonry has its strong points ; at least some that appeal to the inner man, if not to his fraternal sentiments.

Five Commanderies, 1,565 Knights ; gain 77.

Sir Frank H. Thomas, Washington, Grand Commander.

Sir Isaac L. Johnson, Washington, Grand Recorder, (re-elected) and Chairman of Committee on Correspondence.

Next Conclave, Washington, May 10th, 1897.

ENGLAND AND WALES.

The National Great Priory held its annual meeting in London on May 8th, 1896, the very High and Eminent Great Prior, the Right Honorable Earl of Lathom presiding, and a large number of officers and representatives being in attendance.

The Grand Council presented the usual report, which contains little of general interest. The Grand Treasurer's accounts show that they have funds in hand to the amount of £604, of which £120 is held for benevolent purposes.

The Eminent Great Prior having held the high office for the past nineteen years, apparently concluded that it was time to give the boys a chance, and declined to stand for re-election. His decision brought out some highly complimentary resolutions and the Eminent Sub-Prior was promoted to the high office. The abandonment of the former organization known as Convent General necessitated amendments to the Statutes, which were presented in detail in the report of the Council, and came up for adoption. The only adverse criticism was in regard to abolishing the title of Sir Knight, it being held that it was a "mere form of address from man to man and from Knight to Knight." A motion to dispense with the title prevailed by a large majority. During the discussion one of the officers expressed himself as follows:

"Speaking generally, I think that it is a pity not to have uniformity in Masonry, but it is no use talking about what is common sense, we must abide by the old state of things and it is therefore a mistake to suddenly ask us to alter them."

The election of Eminent Prior seems to have been by acclamation, after having been duly nominated, which appears to be at variance with our customs on this side of the water.

One new Preceptory has received a Warrant during the year.

After installation the usual alms were collected and the Great Priory closed in due form.

The usual Priory of the Order of Malta was opened and an even dozen of Sir Knights received the Mediterranean Pass and were admitted into the Order. The closing of the Priory was followed by the customary banquet.

Another meeting of the Great Priory was held on December

13th, 1895, the Very Eminent Provincial Prior for Hampshire, Sir W. W. B. Beach, M. P., presiding. Business light and of local interest generally. One Preceptory having satisfied the Council that it had had a continued existence for over one hundred years, was granted "a Centenary Warrant with permission to the members to wear the Commemoration Jewel."

After the Great Priory closed a Priory of Malta was opened and several Sir Knights received into the Order. The customary banquet closed the proceedings.

No report on Correspondence and no statistics that are available.

The Earl of Euston, Very High and Eminent Great Prior.

The E. Knight R. Loveland Loveland, Chancellor.

FLORIDA.

SECOND ANNUAL CONCLAVE.   Jacksonville, May 14th, 1896.

SIR WILLIAM A. McLEAN, R. E. Grand Commander.

Eight Grand Officers and representatives of five Commanderies were present. Four Grand Representatives were courteously welcomed and appropriately acknowledged the high honor that had been thrust upon them.

The Grand Commander presents a brief address. Official business has been light, five dispensations being the sum total. He deeply regrets that the lack of a seal and the necessary blanks has prevented a general exchange of representatives with the other Grand Bodies, and fears that this seeming indifference will lead to a lack of regard by the sister jurisdictions. We are sure that he overestimates the gravity of the situation and believe that his fears are not well founded. He reports that the two Commanderies chartered at the last Grand Conclave have been duly constituted.

The Finance Committee find that the Grand Commandery is in funds to the extent of $96.

Business light and of local interest only. A resolution was adopted empowering the Grand Commander to appoint a Committee on Foreign Correspondence, which provision is to become a standing regulation. No report appears this year, however.

Five Commanderies, 196 Knights; gain 58.

Sir Wilber P. Webster, Jacksonville, Grand Commander.

Sir William A. McLean, Jacksonville, Grand Recorder and Chairman of Committee on Foreign Correspondence.

Next Conclave, Jacksonville, May 13th, 1897.

GEORGIA.

THIRTY-FIFTH ANNUAL CONCLAVE.   Columbus, April 15th, 1896.

SIR JOSEPH K. ORR, R. E. Grand Commander.

The officers of the Grand Commandery having been escorted from their headquarters to the Asylum where the Conclave was to be held were treated to an address of welcome by P. C. Thomas J. Chappell, to which Deputy Grand Commander Wm. H. Fleming made a suitable response. Refreshments were next in order, after which the Grand Commandery settled down to the labors of the Conclave.

One Grand Officer failed to materialize, but every Commandery was represented and in addition 25 Grand Representatives graced the occasion, North Carolina's being among the number.

The Grand Commander's address is an interesting and poetic effort, giving a full account of his official acts.

A fitting tribute is paid to the memory of Past Grand Commander Allen L. Cutts.

No decisions called for and the dispensations, which are not given in detail, were to permit conferring the Orders in less than the statutory time.

The growing observance of the Christmas Toast is noted and approved and a lengthy account given of its celebration in "full form" by Georgia Commandery of Augusta.

The Triennial has due mention and the hospitality the Georgians received at Boston would seem "to forever refute any fancied charge of Puritanical coldness."

"Georgia had comfortable headquarters and kept open house for five days. The rather too complimentary press notices brought us a good business; nearly three thousand visitors honored us by their presence. Our register shows that these came from Maine to California. A distinguished frater from the latter State, evidently a student of agriculture, after his second cup, complimented us on the flavor of the tea so peculiarly indigenous to Georgia soil. Owing to the lack of diversity in our menu, many of our visitors went off loaded with sentiment, of this we had quite a variety."

Reading the last sentence "between the lines" as it were, one would infer that it was the same *tea* under a different name.

He is not able to announce the marvelous growth of the Order at home that is witnessed in more populous sections, but good times and the destined tidal wave of immigration are expected to effect a large increase in home membership in due season.

A glowing account is given of his official visitations, every Commandery having been favored with the presence of the Grand Commander. He found little that called for adverse criticism and we are sure that no fault could be found with the courtesy and hospitality that were predominant.

We fully endorse the opinion he expresses in the following :

"The next hour was a social symposium not soon to be forgotten, proving most conclusively that it is possible to have a delightful commingling of kindred spirits without the presence of the flowing bowl "

The cash in the treasury has shrunk nearly one-half, during the year, being now $434. It is probable that the Triennial is responsible for this state of affairs and that they will not have cause to feel lonesome when other jurisdictions are heard from.

The Triennial Committee humorously report that the Triennial has come and gone, likewise the appropriation. The flattering comments lead them to believe that their labors were not in vain. They spent more than the appropriation but made up the deficiency out of their own pockets, and "having no desire for re-appointment or vindication," hope that the account may be called square. They were discharged with thanks.

The usual devotional services were held in the evening, being conducted by Grand Prelate Samuel Hape in a very impressive manner. A selected choir of twenty-two voices added to the impressiveness of the occasion. An able and eloquent address on Templar Manhood was delivered by Rev. and Sir Knight R. B. Headden of Rome, which is printed in the proceedings.

Portraits of Past Grand Commanders Thos. Ballantyne and C. T. Watson embellish the volume.

No occasion of the sort is considered complete in this jurisdiction without a barbecue, which was the culmination of an excursion to Warm Springs, tendered the visiting Sir Knights and ladies by St. Aldemar Commandery of Columbus.

Sir Roland B. Hall presents his eighth Report on Correspondence, filling 88 pages with a genial and entertaining review of the doings of 44 Grand Bodies, including the Grand Encampment. North Carolina for 1895 has courteous mention.

There is much that we would like to quote but we must content ourself with his closing words:

"To the Eminent Templars and bright scholars of the 'Corps' who may observe us with less partiality than those of our own 'household' we say, in the language of the son of the Emerald Isle, 'Be aisy, aud if you can't be aisy, be as aisy as you can.'

"With a heart full of love for all who worthily wear the insignia of the Order, we write, 'Consumatum est.' "

Ten Commanderies, 692 Knights; gain 9.

Sir William H. Fleming, Augusta, Grand Commander.

Sir Samuel P. Hamilton, Savannah, Grand Recorder, (re-elected.)

Sir Roland B. Hall, Macon, Correspondent.

Next Conclave, Rome, May 12th, 1897.

INDIANA.

FORTY-SIXTH ANNUAL CONCLAVE.   Indianapolis, April 16th, 1896.

SIR WALTER M. HINDMAN, R. E. Grand Commander.

Three Grand Officers were missing but three representatives from each Commandery in the jurisdiction were present. North Carolina was not in the list of jurisdictions whose representatives were welcomed by the Grand Commander.

The Grand Commander announces a healthy growth in spite of the general depression, the net gain being 99. We are moved to ask, where was "The Hundredth Man?" and are also reminded of the story of the boy who was boasting of the big haul of pigeons his father had netted the day before, the exact number being 999.

To the skeptical query, "Why did you not say a thousand and done with it," the reply came, "Do you suppose I would tell a lie for one pigeon?"

Fraternal dead receive appropriate mention, among them being Past Grand Commander Andrew H. Hamilton.

Numerous dispensations were granted for a great variety of purposes, but he says that he "endeavored to be governed by the construction that an emergency must exist." We note that balloting out of time and conferring the Orders without a uniform was not considered "an emergency," the brothers having been Masons for over forty years. As one of the candidates had reached the advanced age of 79 we are disposed to consider it an emergency when the uncertainty of life is thought of.

The Constituting of a new Commandery is reported.

The half-dozen decisions reported were approved and with one exception call for no comment. A Commandery was opened preparatory to visiting the Triennial and proposed to remain open until its return. The date for the Stated Conclave fell during its absence and as the Generalissimo would be at home they desired to know if he could hold the Conclave. The Grand Commander very properly says that he cannot, and the Committee on Jurisprudence say further that:

"In their opinion there is no authority for opening a Commandery for the purpose of an excursion or journey. The Commandery as a body being absent from the jurisdiction by official permission of the Grand Commandery, no business can lawfully be transacted by the members remaining at home."

The Triennial receives attention and we note that all of the Commanderies were represented by 455 Sir Knights and nearly the same number of ladies. The gentler sex is in such a pronounced majority in Massachusetts that the failure of each Sir Knight to bring a lady was probably not noticed.

The Grand Treasurer reports having $5,589 to his credit, a falling off of one-third during the year.

The Grand Recorder has his salary raised $50 per year, conditioned on the services being "faithfully performed," which we are certain has always been the case. He has performed a very meritorious work in making a collection of portraits of the Past Grand

Commanders, all of which have been procured and appear in the proceedings. We are pleased to see that the portrait of Grand Recorder Smyth is accorded a place.

The Triennial Committee reported that they had successfully carried out the work devolving upon them and had spent a little more than nine-tenths of the funds placed in their hands. A committee was appointed for the coming Triennial, who became the residuary legatee of the former committee's assets.

A resolution was adopted in condemnation of the Turkish Atrocities.

A dispensation was granted to form a new Commandery.

The Report on Correspondence comes from the pen of Sir Knight Nicholas R. Ruckle. He has reviewed the proceedings of 43 Grand Bodies, including the Grand Encampment, in his usual happy manner, and this is his(?) effort. The report fills 128 pages, beginning with an interesting treatise on the genesis, growth and characteristics of Reports on Correspondence, from which we cull a few choice extracts:

"These reports, in a few years past, have been the medium for the presentation of much that is valuable in Templar matters, both historical and argumentative. The reports of the different jurisdictions vary in style, both in printing and preparation, corporally and spiritually One is written where a hammock swings under a leafy oak. Another is indited as the author wends his way around the world. Several are evidently measured off on the leaves of a scratch pad; while reading others you can imagine you hear the bang of the type-writing machine. You can smell the shop in many, or sniff the printer's ink, and each bears certain thumb-marks of identity.

Some reviewers, as it were, sitting serenely on High Olympus, judge the world below without concern; others grace every page with words of courtesy and gracious titles of esteem. The writing of a review is, to many, a labor of love, and to an equal number, a task of dogged perseverence. A few write for honor, many for duty; none for profit Many bear in mind the friendships to be gained and the distinction to be earned; all write with the belief that their labors are a benefit to the Craft.

To one reviewer all Templarism is elevating. The other sees the 'danger in the flowing bowl' and finds the 'cross' and 'welcome,' where no one else looks for it, over the door of the saloon.

The reports, all written by men of ability and Templar standing, cover a wide range of literary ability, and evidence different qualities of temperament and temper in the writers. As a rule, they are written in dignity and sincerity; all with a high sense of honor and with a desire for the advancement of the best interests of the Order."

North Carolina for 1895 has full and courteous notice. He

credits us with a disposition "to throw 'cold water' upon the Christmas ceremonial," and says:

"We think that the struggling brother ought to be eliminated, and not have an opportunity to partake of the Christmas or any other libation."

It is merely the business instinct cropping out dear Frater, as you would naturally expect in a purveyor of that indispensible fluid. But seriously, while far from being a teetotaller, we believe that "if alcohol were unknown one-half of the sin and a large part of the poverty and unhappiness of the world would disappear."

Interesting and instructive statistical tables form the conclusion of the report.

Thirty-seven Commanderies, 3,493 Knights; gain 99.

Sir Winfield T. Durbin, Anderson, Grand Commander.

Sir William H. Smythe, Indianapolis, Grand Recorder, (re-elected.)

Sir Nicholas R. Ruckle, Indianapolis, Chairman of Committee on Correspondence.

Next Conclave, Anderson, April 21st, 1897.

ILLINOIS.

FORTIETH ANNUAL CONCLAVE.   Chicago, Oct. 25th, 1896.

SIR AUGUSTUS L. WEBSTER, R. E. Grand Commander.

Grand Officers all present and the representatives of 63 Commanderies. Thirty-four Grand Representatives stood up and were counted, North Carolina's being among the number.

Sir George M. Moulton, V. E. Grand Captain General of the Grand Encampment, was introduced and having been welcomed by the Grand Commander, responded in a few well chosen words.

The Grand Commander's address, with correspondence and some other papers, fills 26 pages. Fraternal dead are duly mentioned, the most noted among them being Sir Knight Vincent L. Hurlbut, Past Grand Master of the Grand Encampment.

One Commandery has been formed under dispensation and one constituted.

A large number of dispensations were called for, as would naturally be the case in a jurisdiction of this size, but they all appear to have been justified and passed the overseers. Numerous decisions were rendered and we note that he decided that where two or more Commanderies had concurrent jurisdiction the consent of all was necessary to waive jurisdiction. The Jurisprudence Committee say that this is not in accordance with their statute law and reverse the ruling. He also decided that a Sir Knight holding a demit from an Illinois Commandery and now residing in Massachusetts could not deposit the demit in, and become a member of his old Commandery. The Committee reverse this decision, as follows, with a quotation from their Statutes:

" 'The jurisdiction of Commanderies over an unaffiliated Knight Templar extends only to discipline.' No so-called personal or territorial jurisdiction exists. It is within the personal knowledge of a majority of this committee that Sir Knights, created and residing in Illinois, have taken demits and joined Commanderies in adjoining States as a matter of personal convenience. We do not recall any objection to this made by the Grand Commandery, and see no reason why we should voluntarily restrict ourselves in this regard."

The Grand Recorder inserts a note directly following the above quotation, calling attention to the action of the Grand Encampment at the last Triennial, in relation to a similar case. Grand Master McCurdy held that :

"An unaffiliated Sir Knight can apply for affiliation only in the Grand Jurisdiction where he resides."

This decision was approved by the Jurisprudence Committee, whose report was adopted by the Grand Encampment, and if this body is the court of last resort it would appear that the Grand Commander was on top in this fall.

Chicago Commandery proposed to make 111 Sir Knights life members and draw on the treasury of the Commandery for $5,500., to cover the amount of the required fees, in order to evade their statute law that life membership cannot be conditioned on the continuous payment of dues for a certain number of years. Asking if they can lawfully do this they are told that "it is at variance with the law of the Grand Commandery on the subject of 'Life Membership,'" it being "a clearly established law of our Grand Commandery that a fixed sum of money must be paid into the treasury of the Commandery, by each individual Sir Knight in order to lawfully constitute him a life member."

The customary reports of the Grand Inspecting Officers, who have visited the several Commanderies, appear in full and indicate a generally creditable condition of affairs, with courtesy and hospitality abounding.

A committee was appointed to purchase for the Grand Commandery "a silk regulation flag of the United States," in order that with the banner of our faith may be carried the flag of our language and common country. It was also resolved that each Commandery of the jurisdiction be requested to do likewise. This would appear to establish the flag in this jurisdiction.

The Grand Treasurer reports his cash as being $7,590, an increase of one-fifth during the year.

They do not believe in multiplying Commanderies unless it appears that the new ones are going to be especially vigorous without endangering any of the old ones, so dispensations were refused to three aspirants.

They are inclined to think it time that California should make amends for the "invasion of jurisdiction" made some years ago, and the M. E. Grand Master is to be asked to see that the Grand Encampment action in the matter, at the last Triennial, is made effective.

A fine steel-engraved portrait of Past Grand Master Vincent L. Hurlbut appears as a frontispiece.

Sir Knight John Corson Smith comes to the front for the eighth time with a Report on Correspondence, which fills 142 pages, and reviews the proceedings of 44 Grand Bodies. We cannot say that this is his best, for it goes without saying that all have been superlative. North Carolina for 1896 has courteous notice, and we quote:

"Informs us that we don't know Sir Knights Durham and Southgate, or we would not intimate that their beverage was anything but water. Our only regret is that we have not met them personally and that we were too ill while in Asheville last winter to run down on them and partake of that North Carolina beverage which flows from its mountain rills. We do know that it is pure and clear as well as life-giving to all who use it."

He appears to have "mixed those children up," (the place and the person,) and had it been done by any one who would naturally be expected to be acquainted with the geography of the State, we should have assumed it to have been the result of too frequent indulgence in "that North Carolina beverage which flows from its mountain rills." (stills?) The sojourn at Asheville was undoubtedly the inciting cause of the beverage effusion, as that locality is right in the heart of the "rill" country. If he will come soon enough he will find Sir Knight Southgate *in* Durham, and we can assure him a cordial reception.

He notes that their representative was absent from the conclave. Why bless your heart, dear Frater, he has never attended but one conclave since the Grand Commandery was organized and that appearance was in 1882, and in his own city.

Fifty-four pages of our Frater's report are taken up with an account of his sojourn in Scotland when on the home-stretch of his trans-oceanic-continental trip of two years ago. It is profusely illustrated with views of Scottish scenery, buildings and ruins of historic interest. Not the least interesting are two pages of reproductions of Master Mason's Marks, found on the stones in St. Giles Cathedral and Melrose Abbey. As would naturally be the case a liberal amount of space is given to one who is always associated with anything that is Scotch, Robt. Burns, and numerous illustrations appear of places he has made historic, with liberal quotations from his poems. We leave this portion of the report with reluctance and have only room for his very explicit utterance on the question of "perpetual jurisdiction," with which we are fully in accord:

" Few are the questions calling for any special mention in this introduction and we are glad of it. The first is the Grand Encampment law of perpetual jurisdiction, and the earlier that is repealed the better. The claim over a rejected candidate is indefensible. Does a carpenter claim a stick of timber he has refused to receive from his lumber merchant? Does an operative mason lay claim to a stone that has never been taken from the quarry and that he has even refused to have turned over from its native bed? Or does a girl have perpetual claim for alimony upon a rejected suitor? As much justice in the one as in the other The idea of a perpetual claim upon anything never paid for, and rejected when presented, is too absurd for any reasonable persons to present and the sooner stricken from the Code the better. "

Sixty-six Commanderies, 9,518 Knights; gain 132.
Sir Edward C. Pace, Ashley, Grand Commander.
Sir Gilbert W. Barnard, Chicago, Grand Recorder, (re-elected.)
Sir John C. Smith, Chicago, Committee on Correspondence.
Next Conclave, Chicago, Oct. 26th, 1897.

IOWA.

THIRTY-THIRD ANNUAL CONCLAVE.   Templar Park, July 14th, 1896.

SIR THOMAS B. LACEY, R E. Grand Commander.

Only one Grand Officer was missing at roll-call, but 24 of the 56 Commanderies were unrepresented. However, 19 Grand Representatives helped fill the aching void, our own jurisdiction being among those represented.

The Grand Commander's address is an entertaining recapitulation of the year's work. Fraternal dead are duly noted, their own body being afflicted in the decease of Sir Knight Frank E. Fuller, Grand Sword Bearer.

A glowing account is given of the official trip to the Triennial and the resulting pleasures.

Decisions few and of local interest only. He reports having issued several dispensations, all of which have "been confined strictly to the laws governing this subject."

Two Commanderies were constituted, but no new ones were called for, which he is disposed to consider a gratifying state of affairs, believing it "wiser to strengthen existing Commanderies than to weaken them by forming new ones in advance of reasonable necessity."

A satisfactory growth during the year is reported. He notes the general observance of Easter and Ascension Days and well says:

"It is to be hoped, however, that the officers of subordinate Commanderies will use good judgment, and prevent the ceremonies of these days from leaning too strongly towards mere public display."

He notes the fact that there is a growing interest in their beautiful and attractive Templar Park.

Their treasury is burdened with $407, being a slight increase during the year.

A revised Constitution and Statutes was reported by a committee that had had the matter under consideration, and we note that Easter Sunday and Ascension Day are made days of special observance and the Commanderies are given authority "to appear in public without special dispensation therefor." We are of the

opinion that this will be found at variance with the Grand Encampment law on the subject of appearance in public. (Title XII,
Section 31.)

The Triennial Fund indicates that they run over the appropriation, but the Grand Commander came to the rescue and we are
pleased to see that an appropriation was authorized to reimburse
him.

We find no mention of the usual festivities connected with the
conclave, but presume that it has now become an old story and
not deemed worthy a place in the proceedings. A view of Templar
Park appears, as well as portraits of Grand Commander Lacey and
our highly esteemed Fratre, J. C. W. Coxe, the genial reviewer.
The Grand Commander is also favored with a biographical notice.

The Report on Correspondence reviews the proceedings of 36
Templar Grand Bodies, including the Grand Encampment, and
contains 67 pages. It is the third number from the pen of Rev.
and Sir Knight James C. W. Coxe, and is written in his usual
discriminating and entertaining manner. We regret that North
Carolina did not arrive in time to be accorded a place, but a
change in printers delayed the appearance of our proceedings just
long enough to miss the connection.

He comments as follows on a resolution appearing in the California proceedings for 1895, which prohibited "the copying of any
part of the rituals of the order adopted by the Grand Encampment," and we train in his company.

"We question the wisdom of any such prohibition, if the various officers
of a Commandery are expected to become proficient in their work. With
but a single copy of the ritual in a Commandery proficiency and efficiency
are well-nigh unattainable. We can see no vital objection to furnishing
each officer with a copy of that portion of the ritual in which he is directly
concerned, holding him responsible for its safe keeping, as the Commander
is held responsible for the custody of the official work."

From his review of Michigan we take the following, and his wish
is ours:

"We also note a dispensation 'to attend Masonic picnic at Grand Lodge,
July 30th.' What was the peculiarly 'Masonic' feature of the picnic? and
why did the fratres specially need a dispensation to permit their attendance? Or was the dispensation intended to cover their 'toggery' rather
than their persons? A dispensation 'to parade on Memorial day' was
refused, and we think rightly; but surely Memorial day has quite as sacred

a claim on loyal Knights Templar as a 'Masonic picnic!' There has been quite too much of tweedle-dum and tweedle-dee hair-splitting on this matter of 'Masonic' occasions. We heartily wish that the next session of the Grand Encampment would make an authoritative deliverance on the subject, defining the limits of the proper application of the word 'Masonic,' and so relieve us from all doubt as to 'Masonic' fairs, picnics, balls, horse trots, and insurance fakes."

Under Tennessee, in reply to a question as to his feeling about some expected Grand Encampment legislation, he says:

"The Grand Encampment strikes us as a well organized circumlocution office, dispensing patronage to a favored few, and giving little of either sweetness or light to the many who make up the Templar hosts; were it relegated to 'innocuous desuetude' there would be small loss and little grief."

Rather sanguinary talk but he may be more than half right. Who knows?

Referring to the requirement in the Washington petition for the Orders, that the applicant should not be engaged "in the manufacture or sale of intoxicating liquors," he says:

"While we are in sympathy with the implied prohibition of this clause, we question the legal right of a Grand Commandery to add new conditions to those prescribed by the Grand Encampment. We would have the Investigating Committee report on the facts involved, and should exercise our personal right when the petition of a liquor dealer came to ballot; but we do not agree with this action of our Washington fratres."

To describe the Triennial, taxes his pen beyond its ability, so he says, but it requires no effort to say:

"As to the actual work of the Grand Encampment, it was a disappointment to those who had looked to it for the solution of vexed questions."

We note that our Fratre is the *whole committee* for the coming year, which is no more than is proper when one does all of the work. Like ourself, he reaches the end of his task "with a feeling of relief," but we anticipate with pleasure another meeting in print and we hope in the flesh as well, at the next Triennial.

Fifty-six Commanderies, 4,343 Knights; gain 170.

Sir Thomas R. Ercanbrack, Anamosa, Grand Commander.

Sir Alfred Wingate, Des Moines, Grand Recorder, (re-elected.)

Sir James C. W. Coxe, Washington, Committee on Correspondence.

Next Conclave, Templar Park, July 12th, 1897.

KANSAS.

TWENTY-SEVENTH ANNUAL CONCLAVE.   Lawrence, May 12th, 1897.

SIR ROBERT E. TORRINGTON, R. E. Grand Commander.

The officers of the Grand Commandery assembled at their hotel and were escorted by several Commanderies to the sound of martial music, (Marshall's Band,) to the Masonic Hall, where the conclave was to be held.

All of the Grand Officers were in evidence with representatives of 37 Commanderies. Eighteen Grand Representatives also graced the occasion with their presence, but none of them held North Carolina's commission.

Sir Wm. H. Mayo, Grand Recorder of the Grand Encampment, was received with the honor due his exalted station, and being welcomed by the Grand Commander, made fitting acknowledgement.

The Grand Commander's address is a high-toned production, and we quote from his opening paragraph.

"Amidst the strife of sects, and the din of theological controversy, the Knight Templar has shown his loyalty to God by his efforts for man's improvement, and as humble worshippers at the shrine of the once despised, but now risen and ascended Nazarene, we have lovingly shown our appreciation of that masterly heroism which lives in the best thought and inspires the sweetest charity of our age. While changes may be taking place in the theories of social life and methods of political government, we, as Knights of the Holy Temple, have but one grand object before us the exaltation of the Redeemer of the world, and the larger currency of those truths which broaden human thought and sweeten human life."

Fine writing but we are afraid that his picture is that of an ideal Sir Knight, rather than the average one, we are sorry to say.

Dispensations few in number and call for no adverse comment. No decisions reported, as all questions asked were answered by reference to the Code. He is happy to report that the Masonic Home "will soon become a reality in all its beauty and benefience in our own jurisdiction."

He notes that several Commanderies have supplied themselves with the United States flag and appears to be in full accord with the idea. Their Triennial experience has enthusiastic mention. He gravely announces that "depot platforms are always crowded as we passed through," which may be construed as the reader fancies.

Referring to the orders he has issued, he says that he "did not deem it advisable to occupy space in our proceedings with matters that do not directly concern the progress of our work," which is an example worthy of imitation. The Commanderies which have been inspected by himself or his deputies are reported as showing a fair degree of prosperity and in many cases an interest in the work far above the average.

A fine steel engraved portrait of Grand Commander Torrington appears as a frontispiece and the Grand Recorder serves him up in a biographical sketch.

Their cash on hand amounts to $2,540, being only about two-fifths as much as was shown by the last report. The Triennial seems to have been responsible for this state of affairs. Some things come high but we must have them.

The Triennial Committee managed matters so judiciously that they had about fourteen per cent. of their fund remaining, which will come in handy at Pittsburgh.

A well written Report on Necrology was presented by Grand Prelate Busser. The Grand Recorder drew a prize in the shape of a fifty per cent. increase in his salary, which we suppose is to compensate him for the admirable Report on Correspondence he submitted.

Dispensations were ordered issued to form three new Commanderies. A committee was appointed to memorialize the President of the United States on the subject of the Armenian atrocities.

After the closing of the Grand Commandery they had a "Sandwich," which seems to have been made up of a dress parade, an exhibition by the drill corps present and a banquet, the tables being waited upon by the wives and daughters of the Sir Knights of the local Commandery. "Jack the Kisser" does not seem to have been present, but Samuel the Busser was in evidence and the tribute paid by him to the fair waiters virtually paralyzed the pen of the scribe, whom we assume to be the Grand Recorder.

Sir Knight A. M. Callaham presents his second Report on Correspondence, which fills 135 pages, and reviews the proceedings of 44 Grand Bodies in a judicious and entertaining manner.

North Carolina for 1895 has its full proportion of space and our
work is quoted from at length. Quoting Munson's banquet
effusion with its statement of going home "with a full conscious-
ness of having performed our duty to the craft," he says:

> "Well, now, if he had left out the words after full, we might have
> criticised his late hours, etc. but if he had consciousness sufficient to find
> the keyhole when he reached home we will not raise a row about it this
> time."

Answering our question, "where does the 'populist' come in,"
he says:

> "To the best of our knowledge, Sir Chase, he has not 'come in.' We
> have never seen him in our Grand Commandery. In fact, he does not seem
> to be 'in it' this year, even politically."

The Triennial receives due attention, but he takes little stock
in any business of importance being attended to unless the legislative sessions are held the week preceding or the one following
the "vast gathering together of the hosts for a good time." The
failure of the Grand Encampment to accomplish more than it
succeeded in doing is scored in no measured terms.

Several pages are devoted to "Excerpts and Comments," which
bring together in compact form the views of the brainiest Correspondents on some of the live questions of the day. He does
not give us his own sentiments except on "perpetual jurisdiction,"
which he believes in, qualified as appears in the following:

> "We do not believe in a unanimous ballot, however. There is a middle
> ground which will protect the lodge and protect the candidate.
> We believe that any member has the right, yea, *it is his duty*, to cast the
> black ball when he believes the candidate unworthy. * * * * *
> Now when the lodge is asked for a waiver of jurisdiction, *it is known that
> there was some reason for his rejection.* Is it not fair and right there
> should be some precaution against allowing unworthy material to escape by
> acting in too great haste?" * * * * * Always give the benefit of the
> doubt to your lodge. Two many wear the insignia of the fraternity *and too
> few Masons.*"

We regret that the limitations of space prevent our quoting
farther on this subject.

Forty-two Commanderies, 3,247 Knights; gain 71.

Sir William C. Holmes, Parsons, Grand Commander.

Sir A. M. Callaham, Topeka, Grand Recorder, (re-elected,) and
Correspondent.

Next Conclave, Junction City, May 11th, 1897.

KENTUCKY.

FORTY-NINTH ANNUAL CONCLAVE.   Richmond, May 27th, 1896.

SIR SAMUEL H. STONE, R. E. Grand Commander.

The several subordinate Commanderies present, with the Cadets from the University and the "Little Commandery" from the Masonic Widows' and Orphans' Home, escorted the Grand Commandery to the chapel of Central University, where, after an address of welcome and its response, the Office of Public Worship was conducted by Rev. and Sir Knight Thomas U. Dudley, who afterwards delivered an impressive and appropriate sermon. The address of welcome appears in print, but the response and sermon were not to be had, as the inspiration of the occasion was their main incentive and when a copy was called for a month later it was as difficult to obtain as to recover the lost efervesence of champagne.

The Grand Officers were at their posts without exception and only two Commanderies were unrepresented. The 27 Grand Representatives present included the one holding the commission of North Carolina.

The Grand Commander's address gives a very detailed account of the business of the year, which has been a prosperous one. Fraternal dead are briefly noted. Numerous dispensations were granted and a half-dozen were refused, good reasons appearing for either action. He mildly disapproves of granting dispensations to ballot out of time, believing that the 30 day limit is a good one.

A number of official visits were made and he is pleased to report that zeal for the Order is increasing in every section he has visited. He reports with satisfaction that no requests for the establishment of new Commanderies have been made and believes that the multiplication of new Commanderies has been one of the main reasons for the present unfortunate condition of several Commanderies.

The Triennial comes in for extended notice and he reports the Masonic Home as being in fine condition and doing a good work.

The Grand Recorder's report contains three entertaining communications from Grand Representatives, one of whom freely expresses his belief "that the system of Grand Representative amounts to little, if anything." His resignation does not appear, however.

We regret to see that they are in financial straits, the Grand Treasurer's report showing that they are entirely destitute, so far as book-keeping can be credited. Triennial expenses and a large number of Grand Commander's jewels account for the shrinkage of assets during the year.

"Addenda" gives an account of the social features of the Conclave, which were many and varied, and we have no doubt that the Sir Knights will ever cherish vivid recollections of the hospitality of their entertainers.

For the twenty-third time Sir Knight Charles R. Woodruff comes to the front with one of his admirable Reports on Correspondence. Forty-six Grand Bodies pass in review and the result fills 132 pages.

North Carolina for 1895 has courteous notice to the extent of three pages. Referring to our mention of North Carolina's Representative not being in attendance upon the Conclave, he says:

"Since the above comment was made, and in the early days of winter, Sir Knight Wicks calmly passed away from among us, and 'the places that once knew him will know him no more forever.'

The Grand Commandery of North Carolina has lost a Grand Representative in Sir Knight Wicks, who was truly the Christian gentleman in every phase of his amiable character. A life-long acquaintance with our dear friend and Brother, and an intimate association with him of many years, renders his loss very sad and touching to the writer hereof, who has rarely been called to share a deeper grief, or a more serious cause for mourning and regret."

A careful reading of this interesting report finds nothing to join issue upon and we bid our esteemed Fratre adieu for another year.

Twenty-five Commanderies, 1,931 Knights; gain 19.

Sir Reginald H. Thompson, Louisville, Grand Commander.

Sir Lorenzo D. Croninger, Covington, Grand Recorder, (re-elected.)

Sir Charles R. Woodruff, Louisville, Chairman of Committee on Fraternal Correspondence.

Next Conclave, Hopkinsville, May 19th, 1897.

LOUISIANA.

THIRTY-THIRD ANNUAL CONCLAVE.   New Orleans, February 14th, 1896.

SIR M. L. SCOVELL, Acting Grand Commander.

Ten Grand Officers and the representatives of four Commanderies were present. There were also present 19 Grand Representatives, representing 27 Grand Jurisdictions, North Carolina being one of the number.

R. E. Sir Charles F. Buck, Grand Commander, being absent, on account of Congress being in session, his address was read by the Grand Recorder.

He reports a fair degree of prosperity during the year just ended. Their official circle has been unbroken by death. Peace and harmony have prevailed to the extent that no decisions have been called for. A few dispensations were granted, to permit balloting out of time, but the desire to attend the Triennial seemed to be a good reason and he hopes his action will "not be considered as a precedent for future conduct."

The Triennial has due mention and he says:

"Louisiana, few in number and simple in display, stood with the best of them, in the sentiments which they inspired. The union of 'Dixie' and 'Yankee Doodle'—was made a palpable fact and the patriotism that spoke from the rocks of Plymouth was re-echoed from the hearts of Chalmette."

The business of the Conclave was light and of local interest only. A ringing series of resolutions on the Armenian atrocities were adopted.

The Grand Treasurer reports his cash balance as being $409. About one-sixth less than the amount in hand at the beginning of the year.

Sir Knights J. Q. A. Fellows and Richard Lambert present the Report on Correspondence, which, with the included tables, fills 30 pages.

It is prepared on the topical plan, following the example of Sir Knight Moore of Alabama. As would naturally be expected from a reviewer of the calibre of Sir Knight Fellows, the report is a brief but comprehensive setting forth of the views of other correspondents on the topics selected for review. The subject of "non-

. affiliation" occupies a large portion of the space and we gather
that he does not believe that suspension from Lodge or Chapter
for non-payment of dues affects standing in the Commandery.

He considers that "Frater" has been adopted as an English
word, by Knights Templar at least, and that being the case its
plural should be formed by adding *s*, according to the rules of
grammar. He is at variance with Sir Knights Moore and Wait on
this matter, but has Sir Knight Mayo on his side. We have
already put ourself on record as believing "Fratres" to be the
correct form, not considering that the singular form has become
Anglicised.

On the subject of life membership we extract the following as
corroborating the view that we have formerly expressed. The
text being "That a Mason who pays twenty years' dues in his
Lodge much exceeds the average":

"We know it does. Several years ago we took the Lodge having the
most permanent and continuous membership in Louisiana, and found, after
a careful calculation, *that the average was less than ten years.* The brother
who has paid continuously ten years, may get tired of it, and feel inclined
to demit, or some financial or bodily misfortune has befallen him, suffer
himself to be dropped or suspended for non-payment of dues, whereas, if
he knew, that by five or ten years longer he would become a life member,
he would remain, and if flush in money pay the whole in advance. Such
has been the case with both Lodge and Chapter, to which the writer
belongs, and the Chapter on four dollars per annum dues for ten years,
which constitutes a life member, has upwards of $16,000 funds invested."

Four Commanderies, 328 Knights; gain 23.

Sir M. L. Scovell, Shreveport, Grand Commander.

Sir Richard Lambert, New Orleans, Grand Recorder, (re-
elected.)

Sir J. Q. A. Fellows, New Orleans, Chairman of Committee on
Foreign Correspondence.

Next Conclave, New Orleans, February 12th, 1897.

MAINE.

FORTY-FIFTH ANNUAL CONCLAVE.   Portland, May 7th, 1896.

SIR FREDERICK S. WALLS, R. E. Grand Commander.

Twelve Grand Officers present and 17 Commanderies represented. Thirty-one Grand Represenatives were also on hand, but
North Carolina's was not among the number.

The Grand Commander reports peace, harmony and entire unity as prevailing. Announces in fitting terms the death of Sir Knight William A. Albee, Grand Senior Warden. No decisions were reported. A large majority of the dispensations granted were to permit balloting ahead of time.

A pleasing report is given of their Triennial experiences. Official visitation was indulged in to some extent and the only adverse criticism is, "the rather clumsy and unmilitary manner in which the sword is used in the opening and closing ceremonies, as well as in the work." We reckon that the same criticism would not be out of place in some other jurisdictions we wot of. The other Grand Officers who made visits of inspection present full reports of a generally satisfactory condition of affairs.

·The funds in the Grand Treasurer's hands show a fair increase during the year, being now $1,847.

A committee was appointed to arrange for the coming Triennial and $100. was appropriated as an entertainment fund for the Grand Officers. We note that the last Triennial had a good sized unexpended balance, which will serve as a nest egg for the coming one.

An unpleasant episode with a sister jurisdiction came up for settlement. One of their Companions had been rejected several times as a candidate for the Orders, by the Commandery in whose jurisdiction he belonged. Later on he returned to his former home in Massachusetts and upon application to the Commandery there was duly elected and received the Orders. The Commandery having had their attention called to the matter, promptly apologised and admitted that the state of affairs resulted from gross carelessness on their part. They also declared that they would not recognize the party as a Knight Templar. The Committee on Jurisprudence being asked to consider the matter recommended that the party be denied all Knightly recognition and intercourse until after his application to the Commandery that had rejected him, they should by unanimous secret ballot ask the Grand Commander for the time being to heal him. The recommendation was adopted.

The evening was given up to a supper and smoke talk, Sir Knight Drummond having some words of "commendation of the social ways of our ancient brethren,"

The proceedings are embellished with a steel-engraved portrait of Grand Commander Walls. We are also pleased to see that they do not propose to allow the lineaments of former officers to be forgotten, as the Grand Recorder was authorized to publish portraits of Past Grand Commanders.

The Report on Correspondence comes from the hand of Sir Knight Stephen Berry, and we must congratulate him on reaching his majority, as the one before us is the 21st, he has put forth. The proceedings of 47 Grand Bodies have been corralled and the result of his discriminating examination makes 73 pages of entertaining reading.

North Carolina for 1895 is duly noticed. Commenting on our utterance on Life.Membership, he says:

"It is the abuse of a good thing which has made the trouble. In some cases Commanderies have been crippled by placing life-membership too low, and there is danger of the life-membership fund being dissipated by using it for social purposes. Properly guarded, it would be an advantage to a commandery, but the question is, can all commanderies be intrusted with the power. If the Grand Commandery reserves the power to cancel the contracts, great injustice may be done to those who have paid and had their money used up so it cannot be refunded."

"Properly guarded" is a good qualification and we believe that each Grand Commandery could be trusted to attend to the matter. We also believe that a continuous payment of dues for twenty or twenty-five years should entitle the Sir Knight to be made a life member on the payment of a nominal sum, and we do not believe that it would be any evasion of the Grand Encampment law to so enact. The law does not specify the amount to be paid, nor do we believe that the adding of other conditions would violate it. So far as the general principle or outcome is concerned we are not at all alarmed.

Under Tennessee, referring to the question of allowing one man by unanimous consent to cast the ballot of the Grand Commandery for an officer, he says:

"At a corporation meeting, lately, we asked a Justice of our Supreme Court, who was present, if that method was legal, and he smiled and said, 'you cannot go behind the record.' We are of the opinion that if the body unanimously directs it to be done, and the recording officer is wise in making his record, it will stand fire, until, of course, it is absolutely forbidden."

While it may be all right, we believe that the custom is a bad one, as the time may come when some individual may desire a change, and at the same time will not desire the prominence of making an objection.

Replying to a Vermont criticism of Maine's refusing a Commandery permission to parade on Memorial Day, he says:

" We have never criticised the Vermont custom of celebrating Memorial Day, but our Grand Commandery has always made it a rule not to unite with societies which are not masonic, in their celebrations, and not to adopt their customs. "

Replying to Sir Knight Swain's intimation that he has a "pretty type-writer girl " on his staff, he says:

" He is far astray. We have two guardian angels, one with blue eyes and one with brown, who allow no 'pretty type-writers' or other temptations near their papa. "

Since the above was written one of his 'guardian angels' has been adopted by the " Tar Heel State, " and we seem to see the dimly outlined shadow of the approaching "type-writer girl. " Do not be alarmed Brother, you will find her a cheerful companion.

Commenting on the decease of correspondents, in his conclusion, he says:

" There is no reason why correspondents should not live their three-score and ten. To be sure, great writers like Shakespeare, Byron, Scott and Keats have died young, but that need not frighten us. Still our chronicles have a graveyard look, they are strewn so thick with funeral garlands; but that we cannot help, for as our numbers grow, so must the roll of names spread out for whom the lots are cast by angel hands. "

Nineteen Commanderies, 3,067 Knights; gain 163.

Sir Albro E. Chase, Portland, Grand Commander.

Sir Stephen Berry, Portland, Grand Recorder, (re-elected,) and Chairman of Committee on Correspondence.

Next Conclave, Portland, May 6th, 1897.

MARYLAND.

Twenty-sixth Annual Conclave.   Baltimore, November 24th, 1896.

Sir William H. Clark, R. E. Grand Commander.

The Grand Officers were present with one exception and every Commandery was represented. The Representatives of 30 Grand Jurisdictions were also in attendance, North Carolina's being one of the number.

The Grand Commander's address is a well written and full account of his official actions. A heartfelt tribute is paid to the memory of Sir Charles Von S. Levy, Past Grand Captain General, and the Knightly dead of sister jurisdictions are briefly noted. Two Commanderies were constituted during the year, one of them being expected to " be a power of good in this jurisdiction, " and the other "noted for their great hospitality to all visiting Sir Knights." It might be inferred that no banquet was forthcoming in the first instance, but such was not the case. The following extract tells its own story and certainly indicates a gratifying state of affairs:

" During the past year a simple request or two for my decision as Grand Commander have been submitted—and these of such comparative small import, that a reference to the code was sufficient for my decision, which clearly shows the familiarity of the presiding officers of the several Subordinate Commanderies with the jurisprudence of this Grand Commandery, as well as that of the Grand Encampment of the United States, and also for the peace and harmony of the Fratres within our own jurisdiction. "

Eight of the 16 dispensations issued permitted balloting "upon petitions for Orders within the prescribed time," but as he says "good and sufficient reasons" were presented we will say no more.

Official visitation had due attention and he felt highly pleased with the lavish hospitality extended and the evidence of fraternal feeling existing. He regrets to learn from the Grand Inspector that only about sixty per cent. of the Sir Knights are uniformed. He feels that the lack is detrimental to the best interests of Knighthood and recommends that all Companion Knights be fully uniformed before receiving the Order of the Temple.

The Grand Commander apparently did not hesitate to *order* the several Commanderies stationed near Baltimore to assemble and attend Divine service on Ascension Day, which they did with full ranks and listened to an impressive and eloquent discourse. We are pleased to see that our Grand Commander is not the only one open to criticism in the matter of *ordering*, instead of *requesting* a public appearance of the Order. Better look out,

Frater Carson 'll be after you,
" Ef you don't watch out."

The usual special Conclave was held on Easter Monday for the purpose of installing the officers-elect of the Baltimore Commanderies, which was done in the usual elaborate manner, an attractive musical programme being an important part of the ceremony.

The funds in the Grand Treasurer's hands have remained practically unchanged during the year, being now $1,103.

Very little business came before the Conclave, which only held two evening sessions. It was ordered that the standing resolution in regard to uniforms, adopted some years ago, be strictly enforced. A portrait of Grand Commander Clark appears in the proceedings. We note that one of the Commanderies lately constituted bears the name of a person now living, which we fancy is rather out of the usual course. In fact we know that it is prohibited in one Order and on general principles believe the inhibition to be a good one.

Sir Ferdinand J. S. Gorgas scores this heat, it being his twentieth Report on Correspondence. It fills 79 pages and reviews the proceedings of 41 Templar Grand Bodies. As heretofore, it is a very courteous and entertaining production. North Carolina for 1896 has its due proportion of space and our late Frater Blount is kindly mentioned. Our Grand Recorder's opinion that the Grand Representative system "is of doubtful utility and almost an empty honor" calls out the following, which is a sound and sensible presentation of the case:

"So far as the Representative system is a means of bringing Grand Bodies into closer communication with each other, as this system undoubtedly does, we regard it to be so far useful. No one will deny that a Grand Representative regards the Body he represents as being in closer relationship to him than any other except his own Grand Body, and is ready at all times to act as its champion and promote its interests. We have evidences of this warmer fraternal feeling at every reception held during the sessions of the Grand Encampment, where the welcome extended to representatives by the Sir Knights they represent, is not only cordial, but most sincere, and akin to that extended to their own fratres."

We hope the printers will bear him no ill-will, as he is not backward in calling attention to their supposed misdeeds, saying in one place:

"We do not know who is to blame for our mis-spelt name, but will conclude that it rests upon the printer, who is accustomed to such charges, and upon whom they have no more effect than water thrown upon a duck."

We find the following in reference to Frater Jumper, Correspondent of South Dakota:

"There is quite a difference iu the names 'Temple' and Jumper', but let us lay the blame on the printer, who is accustomed to such charges, and does not in the least mind them.   We shall look in the proof of this report very carefully for the name of 'Jumper', and not confound the name of our esteemed Frater with that of an edifice, if it is a Temple."

Next year it will be in order to account for Frater Hodson of Oregon posing as John *Walter*, instead of John *Milton*. Get a "pretty type-writer" Frater Gorgas, and you will be surprised to see what a change it will make in the antics of the printers, and, incidentally, it may have an influence in your own environment.

Twelve Commanderies, 1,132 Knights ; gain 45.

Sir George Cook, Baltimore, Grand Commander.

Sir John H. Miller, Baltimore, Grand Recorder, (re-elected.)

Sir Ferdinand J. S. Gorgas, Baltimore, Chairman of Committee on Correspondence.

Next Conclave, Baltimore, November 23rd, 1897.

MASSACHUSETTS AND RHODE ISLAND.

NINETIETH ANNUAL CONCLAVE.   Boston, October 29th, 1896.

SIR EUGENE H. RICHARDS, R. E. Grand Commander.

All of the Grand Officers were present and every Commandery represented. Thirty-two Grand Representatives also graced the occasion and we are pleased to chronicle the presence of North Carolina's.

The Grand Commander begins his address with congratulations on the continued prosperity of the Order ; peace and harmony prevailing at home and with their Fratres abroad. Their official ranks have remained unbroken, but several members of the Grand Commandery have been summoned to their reward ; prominent among them being :

"Reverend and Eminent Sir Lucius R. Paige, the oldest Past Commander in the world, and a Mason for over seventy years, passed from us in his ninety-fifth year, September 2, 1896. His life was calm and peaceful, and he was distinguished for his many virtues and his noble character."

Fourteen dispensations were issued permitting public appearance in uniform on sundry occasions, only one being for the purpose of attending religious services. As they were prohibited having music on that occasion we presume the rarity of parading for public worship is accounted for.

He is obliged to report that Massachusetts Commanderies have been conferring the Orders upon Companions from Maine and New Hampshire, each of whom had been several times rejected in their home Commandery. The Massachusetts Commanderies had made ample apologies for what the Grand Commander styles as "great carelessness, to say the least," but the aggrieved Commanderies decidedly declined to release jurisdiction over the two Companions, and the Grand Commander therefore decided that they were not entitled to recognition as Knights Templar. We have already noted the action of Maine in regard to the matter.

The several inspecting officers attended to their duty, every Commandery having been officially visited. Their reports are generally favorable and with few exceptions the Commanderies are prospering and in good financial condition.

The Grand Recorder presents a lengthy report, from which we learn that the average membership of the Commanderies in this jurisdiction is 262; the largest being Boston Commandery, which leads the world with 888 members.

The Grand Treasurer reports $6,388 in his possession, the amount having trebled during the year. The Grand Fund receives a tithe of the income of the Grand Commandery and now amounts to over $24,000.

The business of the Conclave was quite light and of a routine character purely. A dispensation to form a new Commandery was granted and another body of petitioners for a like favor were given leave to withdraw, it being the unanimous opinion of the Committee that the formation of a new Commandery would not promote the interests of the Order.

The usual Semi-annual Conclave was held at Providence on May 28th, 1896, all of the Grand Officers and representatives of nearly all of the Commanderies being present. The Grand Commander has nothing but peace and prosperity to note. The fraternal dead of sister jurisdictions receive appropriate mention. Dispensations are given at length, with the statement that so many Commanderies desired to observe Easter Sunday that he issued a General

Order giving permission. Banners were allowed but music was
prohibited. Sixteen Commanderies, mustering 1,672 Sir Knights,
accompanied by nearly all of the Grand Officers and a large
number of Past Officers, attended a religious service on that day
in the Boston Music Hall by invitation of Rev. Sir Knight George
C. Lorimer, D. D , the services being under his charge. The
Grand Commander says:

> "Easter Sunday was a red letter day for Templar Masonry in this juris-
> diction. The service was glorious and impressive. The music, with a
> chorus of Christian Endeavorers of four hundred voices to assist, the several
> participations by the Sir Knights in the music and services, the immense
> auditorium crowded with Sir Knights and citizens together, inspired all
> hearts with the most exalted sentiments and left a lasting memory in the
> minds of those who were present."

He very properly decides that an assessment levied by a Commandery to meet Triennial expenses was legal, it being done at a
special Conclave and notice of the proposed action having been
sent to all of the members.

The Committee on Jurisprudence suggested that a jurisdictional map would be a nice thing to have and a committee was
appointed to carry out the suggestion.

A fine portrait of Grand Commander Richards appears as a
frontispiece, and the proceedings are still further embellished with
two pages of vignette pictures of the Representatives of other
Grand Commanderies near this Grand Commandery, only two of
the forty being missing.

The Report on Correspondence is the joint production of the
Rev. Sirs Henry W. Rugg and Thomas E. St. John and reviews the
proceedings of 39 Grand Bodies in a scholarly and high-toned
manner, the result of their labors filling 114 pages. North Carolina for 1896 has exceeding courteous notice, and much as we
regretted to part company with Sir Knight Finch we cannot find
any fault with the measure of quality or quantity given us by his
successor, Fratre St. John. We fondly anticipate the pleasure of
meeting him, which quite likely will be before these lines will meet
his eye.

He is rather inclined to question the propriety of one of our
dispensations, but as it was approved by the Committee on Jurisprudence he presumes that we "were satisfied that Templarism was

advanced thereby." The dispensation referred to was to permit Raleigh Commandery "to assist in the rendition of the Story of the Reformation." We are afraid that it would be rather a stretch of the imagination to call it a "Masonic Occasion," and feel that perhaps the less we say about it the better.

Our Brother is a strong disbeliever in the use of the elaborate memorial pages seen in some of the volumes of proceedings, our own among the number. We are in full accord with him on that subject—and they are not put in at our instance. We quote from him as follows:

"To our mind there is nothing grander or more sublime than the plain announcement, with name and date, of the mournful event. The ghastly tombstone adds no element of beauty, and embattled wall and implements of Masonic work give no indication of the hope that the heart is allowed to cherish as one thinks of 'loved ones gone before.'"

Commenting on Sir Knight Carson's paper on "Androgynal Free-masonry" he well says:

"Certain it is that no ritual of the 'Order of the Eastern Star' has anything in it that would furnish the remotest hint of such a performance."

Under Tennessee we find the following with which we are in full accord:

"There may be no special reason why the Order of the Temple should be conferred on Sunday, but considering the character of the ritual, the lessons inculcated, and the general bearing of the Order itself we find nothing at variance with the most devout and reverent worship. Could the candidate, as well as those engaged in conferring the order, accept its teaching with serious thought and resolve to honor in subsequent life the admonitions there given, methinks both the day and the work would be sanctified."

He is a non-believer in dispensations to permit balloting out of time, as witness the following, from Virginia, which we also endorse:

"Why should not a regulation of such importance be scrupulously observed? There is time enough to meet all of the requirements of our constitutional law, and in most cases the emergency is fictitious, or at best the result of some unnecessary neglect. It were better if to all such requests the Grand Commander should say 'no.'"

We lay this report aside, regretting the limitations that prevent our drawing from it to a greater extent.

Forty-five Commanderies, 11,789 Knights; gain 293.

Sir William R. Walker, Pawtucket, R. I., Grand Commander.

Sir Benjamin W. Rowell, Lynn, Grand Recorder, (re-elected.)

Sirs Henry W. Rugg, Providence, R. I., and Thomas E. St. John, Haverhill, Mass., Committee on Foreign Correspondence.

Next Annual Conclave, Boston, October 29th, 1897.

MICHIGAN.

FORTIETH ANNUAL CONCLAVE.   Grand Rapids, May 19th, 1896.

SIR WILLIAM E. JEWETT, R. E. Grand Commander.

Twelve Grand Officers present and representatives from all of the Commanderies. No Grand Representatives in this jurisdiction.

R. E. Sir Frank H. Thomas, Grand Captain of the Guard of the Grand Encampment appeared as the representative of the M. E. Grand Master and was received with the honor appropriate to his station.

The Grand Commander's address is a well written presentation of his official acts, which he gives in detail.

He announces the decease of Sir Robert B. McKnight, Grand Senior Warden, and pays an affecting tribute to his memory, "as a jurist, citizen and Mason."

The past year has been one of prosperity. The Triennial comes in for extended notice.

"This important meeting, undoubtedly the largest in the history of the Order, had a far more than ordinary interest to Michigan Knights Templar from the fact that our beloved '*Hugh*' was to preside, and close his labors in the highest official capacity of Templarism, and which position he had occupied with so much ability and distinction."

A large number of decisions are reported but the greater number of them given by direct references to the Code. We give one, more on account of the novelty of the question than anything else.

"*Question.* A Sir Knight was granted a conditional dimit with the sentence, 'and as such we do courteously commend him to the fraternal regard of all valiant and magnanimous Sir Knights wherever dispersed,' stricken out, because 'we could not, from his past record, give him such a clean recommend, and upon such a dimit introduce himself into an unsuspecting community.' Was it legal?"
"*Answer.* No. No right is given to any Commandery to change the form of dimit as prescribed by the Grand Encampment."

It would seem that the Sir Knight was not a proper person for membership in the Order, but we realize the difficulty in certain cases of getting the necessary testimony to furnish good grounds for exclusion.

Numerous dispensations were issued, the most of them permitting public appearance in uniform for various purposes, Memorial day not being considered such.

Official visitation was indulged in to quite an extent and the results of his inspection seem to be generally satisfactory, although he found that many of the Commanderies were not in possession of a copy of the Constitution and Code of Statutes. This may account for many of the decisions that were called for. On the subject of inspection thus he expresses himself:

"There is no Commandery but what would be benefitted by at least an annual inspection. It is an event to be anticipated and prepared for. These preparations incite a zeal and rivalry among the officers and Sir Knights, the good effect of which is felt for some time thereafter."

He recommends that the Grand Commander be authorized to "appoint each of the three Grand Officers composing his council to inspect such Commanderies as he cannot well visit himself, and report to him. The necessary expenses being allowed." He believes that this would meet the requirements of the case and be a valuable training for future Grand Commanders, as with this system they would have visited in some official capacity every Commandery in the jurisdiction by the time their term of office had ended.

Their funds have shrunk nearly one-third during the year, but they need have no apprehension of want as the Grand Treasurer still has $4,004 to his credit.

The Committee on Necrology, by its chairman, Grand Prelate Blades, presented a long and exceedingly appropriate report.

A Charter for a new Commandery was granted after considerable discussion, contrary to the recommendation of the Committee on Charters.

An appropriation of $500 was made to the Masonic Home.

The election of officers was suspended after the election of Grand Commander, in order that a Past Grand Commander's Jewel might be presented to the one who, in a short time, would be numbered with that faithful band of "has beens." The presentation was made in a happy manner by the Grand Commander elect, and R. E. Sir Jewett was equally felicitous in his response. It was a novel time for such a presentation and would naturally suggest the idea of its being an unpleasant task that should be performed as soon as possible.   We expect to be brought up "with a round turn" a year hence by being told that it is none of our funeral, but *allee samee* it *was* a queer time.

R. E. Sir Jewett's portrait faces the title page and the proceedings are further ornamented (?) with sixteen pages of memorial tablets.   And this is the jurisdiction that finds no use for Grand Representatives ! "My ! My !", as Sam Jones would say, how tastes do differ.

The volume of proceedings is no whit behind its predecessors in appearance and is the most attractive that comes to our table.

The Report on Correspondence fills 265 pages, net, and reviews the proceedings of 41 Grand Templar Bodies.   It is signed by John A. Gerow, "for the Committee," but if any one thinks that the other members of the Committee had anything to do with this, the third child of his brain and pen, they are wofully mistaken. His bright and sparkling humor efervesces on nearly every page and we shall hold him only responsible for the "whole shooting match," and his broad shoulders are well able to bear the burden.

North Carolina for 1895 comes in for a fair share of his attention. He quotes in full Grand Commander Cobb's decision in regard to the itinerant book agent, who desired to become a Knight Templar, and believes the decision to be well founded, although a curious one, saying ;

"He must have been Eugene Hale's 'Man without a country,' and we can only hope that the companion has since located and obtained a home."

He has "mixed those children up" this time surely and it is fortunate for him that the coming Triennial is not to be held in Boston, as the Brahmins of that center of light and learning would be slow to condone such a grievous error as calling their noted author by any other name than *Edward Everett*.

Commending an opinion of our Canadian Frater Robertson he says:

"Out of a Keeley Cure and into a Templar Asylum is hardly the thing without a satisfactory probation."

Answering Frater Birdsey, of Connecticut, on the question of "memorial plates," he says:

"In this view we cannot agree with the illustrious fratres.   The obituary mementoes are absolutely necessary as a part of the history of a jurisdiction and should have a place in the proceedings as a tribute to the worth of those who have gone before. ''

To be sure, but we hold that the tablet gives no additional prominence to the name, even if they are used in our own jurisdiction, for which we are not responsible. If tablets are to be used, have only one as a sort of a preface, or else have a different one on each page.

Under Ohio, commenting on Frater Carson's paper on "Androgynal Freemasonry," he well says:

" The review of adoptive Masonry in France under the government of the Duchess de Bourbon has nothing in keeping with the American Eastern Star Chapters. ''

We would like to draw still further on our esteemed Frater, but time and space forbid, and with our thanks for his kindly mention we bid him adieu.

Forty-four Commanderies, 5,457 Knights; gain 84.

Sir Edward D. Wheeler, Manistee, Grand Commander.

Sir John A. Gerow, Detroit, Grand Recorder, (re-elected,) and Chairman of Committee on Correspondence.

Next Conclave, Detroit, May 20th, 1897.

MINNESOTA.

THIRTY-FIRST ANNUAL CONCLAVE.   Stillwater, June 24th, 1896.

SIR HARRY E. WHITNEY, R. E. Grand Commander.

Twelve Grand Officers were present with the representatives of 19 Commanderies and 21 Grand Representatives, North Carolina's being numbered with the latter.

The Grand Commander notes that the relentless hand of Death has not spared them the past year, Past Grand Generallissimo Neville Staughton, Past Grand Captain General D. R. Sutherland and Past Grand Junior Warden Rish A. Gray having been called hence.

No decisions were called for during the year. A goodly number of dispensations were issued, public appearance in uniform dividing time with balloting inside of the statutory limit.

The Triennial excursion seems to have been a pleasant episode.

The Grand Commander visited every Commandery in the jurisdiction during the year and his very full report shows that they are in a sound and healthy condition, although work has been light with several of them. Any mention of banquetting hospitalities is conspicuous by its absence, but we reckon that such festivities were not entirely lacking.

Their funds have remained practically unchanged during the year, $2,086 being the Grand Treasurer's cash balance at the present time.

The business of the session was quite light and of local interest only. The proceedings contain portraits of Grand Commander Whitney and the veteran Grand Treasurer, Sir John G. McFarland.

Sir Thomas Montgomery comes to the front, for the seventh time, with the Report on Correspondence, which contains 80 pages and notices the proceedings of 43 Grand Bodies. He has very little to offer in the way of criticism, so the chance of differing with him is reduced to a minimum. He is pleased to report that:

" Peace reigns supreme in the Templar world, and the past year has been favored with a remarkable degree of prosperity in spite of the general financial depression. There is nothing, in the opinion of your committee, now agitating the thinkers and writers of the order that is worthy of more than a passing mention, and hence our report this year will be rather shorter than usual. We shall in the following pages only notice briefly the items of business transacted, giving here and there such extracts from addresses and reports which we deem worthy of your attention and thought. It would have been much easier to have made our report as long again, but we hope it will be satisfactory in its present form, and that it will be read carefully by all into whose hands these proceedings may fall. "

North Carolina for 1896 has brief notice, the Grand Commander's tribute to Frater Blount being quoted.

He thinks that Frater Carson's strictures on "Androgynal Freemasonry" should not be applied "to our Eastern Star Chapters, which, to our knowledge, have greatly aided the lodges, especially in the social and charitable feature of their work." We are in full accord with our Frater Montgomery on this topic.

Reviewing California he says:

" We are fully in accord with our worthy frater (Davies) on the question of perpetual jurisdiction, a doctrine we cannot uphold. We yet hope to see it set aside by the Grand Encampment. "

His interesting table of statistics appears as usual.

Twenty-five Commanderies, 2,411 Knights; gain 77.

Sir John H. Randall, Minneapolis, Grand Commander.

Sir Thomas Montgomery, St. Paul, Grand Recorder, (re-elected,) and Chairman of Committee on Correspondence.

Next Conclave, Minneapolis, June 24th, 1897.

MISSISSIPPI.

THIRTY-SIXTH ANNUAL CONCLAVE.   Jackson, February 18th, 1896.

SIR F. P. JINKINS, R. E. Grand Commander.

Eleven Grand Officers present, with the representatives of eleven Commanderies and eleven Grand Representatives, North Carolina not having a part in this triple combination of elevens. Any one addicted to an observance of signs and portents would be likely to lay some stress on this conjunction.

The Grand Commandery was duly opened and then proceeded to the First Methodist Church, where the Offices of Devotion were observed and a sermon delivered by Rev. Sir Irvin Miller, in the absence of the Grand Prelate, his text being, "But whom say ye that I am?" The usual collection was lifted for the Natchez Orphan Asylum, resulting in $27.80, and the Grand Commandery returned to the Asylum and got down to business.

The Grand Commander's address is a brief but well written document. He announces that harmony has prevailed throughout the jurisdiction and that the year has been one of prosperity. He has some enthusiastic words in regard to the advantages of his State as a place to emigrate to, and assures a cordial welcome to all who may come. We quote, with approval, as follows:

"It is a deplorable fact that a great many have passed through our solemn ceremonies and departed from our Asylums no better men, husbands, fathers and citizens than they were before being knighted. They are Templars simply in name; and we are weakened instead of strengthened by this class of membership. The sequence of this condition of affairs is directly traceable to the fact that we do not guard the doors of our Asylums with that circumspection that becomes true Knights."

Fraternal dead receive tender mention, their own body mourning for Sir N. S. Walker, Past Grand Commander.

No decisions appear to have been called for and the dispensations, with two exceptions, were to permit balloting upon applications at the same conclave at which they were received. One Commandery observed Ascension Day.

He regrets that they did not make more of an appearance at the Triennial, but those who attended appear to have had an enjoyable time.

"The people of Boston did everything in their power to contribute to our welfare and enjoyment, and I believe if they manifested any partiality to their visitors, those from the South were the favored ones. Mississippi was not mentioned in the papers at the time, as being in the parade, but we were nevertheless, and I felt as much pride with only a few Sir Knights who had the courage to accompany me, as those Commanderies who numbered their hundreds in the line of march through the streets of the historic city of Boston. Now, let us commence to make arrangements for the coming Triennial at Pittsburg."

He reports having issued a charter to a Commandery that had been working under dispensation.

We deem the Grand Recorder's opening paragraph worthy a place:

"It is with special gratitude that I submit to this Grand Body my Twenty-sixth Annual Report. Since our last Grand Conclave, as most of you know, your Grand Recorder has had a very close call, but the good Lord was gracious enough to spare him yet awhile to meet and mingle with his fraters in these Asylums. He is now next to the head of the list of Grand Recorders in seniority of service—Sir Knight Robt. Brewster, of Texas, leading the column."

We extend our congratulations on his recovery and trust he may fill the office for many years yet. We quote what he has to say about Grand Representatives, which is a more or less vital question.

"The list of Grand Representatives to and from the Grand Commandery of Mississippi needs considerable revision. Some who are accredited from other jurisdictions very seldom attend our Conclaves, and some of those who appear on the rolls of other Grand Commanderies as representing Mississippi might resign the honor to others more zealous."

It might be a good idea to proclaim the position vacant if the incumbent failed to appear at two successive Conclaves, giving the honor to some one who was in attendance.

The Grand Treasurer reports the funds in hands as being $276, being practically unchanged during the year.

The business of the Conclave was of a routine nature and only of local interest.

The Report on Correspondence fills 96 pages and reviews the proceedings of 37 Templar Grand Bodies. It is the sixteenth effort of our esteemed Frater, E. George DeLap, and is fully up to the standard of his previous work in this line.

He is anxious to have some live subject for discussion in sight, as witness the following, from Connecticut:

"Some of the 'Mutuals' will, no doubt, rise to inquire what a Correspondence report has to do with the 'Second Blessing' fad, and we are compelled to reply: nothing at all, but the hope that some one might raise a row about it and make things a trifle less monotonous, induced us to put it in."

Well, his shot will miss fire, so far as we are concerned.

Under Indiana, he has the following remedy for the naturally resulting conviviality at Triennials:

"Either abolish the Grand Encampment, which would be a blessing in many ways, prohibit the attendance of any but members of the body at the place of meeting, and the headquarters feature, which is a fruitful source of intemperance and devilment, or secure a park. as Iowa has done, away from the adjuncts of hell—the saloons—and then prohibit the presence on the grounds of any and all intoxicants, expelling each and every Templar (?) who has it in his room, his pocket or his stomach."

He appears to have very decided pessimistic views, as witness the following from Missouri:

"The *world* is *not* growing better. On the contrary, it looks to us very much like the time for the reign of the devil, for a thousand years, is about here. Nearly everybody belongs to some one of the churches, and have joined under the impression that church membership is equivalent to a through ticket into the New Jerusalem, when the hottest corner of hades is reserved for just this sort of christians, who have the *form* but deny the *power* of godliness."

North Carolina for 1895 has courteous notice and the writer's work receives commendation, much higher than it deserves, we fear. He styles Grand Commander Cobb's address "an excellent paper," and says:

" He made but one decision, and that was, that a cosmopolite is in a bad fix, masonically; that as he has no residence, or fixed abode from choice, that he can't come in until he settles on some spot on the Lord's earth and calls it his *home*. This is doubtless good law, but it is hard on the 'sojourner.' "

He honors our Grand Recorder by quoting from his report, but fails to note that what he quotes was quoted from the writings of the lately deceased Sir Knight Robert Macoy, of New York, to whom it is applied. The result is that our Horace is lying awake nights fearing that the "Mutuals" will accuse him of plagiarism, of which he is entirely innocent.

We regret that we cannot draw still further from Frater DeLap's report, but must bid him good-bye and move on.

Twelve Commanderies, 441 Knights; gain 11.

Sir J. M. Buchanan, Meridian, Grand Commander.

Sir J. L. Power, Jackson, Grand Recorder, (re-elected.)

Sir E. George DeLap, Natchez, Committee on Fraternal Correspondence.

Next Conclave, Biloxi, February 9th, 1897.

MISSOURI.

Thirty-fifth Annual Conclave.   Springfield, April 21st, 1896.

Sir Leslie Orear, R. E. Grand Commander.

Only one Grand Officer failed to appear and only two of their 57 Commanderies were unrepresented. Twenty-seven Grand Representatives put in an appearance, North Carolina's being in line. The Grand Commander fills 30 pages with a minutely detailed account of his official acts, and counsels his auditors to take ample time to deliberate upon the business that will come before them, to the extent of taking an extra day, if one will not suffice. He reports, with gratification, that the growth of the Order during the year has exceeded their expectations, and that peace and harmony prevail.

Fraternal dead of their own and sister jurisdictions receive appropriate mention, their own official circle mourning Sir William A. Thoms, Grand Drill Master and Inspector.

Official visitation was indulged in to a limited extent and he reports having been "received with that cordial hospitality and Knightly courtesy which characterizes the Missouri gentlemen." We would not object to have "some of that in ours."

He gives a very enthusiastic account of the Triennial and owns up to being convinced that "Templar chivalry and hospitality are not confined to any particular part of our common country." He apparently run up against the hospitality and courtesy which characterizes the Massachusetts gentleman, and if he expected

anything else we are mightily pleased that he was agreeably dis-
appointed. He is disposed to question the wisdom of keeping
"open house," and is obliged to report that very little was accomplished from a legislative point of view. Of course he is gratified
that their Grand Recorder has been honored with the same office
in the Grand Encampment, which, as he says, brings the Secre-
tariat of that Grand Body to the geographical center of the Union.,
We should consider it more desirable to have him located at the
geographical center of the Templar membership, and consider our
National Capitol as being the appropriate place.

A large proportion of his dispensations permitted public appearance in uniform on divers occasions. He appears to have turned
down all requests for permission to ballot on petitions for the
Orders without waiting the legal time, notwithstanding the principal
reason was that the applicant desired to go to Boston. We consider
his utterance on this subject worthy of a place.

" I am of the opinion that our statutes, requiring the petition of a Companion for the Orders to lie over for four weeks, were enacted for the purpose affording ample time for investigation into the character and fitness
of the applicant to become a Knight among us. With all the safeguards
afforded us by these laws some are knighted who are slow to appreciate the
beauties of the Ritual or the purposes of the Order. The Grand Commandery has so often animadverted against the practice of allowing petitions
to be acted upon short of the prescriben time, that I construe it to mean
that the Grand Commander should not exercise the privilege of shortening
the time merely for the purpose of allowing the petitioner to be hurried
through our ceremonies in time to be enrolled as a member of a pleasure-
seeking party. These should be made secondary considerations, and the
solemn and deeply impressive ceremonies of these splendid Orders should
never be neglected in the slightest degree, as of necessity they must be,
when crowds of postulants are rushed through with their eyes resting on
the brilliant uniform and a dress parade, in perspective, as the chief incentive to their action, rather than the performance of acts of charity and pure
beneficence."

He declined to call the Grand Commandery together to act as
an escort to the Grand Lodge at a cornerstone laying, "the action
seeming unprecedented." A perusal of the late proceedings of
sister jurisdictions would show that it has frequently been done.

A half-dozen decisions were reported at length, all of which
successfully run the gauntlet of the Jurisprudence Committee.

The Masonic Home comes in for a share of attention and the
good work that it is doing may be inferred from the fact that it is
now sheltering 105, of which number 82 are children. This is cer-

tainly one of the acts of "pure beneficence," to which Templars are pledged.

The Grand Treasurer has $5,458 in his hands, practically the same amount with which he began the year.

The Committee on Triennial had nearly two thousand dollars at their disposal and manages matters so successfully that they were able to return more than one-eighth of it to the treasury.

Portraits of Grand Commander Orear and Past Grand Commander Thomas M. Wannall, with biographical notices of each, appear in the proceedings.

The Report on Correspondence is the nineteenth from the pen of Grand Recorder William H. Mayo, who has filled 81 pages with a review of the doings of 43 Grand Bodies. North Carolina for 1895 has its notice to the extent of a page, all but eight lines being two excerpts, without comment.

Fifty-seven Commanderies, 4,234 Knights; gain 204.

Sir Ira V. McMillan, Maryville, Grand Commander.

Sir William H. Mayo, St. Louis, Grand Recorder, (re-elected,) and Correspondent.

Next Conclave, St. Louis, April 20th, 1897.

MONTANA.

NINTH ANNUAL CONCLAVE.   Butte, Sept. 14th, 1896.

SIR EDWARD D. NEILL, R. E. Grand Commander.

Eleven Grand Officers and the representatives of seven Commanderies were present. Nine Sir Knights, representing thirteen Grand Commanderies, were also on hand but North Carolina did not appear, by fragment even.

The Grand Commander's address traverses the usual ground. His only decision was to the effect that a Sir Knight, unable to be present at the annual Conclave of his Commandery, could not give a proxy to be used in the election of officers. Having been asked to define the term "Christian Religion," he says:

"Though in my mind the answer to this question is very clear, the Order has ever been conservative, and, as we think, rather shirked the courage of its own convictions, in refusing to give any general definition."

After quoting expressions of opinion on the subject, from the proceedings of several jurisdictions, he sums up as follows:

"In view of the above, and calling to my mind some of the many passages of the Ritual, as follows: 'The Immaculate Word,' 'The human skull resting on the Word of God,' 'The lesson by the Senior Warden', 'The ascension scene,' 'The Prelate's address,' 'The presentation of the baldric,' and finally, 'The entire of Malta,' I give my answer by stating 'a full belief in the Apostles' Creed, which we recite upon occasions of public worship.'"

The only dispensation issued permitted balloting on a petition a few days before the full time had elapsed. He says further:

"Several dispensations were asked for the purpose of attending divine worship, but I did not deem it necessary to grant them, as this is strictly a Templar duty, and I do not believe that the laws contemplate the asking of permission to attend to the necessary duties of the Order."

If we understand the Grand Encampment law, and it seems to be perfectly plain, the only "Templar *duty*" provided for is a funeral, and Commanderies cannot appear in public for other purposes without the consent of the Grand Commander. We are assuming in this case that the Sir Knights desired to attend in a body, and if we are in error our criticism is of no effect.

The Christmas Toast received general attention and seven Commanderies observed Ascension Day by attending Divine service. Five Commanderies were officially visited and he is pleased to report that peace, harmony and brotherly love appear to prevail, and the Commanderies are in a healthful and prosperous condition. Public installations are commended as being of great benefit to the Order and tending to promote a courteous and manly bearing, which is so necessary for a uniformed body of men to observe. A conjoint public installation of the officers of a Commandery and the officers of an Eastern Star Chapter is noted, which we fancy will cause a raising of eyebrows by some of the "Mutuals." The ladies of the Chapter set up a supper and the Sir Knights are that much ahead. We should be right well pleased to participate in such an occasion, but are afraid that "it will be never so long first," judging from the growth of the O. E. S. in our jurisdiction.

The Grand Treasurer reports his cash balance as being $561, a slight loss during the year.

As a matter of course, a set of spirited resolutions on the

Turkish atrocities were adopted. We think that our Montana fratres mean business on this line, as Frater Hedges was made Grand Commander, and the consequent sacrifice of the salary attached to the office of Grand Recorder, which office he has held ever since the Grand Commandery was first instituted, shows that he has not been "talking for Buncombe." We bespeak a full measure of success for his efforts. We cannot but help expressing our hearty approval of one of his early official acts, which was re-appointing the Committee on Correspondence.

A fine portrait of Past Grand Commander Neill looks away from the title page of the proceedings, which also contain a 17 page sermon in verse, delivered before Helena Commandery on the Sunday following Ascension Day.

Our esteemed Frater Cornelius Hedges serves up the Report on Correspondence, which fills 87 pages, and treats us to an entertaining account of what he has found of interest in the proceedings of 41 Templar Grand Bodies. He still keeps us in doubt as to the number of reports he has prepared, beg pardon, we should have said *written*, for extracts and quotation marks no more appeal to the eye than did the sound of tools make itself manifest to the ear during the building of King Solomon's Temple. Well, some folks can do that kind of work, but we are not of that kind and have to dish up what we can cook.

The subject of Palestine and its redemption crops out on nearly every page and it certainly is becoming a more vital question as the years go by.

He is rather in favor of having the Grand Encampment a peripatetic body, and well says, in reviewing California:

"On patriotic principles, we like to see these World's Fairs and Templar reunions, that bring together the people from different parts of the country to become better acquainted, and to learn of the attractions and resources of different parts of our great common country. We wish our people spent more in travelling in our own territory and less abroad. We are decidedly opposed to the Templars taxing themselves for years to build a great temple in Washington, that they would only need to occupy once in three years for a single week. Wouldn't it be better to secure some large park near some central part of the country, easily accessible, and let each Grand Commandery have a portion of the space to adorn and equip with conveniences, as their means and taste would suggest."

Under Georgia, we find the following, which we can endorse:

"There never was a constitution so much in need of revision as that of the Grand Encampment, and we think that it would be a good thing for the Grand Master to interdict a parade at one Triennial and give a chance for some wholesome and very necessary legislation."

North Carolina for 1896 receives a very cordial notice, and we quote what he has to say about the first thing that naturally caught his eye in our proceedings:

"Instead of giving us the 'frontispiece' of the Grand Commander, we find where it should be, a notice that the time for the next Grand Conclave had been changed to avoid collision with the Baptist Convention. Did they think that the latter would need all the water in the vicinity?"

We are constrained to say that the water question is the one that will give us the least trouble.

Our Grand Recorder is not passed by, as will be seen.

"Brother Munson continues to earn a $500 salary on $50 a year as Grand Recorder. The ladies of Newbern came in for thanks for courtesies and kind attentions, but Brother Munson was too busy or modest to say anything about it."

We were not privileged to be present on the occasion, as Fratre Hedges discovered, but it has been intimated that "Brer" Munson, who is no "tenderfoot" when it comes to giving thanks to the gentler sex, was busy nursing some *feet* that had been traversing something we occasionally hear spoken of, as the "burning sands."

We regret our inability to tarry longer with Frater Hedges, but the waning light admonishes us that we must to bed, and hoping that October of the coming year will bring a meeting with him in Pittsburgh, we lay Montana on the other end of the shelf.

Eight Commanderies, 348 Knights; gain 25.

Sir Cornelius Hedges, Helena, Grand Commander and Committee on Correspondence.

Sir Edward D. Neill, Helena, Grand Recorder.

Next Conclave, Helena; date not announced.

NEBRASKA.

TWENTY-FOURTH ANNUAL CONCLAVE.   Omaha, April 16th, 1897.

SIR CHARLES B. FINCH, R. E. Grand Commander.

The Grand Officers were present with one exception and 19 Commanderies were represented. The representative of North Carolina was among the 15 credited with being present.

After an address of welcome from the Eminent Commander of
the local Commandery, to which the Grand Commander made a
fitting response, they got down to work. The Grand Commander
is not able to report any phenomenal increase of the Order during
the year past, light crops and financial depression not being
conducive to a growing membership. He is disposed to get all
the satisfaction possible out of the state of affairs, however, holding that:

"These conditions are the fertile soil out of which bloom and blossom
the genuine, true-hearted knighthood. We turn away gladly from these
material discouragements, and fix our eyes upon the hearts of men. Trials
which are common to all arouse the deepest sympathies of our nature, and
weld into a more perfect bond the chain of our fraternal fellowship. Thus
it is that the primary principles which prompted our order are brought into
greater prominence, and made, as never before, the ruling motives of our
lives. Material conditions are transient and the cloud of adversity will
soon lift its gloom."

Fraternal dead receive due notice, their own official circle
remaining unbroken. Numerous dispensations were issued for the
usual variety of causes, all of which passed muster, as did the
several decisions reported. Official visitation was indulged in to
a limited extent.

A glowing account is given of their Triennial experience. The
only unpleasant feature was the refusal of the city authorities to
let them pitch their tent on Copley Square, as had been previously
arranged, but they very gracefully acquiesced in the demands of
a "fin de siecle" civilization and in place of an unconventional
canvas dwelling took up their abode in a five-storied brown-stone
front, where Nebraska hospitality was dispensed to all who favored
them with a call.

Their financial condition is such that the Grand Commander
directed that no report on Correspondence be prepared, and he
also recommended that during the three years preceding the
Triennial a fund be accumulated, if practicable, to meet the
necessary expense of these reunions, believing that they "are
worth more to us by far than all their cost in time and money."

The Grand Commandery funds appear to be $1,121; subject to
a loan of $1,600; which looks as if there would be no Report on
Correspondence the coming year. There was a good amount of

business before the Conclave, but it was of a local nature solely. The Inspector presented a full report, largely in tabular form, but as economy is the word, the office is discontinued until brighter times.

Thirty-two pages of the proceedings are given to a catalogue of the proceedings of other Grand Commanderies to be found in their library. We commend the efforts of Grand Recorder Bowen to procure full and complete files of these works, knowing that the result of his labors will be appreciated more and more each year.

No Report on Correspondence.

A fine steel engraved portrait of Grand Commander Finch adorns the proceedings.

Twenty-three Commanderies, 1,712 Knights; gain 56.

Sir Richard P. R. Miller, Lincoln, Grand Commander.

Sir William R. Bowen, Omaha, Grand Recorder, (re-elected.)

Sir William T. Whitmarsh, Norfolk, Chairman of Committee on Correspondence.

Next Conclave, Lincoln, April 27th, 1897.

NEW HAMPSHIRE.

Thirty-seventh Annual Conclave.   Concord, September 29th, 1896.

Sir Daniel C. Roberts, R. E. Grand Commander.

All of the Grand Officers responded at roll-call, but four of the eleven subordinate Commanderies were unrepresented, which seems a litle strange considering their comparative nearness to the city where the Conclave was held.

The Grand Commander gives, in a very readable manner, a full account of his official acts, which with his various recommendations fills 16 pages.

He reports a fair degree of growth and harmonious relations at home and abroad. One Commandery has been constituted during the year. Every Commandery was officially visited and courtesy and hospitality appear to have been dispensed with a lavish hand. He believes that the inspecting officer should present such criticisms as he may deem proper, if the occasions are to be made of any value to the bodies visited.

He is a non-believer in perpetual jurisdiction, and we quote his views with approval:

"Where rejection was for causes affecting moral character the time should be long enough for a man to make a new record for himself. In cases where a Companion, whose application has been rejected for causes not affecting his moral character, moves into a new jurisdiction, unreasoning spite might follow him to his unjust detriment. In such case I think that the matter of waiver ought not to require a unanimous vote, and that an appeal to the Grand Commandery to set aside the non-waiver would be a reasonable remedy."

Twelve of the thirteen dispensations permitted public appearance in uniform for various purposes, divine service being responsible for only three of them. The only request to ballot out of time was denied. He recommends that the Grand Representative's commissions expire with the triennial of the Grand Encampment, in order to conform with a growing usage.

Nearly all of the Commanderies have provided themselves with a U. S. flag, in conformity with a recommendation adopted at the last annual Conclave. We know that our Fratre Smith of Illinois will be greatly pleased to learn of this.

Every Commandery in the jurisdiction and the Grand Commandery turned out to escort the Grand Lodge of the State on the occasion of a corner-stone laying. It was the most noteworthy parade of the Commanderies that has ever been held, largely exceeding in numbers any previous assemblage of Sir Knights under the banner of the Grand Commandery. This reviewer felicitates himself on having been present on this occasion and his thanks are due and tendered for the lavish hospitality enjoyed.

In closing, the Grand Commander well says:

"There is a measureless blessing in the fellowship of loving kindness; it makes the world wider and warmer and gives a better zest to human life. The Order of Knights Templars stands for this to-day. as always. It stands for unwearied zeal in a brother's cause, and a benevolence as universal as the benediction of Him whose cross we wear."

Business light and purely of a routine nature.

The Grand Treasurer reports a slight decrease in the funds, the amount now being $1,154.

The Code of Regulations proposed at the last Conclave was adopted.

The retiring Grand Commander was presented with the usual

jewel and his portrait embellishes the proceedings as a frontis-piece.

The Report on Correspondence, by Sir Knight A. S. Wait, fills an even hundred pages, 42 Grand Commanderies receiving atten-tion and some of them getting a double portion. It goes without saying that it is a sound document and it is no less interesting than its six predecessors.

He does not agree with his brother reviewers in everything, but he differs in such a courteous way that it disarms if it does not convince. He turns over a new leaf at the very outset by an-nouncing his intention of dropping the word "Foreign," as applied to Correspondence, which we heartily commend.

North Carolina for 1896 has courteous notice to the extent of two pages, and he apparently finds nothing that calls for adverse criticism.

Referring to our sojourn in the State he trusts that we will carry away,

" Pleasant impressions of our people as well as of our mountains and valleys, and that by them New Hampshire and North Carolina will find the ties of mutual regard and fraternal sympathy made firmer and more enduring."

We cheerfully own up to the "pleasant impressions" as we must have been born with them, the Granite State being our birth-place and residence for upwards of a generation. As to the ties between our native State and our adopted one, we are sure that they only need cultivation to become as informal as the traditional hospi-tality between the two Carolinas, the only uncertainty being as to which Governor would be the more impatient.

We find nothing in Fratre Wait's report to join issue on and lack of space prevents our quoting much that meets our approval and is well worthy of a place. In closing he sees but one question likely to produce discussion in the Templar world, and that is the effect upon Templar standing of non-affiliation in the Lodge and Chapter, which he hopes will be finally settled in a manner to ensure future harmony. So mote it be.

Eleven Commanderies, 2,060 Knights; gain 67.

Sir John Hatch, Greenland, Grand Commander.

Sir George P. Cleaves, Concord, Grand Recorder, (re-elected.)
Sir Albert S. Wait, Newport, Chairman of Committee on Correspondence.

Next Conclave, Concord, Sept. 28th, 1897.

NEW JERSEY.

THIRTY-EIGHTH ANNUAL CONCLAVE.   Trenton, May 12th, 1896.

SIR EDWARD MILLS, R. E. Grand Commander.

All of the Grand Officers were present and representatives from 13 Commanderies, with the usual contingent of past officers and permanent members. We do not discover the name of North Carolina's representative among the 25 who were credited with being present.

The Grand Commander's address fills 22 pages and is a detailed account of his official labors. He reports a busy year and that he has visited every Commandery in the jurisdiction. One Commandery was instituted under dispensation. Several dispensations were issued, permitting public appearance in uniform for the purpose of attending religious services, and he recommends that:

"This Grand Commandery recognize Good Friday, Easter Sunday and Ascension Day as Templar Days, and that the Subordinate Commanderies may appear in full Templar uniform for the observance of appropriate ceremonies on these days without special Dispensation for that purpose."

No action of the Grand Commandery can take away from the Grand Commander his sole prerogative of saying when and where Commanderies may appear in public.

Another case a little out of the usual order was to permit a Commandery to hold conclaves without its Warrant, the Eminent Commander having, for its safe keeping, taken it with him when he went to the Triennial and lost it during the festivities. The Grand Commander very properly says that the Warrant should not be taken from the immediate territory over which it holds authority. The Warrant was eventually found and returned to its rightful owners.

He has some vigorous words of condemnation in relation to a request for permission to receive and act on the petition of a candidate who, as investigation developed, had not been exalted at the time the request was made. Of course the request was denied and the action of the Commandery declared irregular, which is none too strong a term.

A full account is given of their trip to the Triennial and the recommendation made that a committee be appointed to arrange for the coming one.

The death is announced of Sir Charles G. Hoar, Past Grand Generalissimo.

Several pages of the address are taken up with the correspondence and orders relating to the Commandery whose Charter was ordered arrested at the last annual Conclave. The Commandery in question appealed to the Grand Encampment, which decided that the Grand Commandery was in the right in the matter, and after a lengthy correspondence, the Commandery still remaining obdurate, the Grand Commander arrested its Charter and ordered that it be declared forfeited. Aside from this unpleasantness, the Grand Commander reports harmony as prevailing and that the order is in a prosperous condition.

The other Grand Officers who have made visits of inspection present full and satisfactory reports, and it would appear that banquetting hospitalities had not fallen into disuse in this jurisdiction.

A portrait of Sir James McCain, Past Grand Commander appears as a frontispiece.

The Grand Treasurer reports that the funds in his hands have increased a goodly amount during the year, amounting now to $1,408.

The Commandery working under dispensation was granted a Charter. The Grand Captain General was instructed to prefer charges against the members of the contumacious Commandery and a committee was appointed to serve the papers and take testimony.

The Report on Correspondence is the fifteenth that has been fathered by Grand Recorder Charles Bechtel. He has filled 61 pages with a considerate notice of the proceedings of 41 jurisdictions. He announces that he has been aided by Sir Peter McGill and very modestly says that any improvement noticed should be credited to Sir Knight McGill. Putting new wine into old bottles is not generally commended and we hope that there may be no disastrous results in this case. There is nothing to indicate the paternity of the various portions of the review and we are at a loss to identify the individual handiwork of the reviewers. They apparently believe that there should be more work and less play at the Triennial, as witness their conclusion:

"There should be some rule adopted that would prevent these large gatherings from interfering with the business of the Grand Encampment. We make this suggestion to the wiser heads of the Grand Encampment, in order that they may devise some means by which business could be transacted."

As in previous reports from this jurisdiction, opinions are so scarce that we find nothing to fall out about and pass on to other fields of warfare. Under Iowa he says: "Keep poking us up, and we will smite, and powerfully at that." We expect that we shall want to run next year, sure.

Sixteen Commanderies, 1,736 Knights; gain 117.

Sir Robert Dingwell, Newark, Grand Commander.

Sir Charles Bechtel, Trenton, Grand Recorder, (re-elected,) and Chairman of Committee on Correspondence.

Next Conclave, Trenton, May 11th, 1897.

NEW YORK.

SIR HORACE A. NOBLE, R. E. Grand Commander.

The Grand Officers were all at their posts and 58 Commanderies had representatives present. Thirty Grand Representatives, including North Carolina's, were introduced by the Grand Senior Warden and welcomed by the R. E. Grand Commander.

The Mayor of Utica tendered the Grand Commandery the freedom of the city in an eloquent and humorous manner and a representative of Utica Commandery extended a Knightly welcome. The Grand Commander made a felicitous response and then delivered his address, which gives a succinct account of his official actions.

He pays a fraternal tribute to the memory of Sir Thomas C. Chittenden, Past Grand Commander, and briefly mentions other Knightly dead of his own and sister jurisdictions.

Only one decision was called for, but a large number of dispensations were issued for various purposes, all of which were passed without comment by the Committee on Jurisprudence.

He notes a material increase in membership during the year in spite of the business depression and considers that this increase is an evidence of prosperity and zeal among the Commanderies. We are with him on the following:

"The number dropped for non-payment of dues shows that we are not carrying on our rolls a large number of Knights who neglect to pay their dues and I commend the action of the Commanderies in adopting this course. No Sir Knight is honest who does not pay his dues promptly, provided he is able to do so, and in case of his inability to pay, the law provides a way in which they can be cared for by the Commandery."

He considers the question of "Representation in the Grand Encampment" as being an important one, and one that deeply affects their Grand Commandery. It is the old grievance of "Taxation without Representation," which he considers "all wrong and entirely contrary to all rules of consistency and fairness." Like every other question of this kind, there is much that can be said on both sides, and we greatly fear that we shall not be able to congratulate him on seeing the desired change brought about, for many a long year. His statement of the case is not quite correct in one particular, as each Grand Commandery has more than "four votes" in the Grand Encampment. The permanent members are no small factor in the voting strength of a Grand Commandery, and a larger proportion of them are likely to attend the Triennial from the large and wealthy jurisdictions than from the small ones he refers to. We have no hesitation in saying that we believe that the large Commanderies should be represented to a greater extent but we should be strongly opposed to a *per capita* representation alone, and we do not agree with him that if the Grand Commanderies are to have equal representation then they should bear the financial burdens of the Grand Encampment in the same proportion.

The Grand Treasurer reports his cash balance as being $10,433, being a slight gain during the year.

A committee was appointed to,

"Formulate and present to the Grand Encampment at its next Triennial Conclave, an amendment to its Constitution making the taxation of Grand Commanderies equal in amount."

The Report on Necrology, from the pen of Sir and Rev. Cornelius L. Twing, makes an important part of the proceedings and is up to the usual high standard of his former efforts in this line.

The Grand Officers present full reports of their visitations, from which it would appear that they found little to criticise, or if they did thought that a discreet silence was the better part. "Knightly courtesies" are frequently mentioned and our readers know what they are as well as we do.

The proceedings contain fine portraits of Grand Commander Noble and Past Grand Commander Thomas C. Chittenden.

The Report on Correspondence is signed by a Committee, of which Sir Jesse B. Anthony is Chairman, but it would require an affidavit to convince us that the majority of the Committee had anything to do with the preparation of the Report. It is fully abreast of those which have previously emanated from this team and fills 135 pages with a pleasing review of the doings of 43 Grand Bodies, including the Grand Encampment.

North Carolina for 1896 has courteous notice. He looks askance at the dispensation permitting a Commandery "to assist in the rendition of the story of the Reformation," but we shall not join issue with him on that, as there is some doubt about its being a "Masonic occasion." He notes, with commendation, the interest taken by our Fratres in that "noble charity," the Orphan Asylum, which he calls a "grand work."

Reviewing the Grand Encampment he expresses the opinion that the rule requiring that petitions for the Orders should not be balloted on until four weeks after reception should be made arbitrary and no dispensation allowed under any circumstances. Of course he firmly believes in increasing the representation of large Grand Commanderies in the Grand Encampment and has some sound arguments to allay the fears of those who might be disposed to indulge "an unreasonable apprehension of a combination to control." He is quite philosophical over the result, however, saying:

"The majority, however, seem wedded to the old way, and they (at present) control the Grand Encampment."

The Triennial is characterized as "a magnificent success in its festivities and pleasures, but a failure in all other respects," which is without doubt a true bill.

Looking over the field as a whole he sums up as follows:

"The tidings from the several camps are of the most encouraging character, and the reputation of the Order to-day is of a more elevated character than ever before. To maintain its high prestige demands of its followers—from the Sir Knight to the Grand Commander—a strict conformity to the obligations enjoined, obedience to the elevated teachings of Templarism, practical exemplification of the duties of pure charity and beneficence, a correct walk and deportment in harmony with the spirit of Christian Knighthood, and a laudable ambition for its pre-eminence in all those essentials which go to make up a good and successful organization."

The usual statistical tables appear and their completeness makes them well worthy of the space they occupy.

Fifty-eight Commanderies, 11,037 Knights; gain 327.

Sir Arthur MacArthur, Troy, Grand Commander.

Sir John F. Shafer, Albany, Grand Recorder, (re-elected.)

Sir Jesse B. Anthony, Utica, Chairman of Committee on Correspondence.

Next Conclave, Jamestown, September 14th, 1897.

NORTH DAKOTA.

SEVENTH ANNUAL CONCLAVE.   Fargo, June 12th, 1896.

SIR CLARENCE A. HALE, R. E. Grand Commander.

The Grand Officers were present with one exception and all of the Commanderies were represented. We note the name of North Carolina's representative in the list of 19 that stood up and were counted.

The Grand Commander's address fills 16 pages with a detailed account of his official acts. He announces that death has invaded their ranks for the first time since the organization of their Grand Body, Sir Marc Anthony Brewer, Past Grand Commander, having been called to his reward. Fraternal dead of sister jurisdictions receive appropriate mention.

A request to observe the Christmas Toast was sent out and every Commandery reported their compliance with the request.

The Triennial has due mention, a clam-bake being a prominent feature of the courtesies tendered them.

Official visitation was indulged in to quite an extent and a generally satisfactory state of affairs is reported. He recommends that any unexpended funds in the hands of the Triennial Committee be made the nucleus of a fund for the purchase of a Grand Commandery Banner, it being a long felt want.

The Grand Treasurer has kept the funds well up to the amount last reported and now has $504. to his credit.

The Grand Recorder gives a detailed account of what has been done in the work of preparing a "membership register" of the Sir Knights.

Considerable business came before the Conclave, but it was generally of a routine nature. An effort is to be made to have an encampment at the time of the Annual Conclave, with a competitive drill, the successful Commandery to become the custodian of the Grand Commandery Banner, until it is won by some other Commandery. The next Conclave is to be held at "Devil's Lake," which is a suggestive name, to say the least, and we should think that they would be likely to have "a monkey and parrot time."

No Report on Correspondence and no mention of any Committee having been appointed. A portrait of Grand Commander Hale appears as a frontispiece.

Seven Commanderies, 427 Knights; gain 25.

Sir William T. Perkins, Bismark, Grand Commander.

Sir Frank J. Thompson, Fargo, Grand Recorder, (re-elected.)

Next Conclave, Devil's Lake; time not fixed.

OHIO.

Fifty-fourth Annual Conclave.   Dayton, October 14th, 1896.

Sir John P. McCune, R. E. Grand Commander.

All of the Grand Officers were at their posts and only one Commandery was unrepresented. Twenty-nine Grand Representatives responded with courteous greetings as their names were read and we note that North Carolina's was one of the number.

The Grand Commander reports a peaceful year with nothing to disturb the even tenor of their onward progress. The death of Sir H. H. Tatem, Past Grand Commander, is announced in fitting terms, and other fraternal dead, in their own and sister jurisdictions are duly noted.

The only decision reported, holds that an unaffiliated Sir Knight cannot be elected to honorary membership. A dispensation was issued to form and open a new Commandery, and numerous other dispensations are reported in a general way. He declined to permit a Commandery to turn out on Memorial Day, and says:

" As the request to appear in uniform on Memorial Day is made every year and as regularly refused, I am led to suspect that some of our Eminent Commanders are not in the habit of reading out proceedings closely, or they would not ask this identical favor from every Grand Commander. "

Possibly they are more familiar with the parable of the importunate widow and expect by "continual coming" to gain their end.

General permission was given to attend Divine service on Good Friday, Easter and Ascension Day and 39 Commanderies availed themselves of the privilege, eight of them attending on two occasions.

A stirring appeal is made for subscriptions to aid in furnishing the Masonic Home.

Inspection of the Commanderies by some Grand Commandery officer is earnestly advocated, and the following is sound doctrine:

"The benefit to be derived from inspections can but be admitted by us all. The fact that a Commandery is to be visited by an inspecting officer induces special efforts ou the part of those in office in our subordinate bodies. Each will endeavor to further perfect himself in the rendition of his work; the records and the finances will be more closely kept and observed by the proper officers, and more attention given by the Sir Knights to the floor work in conferring of the Orders and the opening of the Commaudery.

Ambition to appear well before the inspecting officer will call for close following of detail which would otherwise be neglected because no particular incentive existed for same. Close attention to the minutest details makes a perfect whole, and thus renders the ceremonies more impressive to the candidate and the meetings more interesting to the members."

The funds in the Grand Treasurer's hands have more than doubled during the year, being now $6,924.

The Commandery that had been working under dispensation was granted a charter. A committee was authorized to make arrangements for representation at the Pittsburgh Triennial. A donation of $1,000 was made to the Masonic Home.

An incomplete report from the Committee on Obituaries has a sad significance as it was being prepared by Grand Prelate T. J. Melish, who died in less than three weeks after the close of the Conclave, at which he was present.

The proceedings appear in their usual attractive form and contain a portrait of Grand Commander McCune.

It being the 50th anniversary of Reed Commandery at Dayton, several of the leading Commanderies of the jurisdiction, accompanied by bands of music, came to town the day before, bringing "their sisters and their cousins and their aunts," and held high carnival, with a grand parade, exhibition drill, reception and ball, a glowing account of which appears in a XVI page "Praeludium."

The Report on Correspondence would make a good-sized volume by itself, for it contains 158 pages and is a comprehensive review of the proceedings of 41 Templar Grand Bodies. Sir Enoch T. Carson reaches his majority with this report, as it is his twenty-first. It is written in his characteristic vein and, as usual, is exceedingly entertaining.

North Carolina for 1896 has critical, but courteous comment, to the extent of three pages. He pulls us up with a round turn in the following:

"The Grand Commander has no right to 'order' a Commandery to appear in public; if he should order, there is no penalty for disobeying the 'order'; 'request' is the extent of his authority."

In the face of such authority we shall have to subside, although we had supposed that a way was provided to discipline a recalcitrant Commandery.

He quotes our notice of his paper on "Androgynal Freemasonry," and styles it "funny." Well, perhaps it was, but you know that laughter and tears are sometimes only different masks for the same emotion, and, by the way, this self-same paper affords a text for a good many pages of his review, as his brother correspondents are keeping him busy answering and explaining. He asks no quarter, however, and is abundantly able to hold up his own end in the warfare, although we fear that he is leading a forlorn hope.

Under Louisiana, he says in regard to Templar vs. Templars:

"We have never entered into or discussed the gramatical part of this question; we have contented ourselves with being associated with such literary characters as Walter Scott, Addison, Gibbon and Turner; in fact, with all the distinguished English literary gentlemen of Europe for the past one hundred years. If they are in error, we feel that it is no disgrace for us to be associated with them."

Under Arkansas, referring to a subject that has been more or less prominent for many years, he says:

" As for ourselves, we are not advocating any revision of the ritual—we have had enough of that. We would let bad alone, rather than get something worse. We see no impropriety, however, in proper criticisms on the ritual; they may be of benefit, perhaps, in time to come, when some properly qualified persons may have the revision placed in their hands."

On the subject of the " Templar's Creed " and the proper definition of the term " Christian religion, " he quotes the Apostles' Creed and says:

" It is our idea that this is a true definition of the Christian religion, as accepted by 96 per cent. of the Christian denominations of the world."

He fears that the Grand Master has been too liberal in granting a warrant to form a Grand Commandery in Indian Territory and forcibly says:

" We regard this as one of the rottenborough Grand Commanderies. There certainly was no occasion for it The total membership, as before stated, is only 113."

Commenting on Frater Coxe's view that the Grand Commandery of Washington had no legal right to add new conditions, in the petition for the Orders, to those prescribed by the Grand Encampment, he says:

"Sorry we cannot agree with Brother Coxe. We believe that it lies with the Grand Commandery to pass upon such matters. They may require the petitioner to say in his petition that he is not engaged in the lottery business, as this is prohibited in some of the States, while in others the business is perfectly legitimate. We do not regard it as a new condition at all, it is simply a police regulation, as it were, for a particular district. We know that there are many States where such a law as that in Washington would not pass or be accepted at all."

It may be well to say that the added condition required that the petitioner should not be " engaged in any manner in the manufacture or sale of intoxicating liquors, "

We find the following in his review of Kentucky:

" Right here we join issue with our venerable brother, and say that 'Sir Knight' is not correct, but 'Sir' Walter Scott is the correct use of the phrase. The 'Sir' expresses the knight, and to say 'Sir Knight' Walter Scott would be incorrect. We know that in this Democratic country of ours (perhaps I should qualify that by saying this once Democratic country

of ours), the phrase Sir Knight has come into common use. It is not
'foreign,' it is American. There are a good many phrases and titles used
in our Order that are not in harmony with what Brother Woodruff says is
Democratic. However, with 'Sir Knight,' although it is incorrect, we
believe that there are sixteen to one in the United States (Populists) in
favor of its use. 'Want of Culture' ".

Time and space require that we bid Brother Carson good-bye
until another year.

Sir Barton Smith, Toledo, Grand Commander.

Sir John N. Bell, Dayton, Grand Recorder, (re-elected.)

Sir Enoch T. Carson, Cincinnati, Chairman of Committee on
Foreign Correspondence.

Next Conclave, Toledo, September 8th, 1897.

OKLAHOMA.

The Grand Commandery was organized and the First Conclave
held at Guthrie on February 10th, 1896.

Representatives of three Commanderies met in the Asylum of
Guthrie Commandery and organized with Past Commander Cassius M. Barnes as presiding officer, who also held the proxy of
Grand Master Thomas. The Warrant having been read, various
committees were appointed and a brief recess taken to enable
them to get in their work. The Committee on Credentials duly
reported and were discharged. Election of officers was next in
course, and Sir Knight Barnes having been elected Grand Commander, was installed and proceeded to deliver an address. Rules
and Edicts reported by the Committee were adopted and then,
upon the invitation of Guthrie Commandery, the Grand Commandery participated in a banquet, which practically completed
the work of the Conclave.

We cordially welcome the new-comer and wish for it a prosperous future.

The proceedings contain a portrait of Grand Commander Barnes.

Three Commanderies, 131 Knights.

Sir Cassius M. Barnes, Guthrie, Grand Commander.

Sir Harper S. Cunningham, Guthrie, Grand Recorder.

Next Conclave, February 2d, 1897.

OREGON.

TENTH ANNUAL CONCLAVE.   Portland, October 8th, 1896.

SIR B. F. LIPPINCOTT, R. E. Grand Commander.

Only one Grand Officer failed to appear and five of the six Commanderies were represented. The Grand Representatives class was well filled, 23 being present. We note that five of them hold double commissions and that the North Carolina fraction was on hand.

The Grand Commander reports prosperity and few official acts, on account of the thorough knowledge of the law possessed by the Oregon Sir Knights and their willingness to obey its mandates. No decisions were called for and only two dispensations are reported. It is noted, with thankfulness, that their membership has not been decreased by death during the year.

A banner has been procured with funds raised by the several Commanderies, assisted by the Grand Commandery, which is to remain in the custody of the Commandery that has the best drill corps, as shown by competition.

Their funds have increased a few dollars since the last report, being now $583.

The business of the Conclave was purely local in character. Labor was suspended at high twelve to partake of the hospitalities of Oregon Commandery in the adjoining banquet hall, and a note by the Grand Recorder indicates that they had something superb.

This jurisdiction falls into line on the matter of having the commissions of Grand Representative run for three years only, terminating with the Triennial.

The proceedings contain portraits of Grand Recorder James F. Robinson and John M. Hodson, Chairman of the Committee on Correspondence, both of whom are Past Grand Commanders.

The Report on Correspondence is a spicy and entertaining review of the proceedings of 37 Templar Grand Bodies and fills 72 pages. It is the seventh effort of Sir John M. Hodson and is in no way inferior to his previous productions.

North Carolina for 1896 has courteous notice. He quotes from Grand Commander Liddell's address, which he styles "vigorous and instructive:"

"On the Christmas observance he talks exactly as we feel. We never knew exactly why we felt so about it, but we half suspect now that it is because we came so near being a Carolinian."

Quoting from the Correspondent he says:

"A paragraph from his conclusion indicates that, in common with ourselves, he was suffering from 'that tired feeling,' but vacation will soon be over and we hope to play with him again next year."

Our yard will always be open to him and we trust that we will find a welcome in his.

He sees no objection to each officer having a copy of that portion of the ritual in which he is concerned, saying, under Iowa:

"We have never known an instance of the 'giving away' of any part of our service, and we have known of many copies and helped make them."

We do not believe that any degree of proficiency in the work can be attained if only one copy of the ritual is allowed in a Commandery, and we believe that few, if any, Commanderies get along with one copy, even if they are prohibited from having more, as is the case in California.

He takes a very common-sense view of the flag question, as follows:

"While we would not vote to make it obligatory, yet the display of a nice Union flag by a Commandery will always make us feel a trifle warmer towards its members."

We also make a place for his views on another live question:

"There is to our mind no real good reason for continuing the law of perpetual jurisdiction. We think that it would be well to fix a reasonable time, say five years, when such control should cease. Why not let it go with the grand representative system into 'innocuous desuetude'?"

He takes no stock in Frater Carson's paper on "Androgynal Freemasonry" and very forcibly says:

"There was never any such stuff in any way connected with any Masonry in America that we ever heard of, and to claim that it could have the least proper application to the innocent 'Order of the Eastern Star,' in which many of the wives and daughters of Masons, who stand the peers of any class of ladies in the world in any points of high character and good sense, is the merest trash, and, in our opinion, unworthy of a place in any Masonic publication."

We regret that we have no further room for the bright and incisive opinions of Brother Hodson, with whose views we are generally fully in accord, and part company with the hope that we may meet in Pittsburgh.

Six Commanderies, 415 Knights; gain 11.

Sir Robert S. Bean, Salem, Grand Commander.

Sir James F. Robinson, Eugene, Grand Recorder, (re-elected.)

Sir John M. Hodson, Portland, Chairman of Committee on Correspondence.

Next Conclave, Eugene, October 14th, 1897.

PENNSYLVANIA.

FORTY-THIRD ANNUAL CONCLAVE.   Scranton, May 26th, 1896.

SIR EDWARD B. SPENCER, R. E. Grand Commander.

All of the Grand Officers were present with representatives from 71 Commanderies. Twenty Grand Representatives were also in attendance, North Carolina's being one of the number.

M. E. Sir Warren LaRue Thomas, Grand Master of the Grand Encampment, was received and welcomed.

The Grand Commander begins his report by saying that it is one of prosperity and progress and that the healthy growth of the past year is no exception to their previous history. Official visitation was indulged in to quite an extent and with very satisfactory results. Numerous dispensations were granted, but those for a certain purpose were conspicuous by their absence and we quote his views regarding them:

"I have refused all applications to ballot upon petitions within the statutory limit or at special Conclaves. None but the most urgent and stringent reasons would have induced me to vary from this rule so wisely and firmly established by my predecessors."

The few decisions called for were readily answered by reference to the law on the points at issue.

The Triennial has brief mention, as he thinks that so much has already been said in relation to the kindly courtesy and hospitality received that it would seem like mere repetition for him to enlarge upon it.

Action is called for in relation to the Pittsburg Triennial and the Armenian persecution calls out some vigorous words of comdemnation.

He notes in fitting terms the ravages made by death during the year, prominent among the number being Sir Grant Weidman, Past Grand Commander.

The Grand Treasurer reports their cash assets as being $2,620., a shrinkage of about one-fifth since his last report.

The following resolution in relation to a matter of growing interest was adopted :

"Whereas, It is the sense of this Grand Commandery that the American flag is an appropriate emblem to be borne by Knights Templar of the United States in parade, therefore,
Resolved, That permission be given to subordinate Commanderies in any parade which they may lawfully make to carry a silk flag of our country of authentic design and such size as the R. E. Grand Commander may designate, and that any rule or regulation of this jurisdiction to the contrary thereof be and is hereby repealed."

The Representative to the Masonic Home presents a detailed report and makes a strong plea for more general and extended contributions to this worthy object, it appearing that less than one-fourth of the Masonic bodies of the State aid in its support.

A Charter was granted to form a new Commandery. A Committee on the Revision of the Constitution reported that they had been counting on the Grand Encampment making clear for them the path which they were to follow, and as little had been accomplished at the last Triennial, the Committee wished for instructions. Evidently the Grand Commandery thought that they "should wait with patience" until the Pittsburgh Triennial for the Committee was continued. If the Grand Encampment does not mend its pace the Committee stand a chance of dying from old age before their work is accomplished.

The proceedings are embellished with a portrait of Grand Commander Spencer.

Sir Lee S. Smith presents his third Report on Correspondence. Forty-four Grand Commanderies and the Grand Encampment pass in review and receive courteous attention to the extent of 63 pages of fine type.

North Carolina for 1895 receives due attention, with lengthy extracts from Grand Commander Cobb's address, and he does not hesitate to suggest a remedy for some of the short-comings noticed. Regarding the decision in relation to the itinerant petitioner for the Orders, he says:

" Decision is correct. And yet we must heave a sigh for the poor fellow who has no home. No matter if he does travel all of the time, it seems strange that he should not have some one place which he would at least call home, where he might at least have a spare collar stored. Truly, 'Be it ever so humble, there's no place like home.' "

Commenting on Frater Carson's paper on "Androgynal Freemasonry," he says:

" For our part we have not now, nor never did have, any sympathy with this side issue. True, the seeds of the disease were wafted into Pennsylvania at one time, but good sense and sound judgment pulled up the early sprouts, and it is now foreign to Keystone State soil. To our mind it was but a lame and weak excuse at best offered to females It was not Masonry, and was only intended to somewhat reconcile our wives, mothers, sisters and aunts to our absence at our Lodge, and in our experience they so considered it and appreciated it accordingly."

We suppose Brother Smith refers to the Order of the Eastern Star. As they were enough alive to have a convocation of the Grand Chapter in November 1895, within six months of the time he was writing the above quotation, we are inclined to think that they did not pull up all of "the early sprouts." They may have been winter-killed, however, and Frater Smith correct in his assumption that they are "foreign to Keystone State soil." Our advice to him, is to "watch out " or they may make it lively for him yet.

Seventy-three Commanderies, 11,218 Knights; gain 275.

Sir Samuel S. Yohe, Easton, Grand Commander.

Sir Mont. H. Smith, Philadelphia, Grand Recorder, (re-elected.)

Sir Lee S. Smith, Pittsburgh, Chairman Committee on Correspondence.

Next Conclave, Easton, May 25th, 1897.

SOUTH DAKOTA.

THIRTEENTH ANNUAL CONCLAVE.   Huron, June 12th, 1896.

SIR FRANK A. BROWN, R. E. Grand Commander.

Ten Grand Officers present and ten Commanderies represented. Seventeen Grand Representatives were on hand, North Carolina's being included in the number.

The Grand Commander presents a full account of his official acts; says the year has been one of great activity and momentous incidents. The Christmas Sentiment was generally observed and he fully endorses the custom. A general attendance upon Divine service upon Easter Day is noted and the hope expressed that Ascension Day may also be observed. There may be a limit to the public church-going capacity of the South Dakota Fratres.

Dispensations and decisions were few and call for no specific mention. We note that dispensations permitting balloting out of time have to be paid for, which may account for their infrequency. The trip to the Triennial has enthusiastic mention and we cannot but admire the respect manifested for the Supreme Body, as set forth in the following:

"The business of the Grand Encampment was of the usual order. Little of importance to the Fraternity was before that Body, but what was before it was handled with wisdom. A full report of the proceedings is in the hands of each of the Commanderies, and I would urge you to become familiar with it and to make its contents known to your several Commanderies."

We should be inclined to substitute *much* for "little," and we are certain that some of the Corps would put "little" before "wisdom."

The Triennial expenditures evidently played havoc with their finances, as the Grand Treasurer's cash has shrunk nearly one-half during the year, being now $679.

A Commandery which had been working under dispensation was granted a Charter. A portrait of Grand Commander Brown adorns the proceedings.

A 72 page Report on Correspondence comes from the pen of Sir Samuel H. Jumper. Thirty-eight Jurisdictions receive courteous attention. The following, from his Conclusion, outlines his campaign, but he has occasionally allowed an opinion to escape.

"We have made no attempt to decide any point or criticise any decision or take part in any discussion. We have used the scissors freely, putting in here and there a few of those beautiful gems of thought which we have found all along the pages of the proceedings."

North Carolina for 1895 has full and courteous mention. He disagrees with Brother Cobb on the jurisdictional question, which is now pretty old, believing that the Encyclopedia agent should have been received by the Commandery he petitioned. Referring to the Christmas Observance, we quote his views about the use of wine on the occasion.

"While we abhor the use of intoxicants to excess we think Bro. Cobb carries temperance a little too far. Pure wine in moderation hurts no one. In Dakota many things that we have are good, but the water is not always the best, and we prefer pure sparkling wine. It warms the brain, cheers the soul and makes the heart glad. Let us have it on Christmas and we will do without it the balance of the year."

He quotes at length from Grand Commander Cobb's address and finds a place for Frater Munson's banquet effusion. He is strongly opposed to balloting on petitions before the full time shall have elapsed and we quote one of his numerous forcible expressions on the subject, which appears under North Dakota:

"We do not like to criticise the action of Bro. Hare, but we do believe this power of granting such dispensations should be used as little as possible. Men have a whole life time to become Templars. They will think more of the Order if they find it a little hard to get in. Let them wait the proper time, as nearly all have done before them."

Eleven Commanderies; tabulation of returns incomplete.

Sir James J. Casselman, Huron, Grand Commander.

Sir George A. Pettigrew, Flandreau, Grand Recorder, (re-elected.)

Sir Samuel H. Jumper, Aberdeen, Committee on Correspondence.

Next Conclave, Mitchell, June 11th, 1897.

TENNESSEE.

THIRTY-FOURTH ANNUAL CONCLAVE.   Jackson, May 14th, 1896.

SIR ORION L. HURLBUT, R. E. Grand Commander.

The Grand Commandery was escorted by Jackson Commandery and visiting Commanderies to one of the city churches, where they were eloquently welcomed by Sir Robert W. Haynes, Deputy Grand Commander, in behalf of Jackson Commandery and the citizens generally. After the Grand Commander had made courteous acknowledgement the usual devotional services were observed. It being Ascension Day they were made more than usually impressive by the magnificient music rendered, the large audience in attendance and an eloquent sermon delivered by Sir and Rev. W. A. Freeman, Grand Prelate. On the conclusion of the services the Grand Commandery was escorted to the Masonic Temple and began the labors of the Conclave.

Twelve Grand Officers were present with the representatives of thirteen Commanderies. Twenty-four Grand Representatives in attendance were introduced and cordially received as a respectful courtesy to the Grand Jurisdictions they had the honor to represent. The position apparently means something in this jurisdiction and we are pleased to see that North Carolina was represented on this occasion.

A Committee representing the Grand Commandery of Virginia was received with the honors due the exalted rank of its members.

The Grand Commander's address is quite brief but to the point. He says that the past year has been a continuation of the period of waiting for better times begun three years ago, and that in point of numbers they have barely held their own. He gets all possible satisfaction out of this state of affairs, as witness the following:

"This period of waiting has not been without its advantages   There is a strength that is born of waiting that is more stable than that of rapid, pushing progress, and I feel that this strength is ours, and that when the dawn of a new era of prosperity, already brightening the Eastern sky, becomes bright day, that we shall resume our forward movement with tried and tested columns, bearing our banner—the Banner of the Cross—onward and upward toward the summit of our ambition, the final approval of the Great Captain of our Salvation. "

He must have been a " hard-money " man to be looking for a brightening in " the Eastern sky. "

Dispensation business was light and we note that he declined to permit a Commandery to confer the Order of the Temple on Sunday.

A plea is made for an enlargement of the Widows and Orphan's Home, which is now sheltering an even hundred and has 43 applicants for admission, none of whom can be accommodated.

Of course the Triennial comes in for mention, but he considers it beyond the power of words to attempt any description of the entertainment features.

The Grand Treasurer reports his cash balance as being $858,

subject to some outstanding bills, being a decided improvement in their finances during the year.

A Charter was granted to several petitioners who desired to form a new Commandery.

The Grand Commandery has put itself on record in unmistakable terms on the liquor question, and any Sir Knight engaged, as principal or employee, in the business of manufacturing or selling spirituous or malt liquors, to be used as a beverage, must quit the business or be subject to suspension or expulsion, after the offence has been duly proved. Commanderies failing to strictly enforce this law will be liable to a forfeiture of Charter.

A fine portrait of Grand Commander Hurlbut faces the title page.

"Between" is an account of a musical entertainment and banquet in honor of the visiting Sir Knights, in which the ladies were excluded. Brother Foster apparently felt that his pen could not do the subject justice and made use of the account of a professional news-gatherer, whose adjectives gave out by the time he had reached the home stretch and led to the criticism that "the half had not been told."

The Report on Correspondence is the second one fathered by Sir W. F. Foster, Grand Recorder, and is a careful and entertaining review of the proceedings of 44 Templar Grand Bodies, several of them getting a double portion, and fills 102 pages.

North Carolina for 1895 has courteous notice and we doff our chapeau to Brother Foster for his kindly words of commendation. He notes that their Grand Representative did not attend the Conclave and all that we can say is, that he has not been seen at the annual conclave for many years.

Our Grand Commander's decision on the itinerant's petition meets with approval, and Brother Munson's "appetizing foot-note" is quoted in full.

Culling an extract from his conclusion we lay aside this interesting report, with the remark, "them's our sentiments."

"Well, our Report is finished, 'copy' is about to go to the printer, and we confess that the work is not at all satisfactory to this writer. But we are consoled by the remark of a kind but somewhat cynical friend, who says, 'O don't bother! nobody will read it anyhow.' His remark is too true. The fact is to be greatly regretted that these Reports upon Correspondence, prepared by the patient thought and study of some of the most competent writers in America, are not more accessible to the entire membership of the Order, and more highly prized by them as of great value for the condensed information which they contain. "

Fifteen Commanderies, 1,090 Knights; gain 25.

Sir Robert W. Haynes, Jackson, Grand Commander.

ᛐ Sir Wilbur F. Foster, Nashville, Grand Recorder, (re-elected,) and Correspondent.

Next Conclave, Clarksville, May, 1897. Date not fixed.

TEXAS.

Forty-second Annual Conclave.   San Antonio, April 22d, 1896.

⟋ Sir John McDonald, R. E Grand Commander.

Only one Grand Officer failed to be present and 25 of the 31 Commanderies were represented. It does not appear to have been a good year for Grand Representatives, as only 13 were reported in attendance, and we fail to find the name of North Carolina's, although credited to the city in which the Conclave was held.

The usual public ceremonies took place in the Opera House before the Conclave was opened, a welcome being extended by a resident Sir Knight in behalf of the city, and the Grand Prelate, Sir J. C. Carpenter, delivering an elevating address on the beneficence of a divine and overruling Providence.

The Grand Commander begins his address with the welcome news that they have reason to rejoice in the prosperity of the Order which has marked the past year.

He announces the death of Sir James Sorley, Past Grand Commander and Past Grand Captain General of the Grand Encampment, a special Conclave of the Grand Commander having been called to attend his funeral.

Not being able to officially visit all of the Commanderies he appointed an extensive staff of deputies, who made due report, showing that, almost without exception, the Commanderies are in prosperous condition.

He decides that it is not obligatory on the Sir Knights to attend the Christmas Observance, it being "a recommendation of a Committee, not an order from the M. E. Grand Master."

His report indicates that they had an enjoyable time at the Triennial, a good-sized delegation having attended.

Twenty of his thirty-one dispensations permitted balloting out of time and the balance allowed public appearance in uniform, escort duty being slightly in the lead of attendance upon Divine service.

They are well off financially, as the Grand Treasurer reports $2,156 in his custody, which is an increase of nearly fifty per cent. during the year.

V. E. Sir Henry B. Stoddard, Grand Generalissimo of the Grand Encampment, was announced and having been received with the honors due his exalted rank, was introduced as the representative of the M. E. Grand Master.

A Committee was appointed to procure and present suitable jewels to the two oldest Past Grand Commanders, Sir Robert M. Elgin, Correspondent, being one of those honored. An appropriation of $1,000 was also made to the Masonic Widows and Orphan's Home.

Having learned of the death of Sir Francis Jewett of Lowell, Mass., to whom the Texas Fratres were indebted for many courtesies during the Triennial, appropriate resolutions were adopted and copies ordered forwarded to his Commandery and the Grand Commandery of Massachusetts.

Sir Robert M. Elgin, as Chairman, presents an excellent Report on Correspondence, which fills 63 pages, and is the result of his "wading through the Proceedings" of 40 Grand Jurisdictions. North Carolina for 1895 has courteous mention and he sees indications "that the Sir Knights of the Old North State are zealous and fully alive to the interests of the Order."

We are more than glad to learn of his kindly feelings for us, as evinced in the following, and wish he would come up and let us have a look at him.

"North Carolina is a sort of grand-mother to us and we feel more than ordinary interest in anything pertaining to the State. It was the birthplace of our mother and of her ancestry away back in colonial times, and memories of early childhood are associated with things of which she told us about her native State."

He approves Grand Commander Cobb's decision on the "so-journer" question.

There is much in this report that we would like to use, but contenting ourself with a portion of his conclusion we will say farewell for another year:

"We are fond of discussion, but averse to controversy; a lover of wit, but opposed to sarcasm, and while we may sometimes have to differ with our friends, not unfrequently love those best with whom we least agree upon particular points. So, with good will and fraternal feelings to all, will close with the hope that we may all be spared to meet again in this arena next year."

Thirty-one Commanderies, 2,129 Knights; gain 49.

Sir J. F. Brinkerhoff, Waco, Grand Commander.

Sir Robert Brewster, Houston, Grand Recorder, (re-elected.)

Sir Robert M. Elgin, Houston, Chairman of Committee on Foreign Correspondence.

Next Conclave, Houston, April 21st, 1897.

VERMONT.

FIFTY-FOURTH ANNUAL CONCLAVE.   Burlington, June 9th, 1896.

SIR SILAS W. CUMMINGS, R. E. Grand Commander.

Three Grand Officers failed to put in an appearance, but all of the Commanderies were represented and no less than 32 Grand Representatives, North Carolina's included, added dignity to the occasion, if any was needed.

The Grand Commander extends congratulations on a largely increased membership and the existing peaceful relations among themselves and with sister jurisdictions.

Fraternal dead receive appropriate mention, their own official circle being unbroken.

A full report is given of their Triennial experience, which appears to have been a complete success, and the hospitality and courtesies received "have left memories the sweet fragrance of which will ever remain with us."

Official visitation had its full share of attention and a glowing account is given, much being found to commend and little, if anything, to condemn. Banqueting hospitalities were universal, the only variation noticed, being that sometimes they preceded instead of followed the inspection ceremonies. We consider his summing up worthy of quoting:

"The highest degree of efficiency is found in those Commanderies where the strictest discipline is maintained and military bearing is enforced.

The memorizing of the Ritual being first thoroughly accomplished, which I have found in most Commanderies, I would strongly recommend and urge upon each Eminent Commander, the great importance of more frequent drills; and don't be afraid of being called a martinet, because you exact strict discipline, while the Commandery is at work in its Asylum, as well as when on duty in public.

To the members of our Subordinate Commanderies, I would appeal for a larger attendance on our regular stated conclaves. It is a duty you owe to yourselves and your officers, even if it requires the overcoming of inertia, or, at times, a sacrifice of personal comfort."

Several dispensations were issued but the details are not given. The usual general permission was given to appear in uniform on Memorial Day as an escort to other organization observing the day.

No decisions were called for, as no questions arose that the laws did not plainly answer.

The Grand Treasurer reports $873 on hand, their funds having shrunk about one-third during the year.

A petition was presented for a dispensation to form a new Commandery and the request was granted after due investigation.

A portrait of Grand Commander Cummings appears as a frontis-piece.

Sir Kittredge Haskins presents his third Report on Correspond-ence, in which he has reviewed the proceedings of forty-two Grand Jurisdictions, including the Grand Encampment, the result filling 78 pages. Like his former efforts, it is a discriminating and courteous production and well repays a close perusal.

North Carolina for 1895 has due attention, with kindly mention for the Correspondent.

He has no use for the dogma of "perpetual jurisdiction," and is a firm believer in public appearance in uniform on every proper occasion. As a matter of course he is for the flag every time, but we are not going to quarrel with him about that, or about any-thing else for that matter.

Ten Commanderies, 1,458 Knights; gain 62.

Sir Robert J. Wright, Newport, Grand Commander.

Sir Warren G. Reynolds, Burlington, Grand Recorder, (re-elected.)

Sir Kittredge Haskins, Brattleboro, Chairman of Committee on Correspondence.

Next Conclave, Burlington, June 8th, 1897.

VIRGINIA.

SEVENTY-FOURTH ANNUAL CONCLAVE.   Richmond, November 26th, 1896.

SIR JOHN T. PARHAM, R. E. Grand Commander.

Ten Grand Officers present and eighteen Commanderies represented. Sixteen Grand Jurisdictions were also represented, North Carolina being one of the number.

The Grand Commander announces that the Order is in a prosperous condition with harmony prevailing, their difference with Tennessee, in regard to jurisdictional rights, having been settled satisfactorily.

Their official circle was broken during the year by the death of Sir and Rev. George W. Dame, Grand Prelate. In accordance with the request of the Grand Commander, Dove Commandery escorted the Grand Lodge on the funeral occasion.

He finds that some of the Commanderies are dissatisfied with the law requiring officers of Commanderies to be elected without nominations and recommends that it be so modified as to leave it optional with the Commanderies to elect with or without nominations.

Ten of his twelve dispensations permitted balloting "on petitions for the orders, without waiting the regular time of one month." Only two decisions reported, which are of local interest only.

The Grand Treasurer's cash balance is $63, being about one-fifth of the amount reported last time. We note a special donation of $200 to the Masonic Home Library, which cuts quite a figure in the expenditures.

An interesting report on Education at the Masonic Home is presented, which gives a good idea of the grand work being accomplished by this worthy institution. The usual full reports also appear of visitations by the "staff" to the several Commanderies.

The committee, to whom was referred the Grand Commander's address, approved his recommendation that the Commanderies be allowed to use their discretion in regard to nominating officers before election and the Grand Commandery made the desired change in the law. Regarding the dispensations issued, the committee say:

"We would suggest that, in our opinion, dispensations for the conferring of orders without waiting the specified time required by law, should be granted only after mature deliberation and investigation, and with the conviction that they are essentially necessary. "

The "Line of Knights, " to use a Maryland term, were made a committee " to secure quarters and provide entertainment" for the Grand Commandery at the coming Triennial.

No Report on Correspondence appears, nor can one be looked for the coming year, as no Committee was appointed.

Twenty Commanderies, 1,481 Knights; gain 24.

Sir E. H. Miller, Danville, Grand Commander.

Sir James B. Blanks, Petersburg, Grand Recorder, (re-elected.)

Next Conclave, Petersburg, 1897.   Date not given.

WASHINGTON.

NINTH ANNUAL CONCLAVE.   Seattle, June 3d, 1896.

SIR HORACE W. TYLER, R. E. Grand Commander.

The Grand Officers were present with one exception and every Commandery was represented. Twenty-one Grand Representatives were also in attendance, North Carolina's being one of the number.

The Grand Commander presents a very full account of his official labors. Fraternal dead have fitting mention, their own body having sustained no loss during the year. Correspondence and decisions are reported as being light and little worthy of mention. Only four dispensations are reported and none of them relate to balloting.

The Christmas Toast appears to have been generally observed. General permission was given to attend Divine service on Good Friday, Easter and Ascension Day and seven Commanderies report having observed some one of the occasions.

His intention of visiting officially every Commandery bore fruit to the extent of four and the reports indicate a satisfactory state of affairs and an enjoyable time.

He waxes enthusiastic on the flag question and recommends that every Commandery in the jurisdiction procure an American flag as a part of its equipment.

The Grand Treasurer's cash balance is $1,040, being a large increase over the amount last reported.

A committee was appointed to draft resolutions of sympathy with the persecuted Armenians, but we do not find the result of their labors in the proceedings and are in the dark as to the extent of the feeling on the question in this jurisdiction.

A portrait of Grand Commander Tyler embellishes the proceedings.

Sir Yancey C. Blalock, as chairman, presents his fifth Report on Correspondence, which deals with proceedings of 39 Grand Jurisdictions, four of them having a double portion, and fills 122 pages.

It is built on the same lines as his previous efforts and as an expression of the other reviewer's ideas, is a verbatim success, but we find in it very little of Brother Blalock.

North Carolina for 1895 and 1896 is accorded due notice, and we infer from the following that he is not an ardent believer in the Grand Representative system:

"The Grand Recorder recommended abolishing the Grand Representative system, but the committee did not agree with him and the 'farce' is still in vogue in that Grand Jurisdiction."

Under Iowa we find the following, which outlines his line of action:

"Harmony being one of our principles, we think it best to keep quiet on our side of the fence as yet, for we weigh a ton to the square inch when we get 'riled' and possibly might make trouble."

He does not favor giving pro rata representation of Commanderies in the Grand Encampment, according to what follows, quoted from New York:

"We cannot agree with our Frater, as we think that it would be following the example of many secret orders of comparatively recent organization, and besides there are enough members in the Grand Encampment at present.   If an important measure comes up for discussion, and even one member from each State wishes to be heard on the question, when would any business be transacted—take the last Triennial, for instance."

He is evidently a little "riled" when he gets to Frater Carson's views on "female Masonry," and we quote:

"We infer our worthy Sir Knight must have received a severe curtain lecture from some 'female Mason,' or mayhap been refused admission into their 'venerable order.'   We are proud to say that we are a member of the Order of the Eastern Star, and as their principles and teachings are taken from the Holy Bible we fail to see anything 'derogatory to the venerable, dignified Order of Freemasonry' and strenuously object to being called a tramp Mason by a 'crank' who chooses to sit in judgment upon the members of the Order of which he knows almost nothing   We fail to see anything derogatory to any one associating themselves with the wives, sisters, mothers or daughters of Masons, especially when such association is for the purpose of promoting 'Brotherly Love, Relief and Truth, Kindness and Forbearance.'   We are willing our 'worthy and venerable' frater should have his opinions and state them, but when he calls us such names and consigns us to such oblivion, woman-like, we will have something to say, and almost wonder if our Brother ever had mother, wife, sister or daughter."

We are more than glad to see such a vigorous expression of opinion and it fully makes amends for all that he has not said on other questions.

Nine Commanderies, 592 Knights; gain 7.

Sir George E. Dickson, Ellensburg, Grand Commander.

Sir Yancey C. Blalock, Walla Walla, Grand Recorder, (re-elected,) and Chairman of Committee on Correspondence.

Next Conclave, Tacoma, June 2d, 1897.

WEST VIRGINIA.

TWENTY-SECOND ANNUAL CONCLAVE.   Charleston, May 13th, 1896.

SIR W. H. H. Holswade, R. E. Grand Commander.

Eleven Grand Officers present and ten Commanderies represented.   Eighteen Grand Representatives were introduced and welcomed, but no one responded for the "Tar Heel" jurisdiction.

The Grand Commander presents a detailed statement of affairs, from which it would appear that he had not been idle during his official term.

The Triennial has eloquent mention and he considers the year that witnessed it a memorable one in the history of the Order throughout the land. Their experience at the "Hub" seems to have been a pleasant one.

"Our sojourn in the modern Athens was of the most pleasant nature; in fact, a continual round of receptions and sight-seeings, but as all things earthly have an ending, so had this most pleasant diversion, and, with hearts brim full of unalloyed pleasure and renewed devotion to our order, we departed for our homes."

Wonder if they got "brim full" of that local dainty, known as beans? "There were others" who were apparently "brim full" on that memorable occasion, but of what, we are not prepared to say.

The death of Past Grand Commander Frank Rex is announced and other fraternal dead have brief notice. He reports one Commandery as having been constituted.

An even dozen of dispensations were issued, of which seven permitted public appearance in uniform, only one being for the purpose of attending Divine service.

He very properly decides that a Commandery having granted a demit to a Sir Knight cannot reconsider its action. The demit is the due of the Sir Knight on request, without any action of the Commandery, provided he is square on the books and with no charges standing against him. The discovery after the demit has been granted, that his moral character is not above reproach does not permit of any retractive action. The appearance of a squad of Sir Knights in uniform for an exhibition drill at a charitable entertainment is held as not being sanctioned by law or precedent.

On account of ill health he was obliged to forego the pleasures of official visitation, but the reports of the other Grand Officers, to whom he delegated the duty, are very gratifying, a goodly increase in membership being reported, in spite of the business depression, with peace, tranquility and prosperity prevailing.

The Grand Treasurer reports only $294 to his credit; about one-fifth of the sum he had at the beginning of the year. We suspect that the Triennial and new banner they indulged in caused the shrinkage.

The business of the Conclave was exceedingly light and of local interest only.

The Report on Correspondence is the work of Sir Albert B. White, who has filled 126 pages with a bright and genial review of the proceedings of 43 Grand Jurisdictions. It is his first effort in this line and he has scored a home run on his first strike, but we regret to see that he is not going to the bat again.

Frater White owns up to being a newspaper man, which will account for the ease with which he builds up a report and gives him a great advantage over the average member of the Corps

Joining issue with Frater Moore of Alabama, on attending church service in uniform, he says:

"If the Knight Templar uniform should not be worn to church services, when and where upon this mundane sphere should it be worn? Or should it be a great secret, only communicated to the eyesight of the select few at the base of the triangle? Every one should dislike display for display's sake, but the cross of Knighthood on chapeau, baldric, belt, sword and sleeve enobles the wearer and lifts the uniform out of the class of millinery or clown's dress into the rank of something nobler and higher. If *hoi polloi* do not see but the waving of plume and shining of nickel, so much the worse for the Commandery whose *personnel* is not such as to command respect and cause the onlooker to ask, 'What does this mean?' Too frequent display is to be depreciated, since 'our ways' are imitated and burlesqued by other orders. But service in God's house by those wearing the Templar uniform can never be inappropriate."

In his review of Maine for 1895 he comments as follows on the dispensations issued:

"He was pretty free with his dispensations, one being to 'parade in uniform on occasion of visit to Melrose, Mass.'; another 'to appear in full costume on occasion of visit to Portland, June 2d;' another to appear in uniform 'for an excursion to Green's Landing.' We presume that these were 'Masonic occasions,' for he denied an application 'to appear in uniform in a Fourth of July parade.'"

There is apparently quite a difference of opinion in regard to what are "Masonic occasions," and the Grand Encampment could hardly put in its time to better advantage than in formulating a definition of the term, but we are afraid that the parading days of those now on the stage would be over, long before anything could be expected to issue from this source, judging from the paltry results of their labors at Boston.

Commenting on the Triennial, under Massachusetts, he says:

"The whole Conclave was admirably managed, and if the Grand Encampment failed (as it did) to transact the business that called it together, the fault cannot be laid at the doors of the Massachusetts men."

He lets us know "where he is at" on the flag question, when, having quoted Frater Wait's observation that the display of the national flag by Templar bodies is of questionable appropriateness, he launches forth as follows:

"'Questionable appropriateness'. That is ridiculous. If it isn't appropriate, then why have we a 'Grand Encampment of the United States?' Why not call it the 'Grand Encampment of the no-flag, no country, but the wide universe?'"

We own up to being just obtuse enough to miss the point in his reasoning.

North Carolina for 1895 has courteous notice and we regret that we are not to have the pleasure of further association with Frater White.

Eleven Commanderies, 878 Knights; gain 97.

Sir John C. Riheldaffer, Wheeling, Grand Commander.

Sir Robert C. Dunnington, Fairmont, Grand Recorder, (re-elected.)

Sir W. W. Van Winkle, Parkersburg, Chairman of Committee on Templar Correspondence.

Next Conclave, Wheeling, May 12th, 1897.

WISCONSIN.

THIRTY-EIGHTH ANNUAL CONCLAVE.   Milwaukee, October 13th, 1896.

SIR GEORGE H. Hopper, R. E. Grand Commander.

All of the Grand Officers were present and 23 Commanderies represented. Twenty-one Grand Representatives were in attendance, but we find no one credited to North Carolina.

The Grand Commander presents an interesting account of his official acts. Few dispensations were called for and the majority permitted ballotiug upon petitions for the Orders before the statutory time had elapsed.

He declined to allow a Commandery to act as escort for the Grand Lodge of Masons at a corner-stone laying, referring them to the statutes, which, he held, prohibited such appearance. The Committee on Jurisprudence did not approve his refusal, holding that it was a Masonic occasion and that the request should have been granted, which we think is "horse sense." They approved

his refusal to permit a Commandery to take a portion of their
Asylum furniture to church on Easter. One new Commandery was
formed under dispensation.

We give one of the two decisions reported:

"My understanding of the different rulings is this: All proceedings
pertaining to petitions previous to the balloting are subject to dispensation,
but the ballot cannot be taken at a special meeting."

We are not going to say that the Grand Commander errs in his
understanding of the law, but we judge from our reading that his
view is not generally held and that the balloting under dispensation does generally take place at a special Conclave. In fact, we
do not see how the time could be shortened if it did not, for the
petition would naturally be presented at a stated Conclave, which
would be the only proper one to authorize the Eminent Commander to ask for a dispensation.

An account of their District Rendezvoux occupies a good portion of his report. The Commanderies turned out with three
exceptions and the Grand Commander was present at four of the
five inspections. He seems to be "on the fence" in regard to the
advisability of keeping up the system, although he feels that much
good has resulted from the coming together of the different
Commanderies. He reports that "every different degree of proficiency in work was displayed, from very excellent to extremely
poor," which we have no doubt would be equally applicable to the
results of such an inspection in other jurisdictions.

The funds in the Grand Treasurer's hands amount to $2,188, a
shrinkage of nearly one-half during the year, of which a large
portion went to pay for their Triennial pleasures.

A Charter was granted to the Commandery U. D. The system
of inspection by District Rendezvous was discontinued and the
Grand Commander requested to appoint an Inspector General, as
provided for in the Statutes.

The Grand Commandery dedicated the new Asylum of Wisconsin Commandery and rounded out the occasion with a reception,
banquet and ball, which is styled "an elaborate affair," fully five
hundred Sir Knights being in attendance with more than that
number of ladies.

Sir William C. Swain comes smilingly to the front with his fourteenth Report on Correspondence, his thirteenth effort apparently not having had any baneful effect on his person or stylus. Having been admonished to be brief he has restricted himself to 68 pages, but the doings of 43 Templar Grand Bodies are reviewed in his characteristic and artistic manner, and the brevity of his effort only makes us sigh for more.

Commenting on an Indiana decision that a certain Commandery having duly opened and gone on a pilgrimage to the Triennial, their stated Conclave could not be held in their absence, he says:

"We grant that a Commandery cannot be open in two places at the same time; but, on the other hand what right has a Commandery to be open in another location, and in another State, from that named in its Charter? The Committee on Jurisprudence take the same view, but add, that, the Commandery as a body being absent, 'no business can be lawfully transacted by the members remaining at home.' But we are of opinion that, if a sufficient number, with a proper officer to open, remained at home, the Commandery was not absent as a body."

We reckon he is not far out of the way, if the Charter was left at home, as it should have been, but we have noted that one Commandery took its Charter to the Triennial and lost it during the festivities; it was eventually found and returned, however.

Reviewing Iowa he has the following in relation to Frater Coxe:

"He thinks McCurdy's decision, that a dimitted Templar must apply for affiliation in his own jurisdiction, 'a just one, law or no law.' We differ. He might as well insist that he must dimit, when he removes from a jurisdiction, and affiliate in his new location."

We shall have to side with Frater Coxe on this question. While the Sir Knight is affiliated he is in a "City of Refuge," as it were, but when he becomes a sojourner he is, very properly, made subject to certain domiciliary laws when he desires to settle down again.

The temperance question calls forth the following under Kansas:

"We are also a strong believer in the cardinal virtue of temperance, and have no particular love for a saloon keeper, and wouldn't let him into one of our Masonic bodies; but we wouldn't keep him out by legislation. That is one of the questions safely to be trusted to Subordinates. If it is not, they have no just claim to Charters. Our Grand Bodies are acquiescing in the introduction of politics into the Masonic Fraternity by allowing one clause of our political friends to bring in prohibition and those of us who are not prohibitionists are afraid to say anything against it for fear of being classed with the intemperate."

We do not think that because the politicians make a football of
a moral question our Grand Bodies should therefore be debarred
from legislating in regard to it.

North Carolina for 1896 has full and courteous notice, the Correspondent coming in for the major portion. He is credited with
having "generally sensible ideas" and we cordially reciprocate the
sentiment.

He notes the death of our highly esteemed Frater, George W.
Blount, "whom we several times had the pleasure of greeting
through Correspondence Reports, and who made his mark in that
line."

Replying to our comment on the fac-simile of his signature, he
says:

"Well, we do not brag of our fist, but we do not have the ' pretty type-
writer girl,' because it would interfere materially with our thinking facul-
ties. Girls work that way with some people."

Give us your hand Brother. "One touch of nature makes the
whole world kin," and we bid you farewell from necessity, not
inclination.

Twenty-seven Commanderies, 2,902 Knights; gain 54.

Sir Edmond C. Deane, Racine, Grand Commander.

Sir John W. Laflin, Milwaukee, Grand Recorder, (re-elected.)

Sir William C. Swain, Milwaukee, Committee on Correspondence.

Next Conclave, October 12th, 1897. Place not named.

WYOMING.

NINTH ANNUAL CONCLAVE.   Rawlins, May 20th, 1896.

SIR FRANK M. FOOTE, R. E. Grand Commander.

Nine Grand Officers present and all of the Commanderies represented. Ten Grand Representatives responded at roll call, but
North Carolina's voice was not heard.

The Grand Commander's address is quite brief. Reports a year
of tranquility, with no decisions called for and few dispensations
issued. Lack of time prevented his making the official visits
authorized by the resolution adopted at the last Conclave.

Their cash on hand amounts to $559, a gratifying increase during the year. The Grand Recorder reports a general observance of the Christmas Toast.

The business of the Conclave was light and nothing is reported that suggests comment.

A portrait of Grand Commander Foote appears as a frontispiece.

No Report on Correspondence, nor does any excuse appear for its absence this year, as was the case the last time. As the committee is continued we live in hopes that the void will be filled the coming year.

Five Commanderies, 262 Knights; gain 14.

Sir Adrian J. Parshall, Cheyenne, Grand Commander.

Sir John C. Baird, Cheyenne, Grand Recorder, (re-elected,) and Chairman of Committee on Foreign Correspondence.

Next Conclave, Green River, May 12th, 1897.

CONCLUSION.

"Time with his ever rolling flood" has swiftly borne us toward the end of another reportorial trip and the near approach of the annual Conclave admonishes us to pull for the shore and bring our journey to a close.

As announced in our prefatory remarks, we have reviewed the proceedings of 43 Templar Grand Bodies, Arizona being for 1895 and the others for 1896, Indian Territory not having shown up.

No one can be more fully aware of the imperfections of this review than ourself, but, such as it is, it is sent forth with the hope that it will be worthy of the courteous consideration accorded its predecessors.

And now the time has come to say farewell to our brethren of the Corps of Reviewers, for whom, one and all, we entertain the kindliest feelings, but

> "Farewell is a lonely sound,
> Which always brings a sigh,
> So give us rather, when true friends part,
> The good old words, good bye."

Courteously submitted,

JOHN C. CHASE.

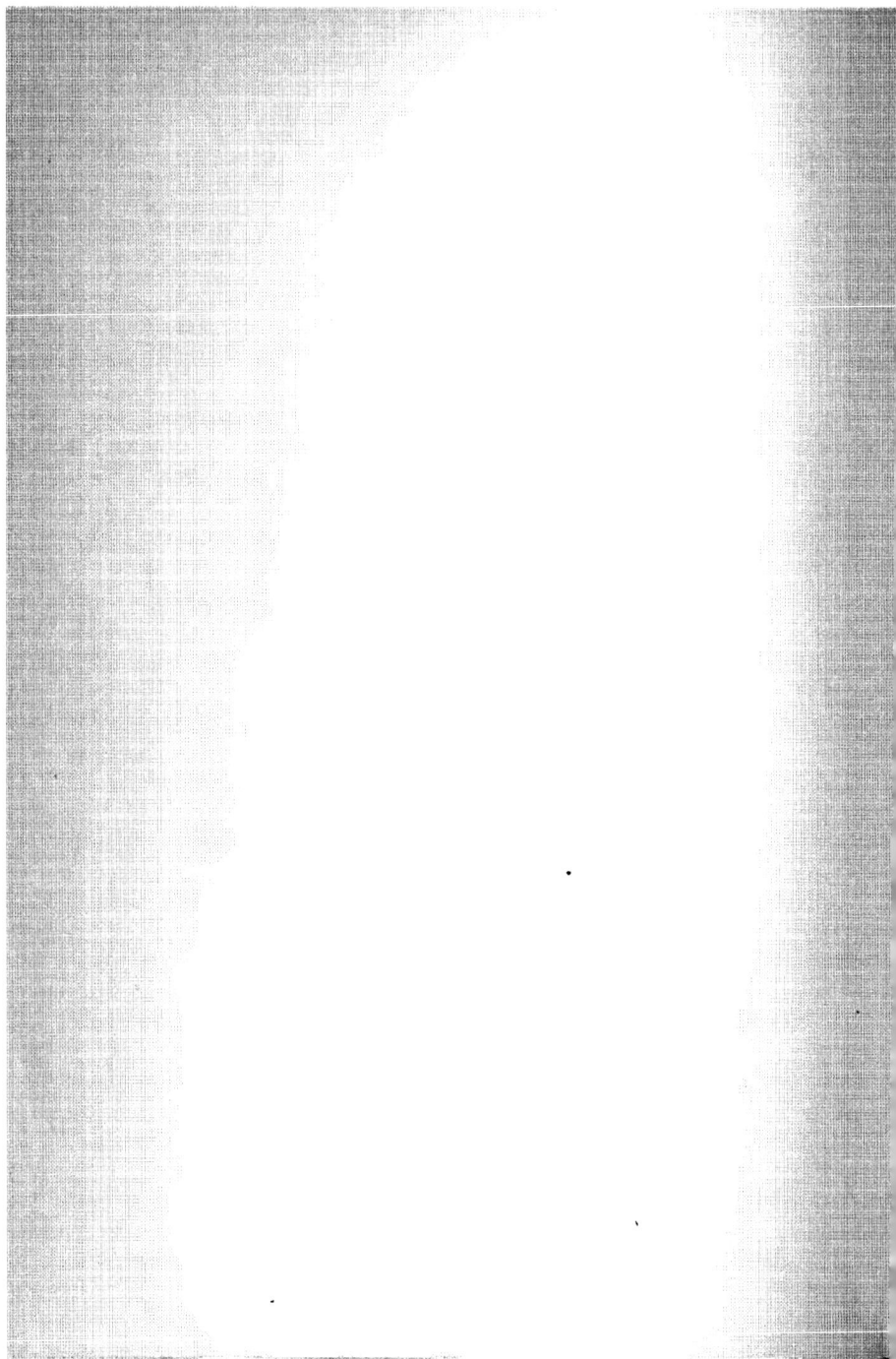

PROCEEDINGS

OF THE

GRAND COMMANDERY

—OF—

KNIGHTS TEMPLAR

OF THE

STATE OF NORTH CAROLINA,

AT ITS

EIGHTEENTH ANNUAL CONCLAVE

HELD AT

RALEIGH,

MAY 18TH AND 19TH, A. D, 1898, A. O. 780.

———•••———

DURHAM, N. C.:

THE EDUCATOR CO., PRINTERS AND BINDERS,

1898.

PROCEEDINGS.

The Grand Commandery of Knights Templar in North Carolina, convened in its Eighteenth Annual Conclave, at the Asylum of Raleigh Commandery No. 4. in the City of Raleigh, Wednesday, May 18th, 1898, at 8:00 p. m., and opened in ample and Knightly form.

COMMITTEE ON CREDENTIALS.

The Grand Commander appointed Sir Knights Ferdinand Ulrich, James Dinwiddie and Robert W. Smith a Committee on Credentials, whose report, as follows, was adopted:

REPORT ON CREDENTIALS.

To the Grand Commandery of the State of North Carolina:

Your Committee on Credentials beg leave to report that they find the following named Commanderies to have paid their dues to this Grand Body, and to be properly represented by their proper officers, as named below.

We also find in attendance and entitled to seats in this Grand Commandery, the officers present and past, as mentioned below.

F. ULRICH,
JAMES DINWIDDIE,
ROBT. W SMITH,
Committee.

GRAND OFFICERS PRESENT.

Joseph H. Hackburn . . . . R. E. Grand Commander.
Mumford D. Bailey . . . . V. E. Deputy Gr. Commander
Walter E. Storm . . . . E. Grand Generalissimo.
William F. Randolph . . . . E. Grand Captain General.
James Southgate . . . . as E. Grand Prelate.
James D. Bullock . . . . E. Grand Senior Warden.
DeWitt E. Allen . . . . E. Grand Junior Warden.
William Simpson . . . . E. Grand Treasurer.
Horace H. Munson . . . . E. Grand Recorder.
John C. Drewry . . . . E. Grand Standard Bearer.
Martin S. Willard . . . . as E. Grand Sword Bearer.
Arthur J. Wills . . . . E. Grand Warder.
Robert H. Bradley . . . . E. Grand Sentinel.

PAST GRAND OFFICERS PRESENT.

Horace H. Munson . . . . Past Grand Commander.
James Southgate . . . . Past Grand Commander.
F. M. Moye . . . . Past Grand Commander.
Walter S. Liddell . . . . Past Grand Commander.
William A. Withers . . . . Past Grand Commander.
Eugene S. Martin . . . . Past Deputy Gr. Commander.
Peter A. Wilson . .   . . Past Grand Generalissimo.

PLANTAGENET COMMANDERY NO. 1—WILMINGTON.

J. C. Munds . . . . Proxy for Em. Commander and Capt. General.
M. S. Willard . . . . Proxy for Generalissimo.

CHARLOTTE COMMANDERY NO. 2—CHARLOTTE.

R. W. Smith . . . . Eminent Commander.
D. E. Allen . . . . Generalissimo.

DURHAM COMMANDERY NO. 3—DURHAM.

James Southgate . . . . Eminent Commander.

RALEIGH COMMANDERY NO. 4—RALEIGH.

D. S. Hamilton . . . . Eminent Commander.
W. H. Bain . .   . . Proxy for Generalissimo.
W. E. Jones . . . . Captain General.

CYRENE COMMANDERY NO. 5—ASHEVILLE.

W. F. Randolph . . . . Proxy for Officers.

PIEDMONT COMMANDERY NO 6—WINSTON.

J. K. Norfleet . . . . .   Proxy for Generalissimo and Captain General.

MT. LEBANON COMMANDERY NO. 7—WILSON.

F. M. Moye . . . . Proxy for Eminent Commander.

IVANHOE COMMANDERY NO. 8—GREENSBORO.

Rev. J. D. Miller . . . . Proxy for Eminent Commander.

ST. JOHN COMMANDERY NO. 10—NEW BERNE.

T. W. Dewey . . . . Eminent Commander.

D'MOLAI COMMANDERY NO. 11—OXFORD.

S. H. Smith . . . . Eminent Commander.

ST. ALDEMAR COMMANDERY NO. 12—ENFIELD.

F. L. Pippen . . . . Proxy for Eminent Commander.
W. F. Parker . . . . Captain General.

ADDRESS OF R. E. GRAND COMMANDER.

The Grand Commander read his Annual Address, which on motion was referred to Sir Knights E. S. Martin, D. E. Allen and W. A. Withers.

Sir Knights of the Grand Commandery of North Carolina:

Deeply mindful of the many blessings vouchsafed us by the Great Captain of our Salvation, we bid you welcome to the Eighteenth Annual Grand Conclave of the Grand Commandery of North Carolina:

When deciding that this Grand Conclave should be held in our Capital City among our beloved Fratres of Raleigh Commandry No. 4, none of us imagined that he would meet in an armed camp and that our peaceful country, so long devoted to Progress and the cultivation of the Arts and Sciences, would be in the throes of a bitter War, but Sir Knights, the World recognizes that we are fighting for civilization and humanity, and the World believes that Right will triumph.

While Ours is a Peaceful mission and our swords intended for the proper rendition of our tactics, yet when necessities require Thousands of Templars clad in the uniform, and fighting in the service of their Country, will shed their blood that "Old Glory" may float at the head of the lines; many ask for a Templar Flag for a Templar Parade, but there is no difference of opinion as to the flag when our Country is assailed.

Sir Knights, It was with profound sorrow, that I issued the following General Order, No. 1 :

NEW BERNE, N. C., October 28th, 1897.

To all Knights Templar of this Jurisdiction :

With a sad heart, I announce that God in His Infinite Wisdom, has summoned to His Presence, Eminent Sir Joseph B. Clark, Grand Warder of the Grand Commandery of North Carolina.

Our beloved Frater was born October 17th, 1858, near Mays Landing, New Jersey, and entered into Rest, October 20th, 1897, at New Berne, N. C. He was made a Master Mason in St. John's Lodge No. 3, and was Worshipful Master of said Lodge at the time of his death. He was exalted in New Berne Chapter No. 46, and was King at the time of his death. He was Knighted in St. John's Commandery No. 10, and was Generalissimo at the time of his death.

What need for me to remind you of his zeal and virtues.—You knew him and loved him.—He was very near and dear to me. He was Raised and Exalted and Knighted under my own hand, and with a tear-dimmed eye and sorrowing heart, I assisted in lowering his body into the grave, near Mays Landing, New Jersey, October 22, 1897.

It is hereby Ordered, that this Communication be read at the head of the lines at the first stated Conclave after its receipt, and that proper record be made of the same

Given under my hand, and the seal of the Grand Commandery, the date above written.   (Signed) J. H. HACKBURN,

Grand Commander.

The Death Angel has also stricken from our rolls. Sir Knight Alfred Martin, who entered into Eternal Life, September 1st, 1897. It requires a more gifted and familiar mind than mine, to fittingly portray the virtues of this good man and zealous Mason.

In our Sister Grand Jurisdictions also, many mighty Monarchs of Masonry have received the Crown promised to those faithful unto death.

Most Eminent Sir Knight Daniel Spry, Grand Chancellor of the Sovereign Great Priory of Canada, died August 13th, 1897.

Past Grand Master, John Q. A. Fellows, passed away at his home in New Orleans on the 28th day of November, 1897. Aged 73 years

Past Grand Master, Vincent Lombard Hurlburt, died at his home in Chicago, July 24th, 1896. Aged 67 years.

Past Grand Master Benjamin Dean, died in South Boston, Mass., on April 9th 1897. Aged 73 years.

Right Eminent Sir Thomas Spangler, Past Grand Commander of the Grand Commandery of Colorado, entered into Rest, December 12th, 1897.

Past Grand Commander James B Wildman of the Grand Commandery of Connecticut, died June 27th, 1897.

Past Grand Commander Jerome B Gorin of the Grand Commandery of Illinois, passed to his eternal rest, September 1st, 1887.

Right Eminent Sir Thomas Newby, Past Grand Commander of Indiana, was summoned to His Presence, June 16th. 1897. Aged 79 years.

Right Eminent Alexander Thomas, Past Grand Commander of Indiana, died in Terra Haute, July 26th, 1897, Aged 68 years.

Past Grand Captain General Sir Eugene Robinson of Michigan, passed into the life beyond, October 28th, 1897. Aged 60 years.

Past Grand Commander Luther Zoan Rogers of Minnesota, died April 27th, 1897.

Right Eminent Sir Thomas Sewell, Past Grand Commander of Nebraska, laid aside his pilgrimage garb, February 28th, 1898.

Eminent Sir John Dwyer, Grand Generalissimo of Nebraska, died at his home in Beatrice, May 7th, 1897.

Right Eminent Sir Joseph S. Wright, Past Grand Commander of Pennsylvania, died May 26th. 1897.

Right Eminent Sir Eugene Stocker, M. D., Past Grand Commander of Pennsylvania, died in Philadelphia, May 23d, 1897.

Right Eminent Sir William Morgan Brooks, Past Grand Commander of Tennessee, died August 7th, 1897

General John Sayles, Past Grand Captain General of Texas died May 22d, 1897.

Past Grand Commander Odell Squier Long. of West Virginia, answered the summons of his Maker, December 26th, 1897. Aged 61 years.

DISPENSATIONS.

By request of Most Eminent Grand Master, W. LaRue Thomas, granted September 22d, 1897. Dispensation to Mt. Lebanon Commandery No. 7, to confer the Templar Degrees upon Companion W. W. Freeman, who had been elected to receive the same by Columbia Commandery No. 2, Columbia, S. C.

Granted Dispensation to Charlotte Commandery No. 2, to elect Officers at a Special Conclave, held December 10th, 1897.

Granted Dispensation, December 16th, 1897 to Cyrene Commandery No 5, to act as escort to the Grand Lodge of North Carolina A. F. & A. M., at the laying of the Corner Stone, of the monument to the memory of Brother Zebulon B. Vance, December 22d, 1897.

Granted Dispensation, January 14th, 1898, to St John's Commandery No. 10, to install officers at a Special Conclave.

Granted Dispensation to Ivanhoe Commandery No. 8, to elect Officers at a Special Conclave held December 8th, 1897.

Dispensations granted March 12, 1898, to Plantagenet Commandery No. 1, to elect and enstall a Junior Warden. The Sir Knight elected to this position having declined to serve.

Granted Dispensation to Piedmont Commandery to act upon Petition of Companion C. F Dalton, within statutory time—he being about to travel for an indefinite time.

Granted Dispensation to Raleigh Commandery No. 4, to act upon Petition of Companion C. M. Cook, within statutory time—that there might be work upon the occasion of the official visit of Very Eminent Deputy Grand Commander M. D. Bailey.

Granted Dispensation April 27th, 1898, to Charlotte Commandery No. 2, to Ballot upon petitions of Companions R. I. Grant, E. W. Koontz, and J. A. Bolich within statutory time upon unanimous request of Charlotte Commandery backed by request of Past Grand Commander Liddell, who had been requested to confer Degrees and could not be present at Stated Conclave.

Received request from Committee appointed by Raleigh Commandery No. 4. Also from several Sir Knights throughout the State that the date of Grand Conclave be changed, as many Sir Knights desired to attend celebration of Mecklenburg Declaration at Charlotte, May 20th, but in each case was compelled to decline as the Statutes of the Grand Commandery of North Carolina gave me no authority to do so.

On November 24th, 1897, I issued the following General Order No. 2 :

To Grand Commandery and Subordinate Commanderies of the Grand Jurisdiction:

There being a vacancy caused by the death of our beloved Frater Eminent Sir J. B. Clark, in the position of Grand Warder of the Grand Commandery, I hereby appoint Eminent Sir Arthur J. Wills for the unexpired term. He will be respected and obeyed accordingly.

Given under my hand and the Seal of the Grand Commandery, the day and year above written.　　　Signed, J. H. HACKBURN,

Grand Commander.

I requested Past Grand Commander Cobb to install Eminent Sir Wills in Cyrene Commandery No. 5, which was done and due report made.

CHRISTMAS OBSERVANCE.

November 26th, I issued the following :

The Committee on Christmas Observance of the Grand Encampment has prepared the following sentiment for the coming Christmas. "To Our Most Eminent Grand Master, Warren LaRue Thomas, a Faithful leader. May his days be long, and may the blessings of our Lord and Master follow him all the days of his life."

The Grand Master sends the following response : "To all true Knights of the Temple : Health and Peace : God bless us every one." You are requested to assemble in your Asylums on Saturday, December 25th, at 12 o'clock, noon, and join in these sentiments remembering that your Grand Commander wishes and hopes that all the joy and happiness possible in human life may abide with you.

Signed, J. H. HACKBURN,
Grand Commander.

APPOINTMENTS FOR OFFICIAL VISITATIONS.

General Order, No. 3.   February 14th.

To the Inspecting Officers and Subordinate Commanderies of this Grand Jurisdiction—*Greeting :*

The following assignments are hereby made for Official Visitations and Inspection: Very Eminent Sir M. D. Bailey, Cyrene Commandery, No. 5; Durham Commandery No. 3; Raleigh Commandery No. 4.

Eminent Sir W. E. Storm, St. John's No. 10; Mt. Lebanon No. 7; St. Aldemar No. 12.

Eminent Sir W. F. Randolph, Plantagenet No. 1; St. George No. 9; DeMolai No. 11.

J. H. Hackburn, Charlotte No. 2; Piedmont No. 6; Ivanhoe No. 8.

This Order will be authority to the Officer designated to issue such notices to Commanderies assigned to him as he may deem advisable and visit said Commanderies.   Signed, J H. HACKBURN,
Grand Commander.

On December 8th, I visited Ivanhoe Commandery No. 8, stationed at Greensboro, conferred the Order of the Temple upon two. This Commandery I found short of Paraphernalia and are not bright in the Ritual, but new members are coming in and they express themselves as determined to place the Commandery among the brightest and best appointed in the State.

On December 9th, I visited Piedmont Commandery No. 6, stationed at Winston. There was a good attendance. The Sir Knights were well uniformed and perfect in the opening and closing; this was my first visit to Winston, and I have the remembrance of many courtesies treasured up and trust the future will bring me the privilege of reciprocating.

On December 10th, I found myself shaking hands with Sir Knights of the Charlotte Commandery No. 10, and Officially visited that Commandery. This is the largest and among the brightest in the State and the Sir Knights were all properly uniformed and filled the several stations in strict accordance with the Ritual; a number of the Sir Knights from this and other States favored us with their presence and we were royally enter-tained with carriage drives and other things necessary when citizens of the two Carolinas meet, winding up with a superb Banquet, which kept wine and wit flowing till low twelve was well behind us

Our Grand Generalissimo and Grand Captain General have written me that absolutely unavoidable circumstances have prevented them making their visitation and I accepted their reasons as good and promised to make this explanation to the Grand Commandery.

I beg to bring to the attention of this Grand Commandery the following communications, from the Grand Commandery of Tennessee:

NASHVILLE, September 17th, 1897.

Right Eminent Sir Knight Horace H. Munson, Grand Recorder, Grand Commandery North Carolina:

DEAR SIR :—The following Preamble and Resolutions were adopted by the Grand Commandery of Tennessee at its last Annual Conclave, to-wit:

WHEREAS, The Maltese Cross has for Centuries been the Official Insig-nia of our Order, and

WHEREAS, We note with much regret the appropriation of this emblem by other secret orders and religious societies, and knowing as we do that their action in thus using an emblem the very name of which is significant of our Order, is absolutely unnecessary, and

WHEREAS, Such conduct on their part is only calculated to mislead and has already caused unnecessary confusion. Therefore be it

Resolved, 1. That this Grand Commandery protests against the action of other secret orders and religious societies in thus unnecessarily appropriating our time-honored significant emblem.

2. That our Grand Commander take such action as may be necessary to memorialize the Grand Encampment on this subject with a view of bringing about a moral influence that will stop other orders and societies from misleading the public by the use of our emblem.

3. That our Grand Recorder correspond with our Sister Jurisdictions on this subject and send a copy of these resolutions   This copy is for-warded as per instruction in Item 3, of said resolutions, and the attention of your Grand Commandery is respectfully and courteously invited, for such action upon the subject as may be deemed expedient.

By Order of the Grand Commandery of Tennessee K. T.

Signed, W. T. FOSTER,
Grand Recorder.

TRIENNIAL.

Your Committee on Triennial, of which I have the honor to be Chairman, has taken no steps toward providing headquarters at Pittsburg. There can be no difference of opinion as to the advisability of North Carolina having suitable appointments at Pittsburg—but unfortunately, we have no funds in our Treasury that can be justly devoted to such purposes, and believing that the Commanderies are not in condition to stand such assessment I see no other way than that our Representatives should pay their own expenses. I do not consider this a hardship for surely the privilege of fraternizing with such a body of men is well worth the money it will cost.

I must here call the attention of the Finance Committee to the necessity of looking into our financial condition: We are now one year ahead of our receipts. In other words, the expenses of this year have to be paid out of next year's income. This matter if neglected may lead us into a very unpleasant situation.

COMMANDERIES.

There are two Commanderies. St. George No 9, and DeMolai No. 11; which are derelict in their dues and returns. I had correspondence with Sir Knight Austin, Recorder of St. George No. 9, and he reported to me that they could not get a quorum.

Eminent Sir S H. Smith, Commander of DeMolai No. 11, wrote me that his Commandery also had difficulty in getting a quorum and asking a Dispensation to receive petitions, with $10.00 fee and waive statutory time on all petitions up to June 15th, or July 1st, I wrote him that the Constitution of the Grand Encampment made the minimum fee $20.00 and that as my term as Grand Commander would expire with this Grand Conclave, I could not issue the Dispensation waiving the statutory time. I urged him to have a representative at the Grand Conclave and hope they will be able to make satisfactory explanations.

CONDITION OF ORDER IN THIS JURISDICTION.

I regret that I cannot report a large increase in our membership. But financial depression is largely responsible—besides we have few large cities in our State and it is almost impossible for a small town to properly maintain a Commandery.

And now, Sir Knights: I return to you the high power which you entrusted to me one year ago.

Before retiring I wish to express my sincere thanks to our beloved Grand Recorder, for the wise Counsel which has ever been at my call, and to acknowledge the unvarying courtesy and obedience from every Sir Knight with whom I have come in contact, even when my course may have seemed arbitrary and stubborn: and I assure you that every act of mine has been governed by an endeavor to see the laws duly and properly observed: You have crowned my life with one of its highest ambitions: You have bound me with ties of love that I trust will ever tighten, and I assure you that every throb of my heart beats appreciative devotion to Masonry and those whom I have found in its charmed circle.

Courteously submitted,

[SEAL.]   J. H. HACKBURN,
                                     Grand Commander.

The Deputy Grand Commander, M. D. Bailey, submitted his report, which, on motion, was referred to Committee on Grand Commander's address.

To the Grand Commandery of North Carolina:

According to orders of R. E. Grand Commander Hackburn, I visited Durham Commandery, No. 3, on the 5th April, at their regular Conclave. There was a quorum present and transacted the regular business of the Commandery. I was informed that they had not been having regular meetings. Was very courtiously received at the train by Sir Slater and Past Grand Commander Southgate. After the Conclave I was very pleasantly entertained at my hotel by the Sir Knights of Durham Commandery, and my short stay in Durham will ever be a pleasant remembrance, and especially so when I consider it was an honor paid to the Grand Commandery of North Carolina.

On April 6th, I visited Raleigh Commandery No. 4, at a special Conclave, called at my request. Although this was a special Conclave, there was a good turnout of the Sir Knights. The Red Cross degree was conferred in a very creditable manner, making a good impression on the candidate. I consider this Commandery in a healthy and growing condition. In fact, some of the Sir Knights are very "robust" already.

I was met at the station by Sir Drewry E. Grand Standard Bearer, in his pleasant style, who escorted me to my hotel and later in company with other Sir Knights, showed me many courtesies. After Commandery had closed, a nice banquet awaited us in an adjoining room, to which we did full justice, and after the usual pleasantries, we adjourned.

April 7th, I visited Cyrene Commandery No. 5, at Asheville. On my arrival at the depot, I was met by Sir Randolph, Grand C. G., and Sir Wills, Grand Warder, who escorted me to my hotel and showed me every courtesy possible. At a special Conclave, a goodly number of Sir Knights were present, as also some visiting Sir Knights from other Grand Jurisdictions. The Red Cross degree was conferred in excellent form, the various officers doing their parts well. It is hardly necessary for me to speak of the courteous manner in which I was received by Sir Knights of Cyrene Commandery, for any Sir Knight who has had the pleasure of meeting those valiant Knights, know what kind of reception they would receive should they go into their midst, especially so, one representing the Grand Commandery of North Carolina. After the Commandery closed, a sumptuous repast was served, and a grand social indulged in by the Sir Knights, visitors from other States taking full part.

In conclusion, I must say that my trip from the time I reached Durham until I left Asheville, was a most pleasant one made so by the different Sir Knights whom I met.

Courteously submittted,
M. D. BAILEY,
Deputy Grand Commander.

GRAND REPRESENTATIVES.

The following Grand Representatives were awarded special honor:

A. J. Wills	Montana.
F. Ulrich	New Jersey.
J. Southgate	Indiana.
Wm. Simpson	Kansas.
F. M. Moye	Minnesota.
H. H. Munson	New York.
W. E. Storm	Vermont.
J. D. Bullock	Wisconsin.
P A. Wilson	Missouri.
W. S. Liddell	Oregon.
M. D. Bailey	Connecticut.
E. S. Martin	Iowa.
W. F. Randolph	Maryland.
J. C. Munds	New Hampshire.
J. H. Hackburn	North Dakota.
W. A. Withers	Wyoming
M. S. Willard	Mississippi.

The Grand Treasurer and Grand Recorder submitted their reports, which were referred to Committee on Finance.

REPORT OF THE GRAND RECORDER.

To the Grand Commandery:

I have the honor of submitting my official report.

May 15. Distributed circulars of Grand Officers.
June 8. Distributed proceedings Annual Conclave.
    11. Drew draft on Grand Treasurer to pay Grand Encampment dues.
Oct. 13. By order of R. E. Grand Commander J. H. Hackburn, I called attention of Subordinate Commanderies to the law requiring summons to issue for the annual election and installation of officers.

Oct. 30. Issued circular of Grand Commander on death of Eminent Sir
J. B. Clark.

Received letter of regret from the R. E. Grand Commander of
Oregon on the death of Grand Warder J. B. Clark.

Nov. 27. Issued General Order No. 2, Grand Commander appointing Sir
Arthur J. Wills Grand Warder in place of deceased Sir
Knight J. B. Clark.

30. Issued circular Grand Commander requesting Christmas observance in connection with toast to Grand Master.

Feb. 14. Issued General Order No. 3 Grand Commander relating to the
the appointment of inspecting officers and visitations.

Mar. 1. Sent blank returns to Commanderies.

GRAND REPRESENTATIVES.

The following Commissions have been issued:

June 23. Henry E. Day, Glendine, Montana.

28. Fred. G. Brest, Prescott, Arizona.

COMMISSIONS RECEIVED.

June 23. J. B. Clark, New Berne, Montana.

Oct. 12. Rev. C. L. Hoffman, Charlotte, Arizona.

Nov. 21. A. J. Wills, Asheville, Montana.

(In place of J. B. Clark, deceased.)

During the Conclave of 1897, I received from Piedmont Commandery
No. 6, the sum of Forty-five Dollars, which I turned over to the Grand
Treasurer, and which is embodied in his report of that year, but my
report having been submitted before the payment to me of above amount,
I forgot to add it to the printed statement. I make this apology as
explanatory to my friends of that Commandery why this credit does not
appear in the printed report of that year. In this connection the law
provides that returns shall be made on the first of the month previous to
that in which the Grand Conclave is to be held. If this law was carried
into effect the reports of both Treasurer and Recorder would be ready at
the opening of every Grand Conclave, thus avoiding the possibility of any
mistake of this character being made.

GRAND RECORDER'S OFFICE.

For a number of years the office and library of the Grand Commandery
has been held in an inconvenient room in the city of Wilmington. By
and with the advice and consent of the Grand Commander, a far better
room has been secured in the Masonic building on Market street, at an
annual rental of twenty-four dollars per year, divided equally between the
Grand Commandery and the Grand Chapter; for fitting up, twenty dollars and seventeen cents, divided as before. In this room one hundred
and eighty bound volumes of Sister Grand Jurisdictions are neatly kept.

At present there are of these latter as follows:

Alabama 3	Maryland 6	Ohio 10
California 7	Massachusetts 10	Oregon 1
Connecticut 5	Michigan 10	Pennsylvania . . 8
Colorado 3	Minnesota 3	South Dakota . . . 1
Canada 2	Mississippi 1	Tennessee 6
Georgia 2	Missouri 4	Texas 3
Illinois 10	Montana 1	Virginia 7
Indiana 7	Nebraska 2	Vermont 9
Iowa 7	North Carolina . . . 4	West Virginia . . . 2
Kansas 4	New Hampshire . . 5	Washington 1
Kentucky 7	New Jersey 5	Wisconsin 7
Louisiana 2	New York 6	Wyoming . 1
Maine 7	North Dakota 1	

PROCEEDINGS OF FRATERNAL BODIES.

The following proceedings have been received during the current year:

Arkansas,	Kentucky,	Ohio,
Alabama,	Louisiana,	Oklahoma,
California,	Michigan,	Oregon,
Colorado,	Missouri,	Pennsylvania,
Connecticut,	Minnesota,	South Dakota,
Canada,	Maine,	Tennessee,
District Columbia,	Montana,	Texas,
Florida,	Massachusetts,	Virginia,
Georgia,	New Jersey,	Vermont,
Illinois,	Nebraska,	Wisconsin,
Iowa,	North Dakota,	Washington,
Indiana,	New York,	Wyoming,
Ind. Territory, '96-'97,	New Hampshire,	West Virginia.
Kansas,		

GRAND COMMANDERY DUES.

The following Commanderies have paid dues, as follows:

April 5.	St. Aldemar No. 12	$ 17.00
11.	Raleigh No. 4	39.00
19.	Piedmont No. 6	44.00
20.	Plantagenet No. 1	48.00
30.	St. John No. 10	25.00
May 5.	Durham No. 3	19.00
14.	Cyrene No. 5	46.00
17.	Charlotte No. 2	63.00
17.	Greensboro No. 8	37.00
		$338.00

Which has been paid to the Grand Treasurer as per receipts.

I am happy to report that all our Commanderies, save ——, have sent in their returns, and that there is an indication that DeMolai No. 11, so long dormant, will soon resume labor under brightened auspices.

Death has again invaded our ranks and consigned to their tombs from

Plantagenet Commandery No. 1—one.
St. John's   "   No. 10—one.
Mt. Lebanon   "   No. 7—one.

The following is the loss and gain for this Templar year:

Plantagenet No. 1 has lost 2
Charlotte   No. 2 " " 9
Durhım   No. 3 " " 2
Raleigh   No. 4 " gained 3
Cyrene   No. 5 "   "   5
Piedmont   No. 6 " lost 1
Mt.Lebanon No. 7 " gained 3
Ivanhoe   No. 8 "   "   5
St. George   No. 9 "   . . . .
St. John   No. 10 "   "   same as last year.
St. Aldemar No. 12 "   "   3

Total gain 5

Courteously submitted,
H. H. MUNSON,
Grand Recorder.

GRAND TREASURER'S REPORT.

WILLIAM SIMPSON, *Grand Treasurer.*

In account with THE GRAND COMMANDERY OF NORTH CAROLINA.

1897.   DR.

June 1.   To balance on hand as per last report . . . $ 80 76
July 16.   " Cash from Grand Recorder 200 20
1898.
April 6.   " "   "   "   " 17 00
     12.   " "   "   "   " 39 00
     20.   " "   "   "   " 44 00
     21.   " "   "   "   " 48 00
May 5.   " "   "   "   " 25 00
     6.   " "   "   "   " 19 00
    16.   " "   "   "   " 46 00
    18.   " "   "   "   " 63 00
    18.   " "   "   "   "   . . . . 37 00— $618 96

1897.   CR.

May 25.	By Cash paid	Educator Company . .	. $	50	00
June 17.	" "	" Dues Grand Encampment . .	17	45
July 15.	" "	" Jackson & Bell Proceedings .	153	81
15.	" "	" H. H. Munson, G. R. expenses	22	83
Dec. 2.	" "	" " " "	30	67
14.	" "	" J. H. Hackburn, Gr. Com . .	27	00
1898.				
April 15.	" "	" H. H. Munson, office expenses	23	21
21.	" "	" H. H. Munson, Gr. Recorder	50	00
May 18.	" "	" Geo. H. King, Secretary .	9	00
20.	" "	" H. H. Munson, expenses . .	9	00
20.	" "	" J. Hackburn	200	00
20.	"	Cash on hand	25	59— $618 96

Courteously submitted.

WILLIAM SIMPSON,
Grand Treasurer.

STANDING COMMITTEES.

The Grand Commander announced the Standing Committees
as follows :

On Warrants and Dispensations: Sir Knights Storm, Parker and
Jones.

On Finance: Sir Knights Munds, Norfleet and Dewey.

On Appeals and Grievances: Sir Knights Withers, Drewry and Willard.

On Next Place of Annual Conclave: Sir Knights Liddell, Ulrich and
Munds.

On Templar Jurisprudence: Sir Knights Southgate, Martin and Liddell.

On Fraternal Correspondence: Sir Knight John C. Chase.

On Necrology: Sir Knights Moye, Miller and Pippin.

Sir Knight W. A. Withers, P. G. C., from Committee on
Grand Commander's Address, submitted the following report,
which was adopted :

To the Grand Commandery of North Carolina :

Your committee in common with the Grand Commandery fully appreciate and respond to the patriotic sentiments expressed by the Grand
Commander in his eloquent and instructive address, and recognize the
energy and ability with which he has presided over the destinies of Templarhood during his term of office.

·We respectfully recommend (1) that that portion of the address relating
to the fraternal dead be referred to the Committee on Necrology.

(2) That that portion of the address relating to dispensations be referred to the Committee on Jurisprudence.

(3) That that portion relating to the communication from the Grand Commandery of Tennessee in regard to the appropriation of the Maltese Cross by other secret societies and others, be referred to a special committee to be appointed by the Grand Commander.

(4) That that portion of the address relating to the financial condition of the treasury be referred to the Financial Committee, with the request that they give careful consideration to the same.

(5) That that portion of the address relating to the two Commanderies, St. George No. 9, and DeMolai No. 11, be referred to the Committee on Charters and Dispensations.

The committee regrets that the financial condition of the treasury will not permit the Grand Commandery to establish headquarters at Pittsburg during the Triennial Conclave of the Grand Encampment, but expresses the hope that our Representatives and many other Sir Knights may be present at Pittsburg to enjoy the hospitality of that city and the fraternal greetings of the Templars of sister Jurisdictions.

Courteously submitted,

E. S. MARTIN,
W. A. WITHERS,
D. E. ALLEN,
Committee.

Sir Knight J. C. Chase, through Sir Knight Southgate, presented his report on Fraternal Correspondence, which, on motion, was ordered printed in the proceedings and the thanks of the Grand Commandery tendered. Adopted.

The Grand Commander appointed a Special Committee on Communication of the Grand Commandery of Tennessee regarding use of Maltese Cross, consisting of Sir Knights Southgate, Martin and Moye.

The Grand Commandery adjourned till to-morrow morning at 10 o'clock.

THURSDAY MORNING, MAY 19, 1898.

The Grand Commandery met pursuant to adjournment, Grand Officers in their stations. The minutes of last night's session read and approved.

The following telegram was received:

2

PROVIDENCE, R. I., May 18, 1898.

Horace H. Munson, Grand Recorder K. T., Raleigh, N. C.:

Courteous greeting to the Grand Commandery, with regrets for my enforced absence. JOHN C. CHASE.

Which was received with the regrets of this Grand Body.

AMENDMENT TO THE CONSTITUTION.

The following amendment to the Constitution presented at our last annual Grand Conclave, and which was laid over under the rules, was adopted :

Resolved, That the Eminent Commander, by and with the consent of Deputy Grand Commander, Grand Generalissimo and Grand Captain General, or any two of them, shall have power to change the time and place of holding the next Annual Grand Conclave appointed by the Grand Commandery at its preceding Annual Grand Conclave, when, in their opinion, circumstances demand it.

Sir Knight F. M. Moye, from the Special Committee on the Communication of the Grand Commandery of Tennessee, presented the following report, which was adopted :

To the Grand Commandery of North Carolina :

The Special Committee to which was referred that part of the address of the Grand Commander relating to the communication of the Grand Commandery of Tennessee in regard to the Maltese Cross, having duly considered the same, now report that, while we fully concur with the Grand Commandery of Tennessee in the sentiments expressed in said communication and heartily desire that the object proposed could be obtained ; yet we are of opinion that there is no remedy for the evil complained of, and therefore recommend that no action be taken by this Grand Commandery in the premises.

Courteously,

JAMES SOUTHGATE,
E. S. MARTIN,
F. M. MOYE,
Committee.

Sir Knight F. M. Moye, P. G. C., submitted the report on Necrology, which was adopted :

To the Grand Commandery of North Carolina :

Your Committee on Necrology beg leave to make the following report: We have heard with feelings of deep emotion the tender, loving, and beautiful tribute paid by the R. E. Grand Commander in his address, to our own and the fraternal dead of our sister Grand Jurisdictions.

While our hearts are sad, and with unaffected sorrow we mourn their loss. it is a sweet privilege to recount the many virtues which beautified and adorned the lives of these noble Fratres. Their earthly pilgrimage is ended, they have crossed the "Dark River" and entered, we trust, the Heavenly Asylum in that beautiful world of light and joy, where a glorious welcome ever awaits the valiant and faithful Templar.

The earthen vase which has contained precious odors will lose none of its fragrance though the clay be broken and shattered."

"The memory of their virtues lingers in our remembrance and reflects its shining luster beyond the portals of the tomb."

We recommend that memorial pages be set apart in the proceedings of the Grand Commandery and the same be suitably inscribed in memory of our own beloved and honored dead.

Courteously submitted,

F. M. MOYE,

J. D. MILLER,

F. L. PIPPEN,

Committee.

Sir Knight W. E. Storm, from the Committee on Charters and Dispensations, presented the following report, which was adopted :

DeMolai Commandery, No. 11, requests remission of Grand Chapter dues. Upon investigation we find this Commandery has been, from good and sufficient reason, practically dormant. We learn the prospects are now brighter for revival and recommend for their encouragement the remission of the dues, feeling assured the dereliction will not again occur.

St. George Commandery, No. 9, fails to make returns or remit dues. A private communication from a Sir Knight of that body reports an inability to get a quorum, and that apparently nothing can be done. We regret exceedingly this condition of St. George Commandery, No. 9, and earnestly desire their early revival. In the face of the above facts, and as no request has been made for remission of dues, and whereas no dues have been paid within the statutory limit, your committee find no other course to pursue than according to our law, and recommend the Right Eminent Grand Commander to order the Grand Recorder to obtain possession of their Charter according to said law.

Courteously submitted,

W. E. STORM.

Sir Knight J. C. Munds, from the Committee on Finance, submitted the following report, which was adopted :

To the Grand Commandery of North Carolina :

Your Finance Committee report as follows :

We have examined the books of the Grand Treasurer and Grand Re-

corder and find them correct. The Grand Treasurer's books show that
he has a balance of $148.99 in bank and $95 cash, making a total of
$243.99.

We find the Grand Commandery to be indebted to the R. E. Grand
Commander in the sum of $200, the immediate payment of which we
recommend. This will leave a balance of $43.99 in the treasury, to sup-
plement which we would further recommend the reinstatement of Knighthood fees of $2 per Knight, also the increase of 25 cents per capita on the
Subordinate Commanderies, and to meet this year's expenditures we
recommend that the R. E. Grand Commander be authorized to borrow
the amount absolutely necessary.

We recommend that the Grand Recorder have the proceedings of this
Conclave printed as he has heretofore done.

Courteously submitted,

JAMES C. MUNDS,
T. W. DEWEY,
JAS. K. NORFLEET.

On motion of Sir Knight W. F. Randolph, Eminent Grand
Captain General Sir Knight E. S. Martin, P. D. G. C., was
requested to furnish a history of Templarism in North Carolina and present it at our next annual Conclave. Adopted.

On motion of Sir Knight A. J. Wills, amended by Sir Knight
W. S. Liddell, the matter relating to uniform buttons, be
referred to a committee to report at our next annual Conclave.
Adopted. The Grand Commander appointed Sir Knights
Storm, Liddell and Wills, said committee.

Sir Knight F. Ulrich, from the Committee on Time and Place
of next annual Conclave, submitted the following report, which
was adopted :

To the Grand Commandery :

Your Committee on Time and Place for holding our next annual Conclave, beg leave to report that Asheville has been selected as the place,
and the second Tuesday in June, 1899, as the time.

F. ULRICH,
For Committee.

Sir Knight James Southgate, from the Jurisprudence Com-
mitteee, presented the following report, which was adopted :

REPORT OF COMMITTEE ON JURISPRUDENCE.

To the Grand Commandery Knights Templar of North Carolina :

Your Committee to whom so much of the R. E. Grand Commander's
address, as refers to Dispensations, beg leave to report that they have the

approval of the Committee, being in accord with the general usage in this State. Your Committee would, however, recommend that the greatest caution be exercised in granting Dispensations to ballot on candidates out of the statutory time, and in no case should this be done except in cases of emergency, of which the Grand Commander should be the judge.

Courteously submitted,

JAMES SOUTHGATE,
W. S. LIDDELL.

The Grand Commandery proceeded to an election of Grand Officers for ensuing Templar year, under the direction of Sir Knights Bullock and Allen tellers, resulting as follows:

MUMFORD D. BAILEY . . .	Winston. . .	R. E. Grand Commander.
WALTER E. STORM	Wilmington . .	V. E. Dep. Gr. Commander.
WILLIAM F. RANDOLPH . .	Asheville . . .	E. Grand Generalissimo.
JAMES D. BULLOCK	Wilson	E. Grand Captain General.
REV. JAMES D. MILLER . .	Greensboro . .	E. Grand Prelate.
DeWITT E. ALLEN	Charlotte . . .	E. Grand Senior Warden.
JOHN C. DREWRY	Raleigh . . .	E. Grand Junior Warden.
WILLIAM SIMPSON	Raleigh	E. Grand Treasurer.
HORACE H. MUNSON. . .	Wilmington . .	E. Grand Recorder.
ARTHUR J. WILLS	Asheville . . .	E. Grand Standard Bearer.
JAMES K. NORFLEET . . .	Winston . . .	E. Grand Sword Bearer.
FERDINAND ULRICH. . . .	New Bern . . .	E. Grand Warder.
ROBERT H. BRADLEY . . .	Raleigh	E. Grand Sentinel.

Sir Knight E. Martin, offered the following, which was adopted:

That the R. E. Grand Commander be requested to apply to the next Legislature for an Act of Incorporation of this Grand Commandery.

Sir Knight W. A. Withers, from the Committee on Appeals and Grievances, presented the following, which was adopted:

To the Grand Commandery of North Carolina:

Your Committee appointed to hear Appeals and Grievances, would congratulate the Fraternity that the acts of the Grand Commander have been so just and so strictly in accordance with law, and that the spirit of fraternalism is so strong between the Sir Knights that nothing has been brought before this committee for consideration.

Courteously submitted,

W. A. WITHERS, Chm'n.,
M. S. WILLARD,
JOHN C. DREWRY,
Committee.

Sir Knight Dewey offered the following resolution, which was adopted :

Resolved, That the thanks of this Grand Body are due and hereby tendered to the Sir Knights of Raleigh Commandery, No. 4, and the Committee of arrangements, for abundant courtesies rendered.

The Grand Commandery proceeded to the installation of Grand Officers elect, by the retiring Grand Commander, J. H. Hackburn, W. S. Liddell, P. G. C., Grand Marshall.

No further business appearing, the minutes having been read and approved, the Grand Commandery closed at twelve o'clock m. in ample and Knightly form with prayer by the Grand Prelate.

MUMFORD D. BAILEY,
Grand Commander.

Attest :
HORACE H. MUNSON,
Grand Recorder.

RETURNS

OF

Subordinate Commanderies,

FOR THE YEAR ENDING APRIL 1, 1898.

- - - ... - ...

.

PLANTAGENET COMMANDERY No. 1—WILMINGTON.

Time of Stated Conclave: Second Wednesday evening in each
month at 8 o'clock.

OFFICERS.

W. N. Toomer . . . . Eminent Commander.
M. S. Willard . . . . Generalissimo.
U. M. Robinson . . . . Captain General.
G. Y. French . . . . Prelate.
J. C. Munds . . . . Treasurer.
H. G. Smallbones . . . . Recorder.
J. W. Jackson . . . . Senior Warden.
Eric Norden . . . . Junior Warden.
W. A. Williams . . . . Standard Bearer.
S. G. Hall . . . . Sword Bearer.
J. C. Loder . . . . Warder.
T. H. Johnson . . . . Sentinel.

SIR KNIGHTS.

Allen, W. W., P. G. C.	Grant, R. H.	McEarchern, D.
Baily, E. P., P. C.	Harriss, G.	McKethan, D. T.
Boatwright, E. P.	Horn, J. M.	Morton, G. L.
Baltzer, E. V.	Heide, A. S.	Munds, J. T.
Chadbourn, W. H., P. C.	Jones, W. C.	Noble, M. C. S.
Chase, J. C., P. D. G. C.	Kenan, W. R.	Price, R. W.
Comfort, C. I.	Knowles, F. M.	Post, Jr., J. F.
Chadbourn, Jr., J. H.,	Latimer, E. L.	Pond, E. W.
Cantwell, J. L.	Lawrence, J. R.	Smith, W. J.
Emerson, T. M.	Munson, H. H., P. G. C.	Storm, W. E., G. G.
Forshee, J. M.	Martin, E. S., P. C.	Scott, A. L.
French, J. McD.	Monroe, J. W.	Stedman, F. H.

CHARLOTTE COMMANDERY No. 2—CHARLOTTE.

Time of Stated Conclave : Second Tuesday of each month.

OFFICERS.

Robert Walter Smith . . . . Eminent Commander.
DeWitt E. Allen . . . . Generalissimo.
Charles M. Kyle . . . . Captain General.
Charles L. Hoffman . . . . Prelate.
George H. King . . . . Treasurer.
George A. Page . . . . Recorder.
Earl A. McCausland . . . . Senior Warden.
Lawrence A. Dodsworth . . . . Junior Warden.
Silas W. Neece . . . . Standard Bearer.
John F. Orr . . . . Sword Bearer,
David Guy Maxwell . . . . Warder.
Edgar M. Purefoy . . . . Sentinel.

SIR KNIGHTS.

Anderson, William	Franklin, T. S	Murrill, Hugh A.
Belk, John Montgomery	Fullenwider, C. H.	Meredith, Geo. W.
Belk, William Henry	Grant, R. Q.	Misenheimer, Jos F.
Bolick, J. A.	Hilton, Sam'l Harrison	Owens, W. W.
Bridgers, W. Luther	Helms, Jefferson Davis	Parks, S. L.
Carpenter, Jonathan B.	Hunt, F. D.	Quinn, M. C.
Curtis, F. O. S.	Hopkin, Chas. L	Ramsay, R. H.
Creasy, Walter Scott	Hennessee, J. E.	Reinhardt, R. S.
Campbell, George	Herring, H. C.	Robertson, J. F.
Clarkson, Heriot	Koontz, E. W.	Robertson, Thos. Ross
Day, Harvey McLelland	Kyle, C. M.	Spencer, Orpehus W.
Dorritee, J. A.	Lipscomb. C. F.	Springs, H. G.
Davis, B. S.	Lawton, Chas. L.	Smith, W. M.
Dixon, Henry McK.	Liddell. Walter Scott	Worrell. W. W.
Eccles, Henry Easton	McDonald, Robt. E.	Woodrum, W. J.
Farrier, John	McAden, John Henry	Williams, W. H.
Fitzgerald, W. H.	Milburn, Frank P.	Young. Earnest F.

DURHAM COMMANDERY No. 3—DURHAM.

Time of Stated Conclave: First Tuesday in each month.

OFFICERS.

James Southgate . . . . Eminent Commander.
James Gattis . . . . Generalissimo.
W. A. Slater . . . . Captain General.
H. J. Bass . . . . Prelate.

T. E. Cheek . . . . Treasurer.
C. C. Taylor . . . . Recorder.
W. L. Wall . . . . Senior Warden.
——— ——— . . . . Junior Warden.
Norman M. Johnson . . . . Standard Bearer.
James W. Blackwell . . . . Sword Bearer.
M. H Jones . . . . Warder.
Wyatt P. Rollins . . . . Sentinel.

SIR KNIGHTS.

Adkisson, L. A.	Carr, J. S.	Parrish, E. J.
Bishop, F. A.	Lee, J. W.	Wilbon, John D.
Blackwell, W. T.	Markham, F. D.	

RALEIGH COMMANDERY No. 4—RALEIGH.

Time of Stated Conclave: First Thursday of each month.

OFFICERS.

D. S. Hamilton . . . . Eminent Commander
A. L. Baker . . . . Generalissimo.
W. E. Jones . . . . Captain General.
B. R. Lacy . . . . Prelate.
William Simpson, P. C. . . . . Treasurer.
W. A. Withers, P. G. C. . . . . Recorder.
M. Bowes, P. C. . . . . Senior Warden.
C. P. Snuggs . . . . Junior Warden.
James Dinwiddie . . . . Standard Bearer.
T. W. Blake . . . . Sword Bearer.
Charles Wallin . . . . Warder.
R. H. Bradley . . . . Sentinel.

SIR KNIGHTS.

Andrews, A. B.	Edwards, C. B.	Thompson, J. W.
Bain, W. H.	Greason, H. B.	Ueltschi, J., Jr.
Baker, B. W.	Heartt, L. D.	Uzzell, E. M.
Busbee, F. H.	Irby, Benjamin	Wait, S. D.
Carpenter, E. F.	Massey, C. F.	Walters, G. N.
Clarke, A. M.	Pescud, John S.	Watson, F. A.
Dobson, J. P.	Potter, E. C.	Weir, W. J.
Drewry, John C., P. C.	Sexton, J. A.	Wetherell, W. P.
Eberhardt, T. L.	Smith Z. P., P. C.	Woodruff, C. A., P. G. C.

CYRENE COMMANDERY No. 5—ASHEVILLE.

Time of Stated Conclave: Fourth Thursday in each month.

OFFICERS.

John A. Wagner . . . . Eminent Commander.
Claudius H. Miller . . . . Generalissimo.
John A. Nichols, P. E. C. . . . . Captain General.
Alfred H. Stubbs, P. G. C G. . . . . Prelate.
Henry C. Fagg . . . . Treasurer.
Marcus W. Robertson . . . . Recorder.
James H. Drakeford . . . . Senior Warden.
Frank T. Merriweather . . . . Junior Warden.
John H. Woody . . . . Standard Bearer.
Rufus J. Sherrell . . . . Sword Bearer.
James G. Colvin . . . . Warder.
William L. Shope . . . . Sentinel.

SIR KNIGHTS.

Brookshire, James M.
Brevard, John D.
Burroughs, James A.
Brookshire, John A.
Bell, George H.
Buckner, Neptune
Cobb, A. H., P. E. C. G.
Collins, David K.
Carter, John H.
Dickerson, Jos. E.
Fletcher, Robt. L.
Fullbright, Cassius S.

Gudger, Hezekiah A.
Gudger, Wm. J.
Herndon, David F.
Jacobs, F. L., P. E. C.
Lawson, Thomas
Lange, John H.
Moore, Charles A.
Moore, Walter E.
Porter, J. A., P. E. G. C.
Randolph, W., P. P. E. C.
Reed, Thos. J.

Reed, Marcus L.
Sprinkle, Wm. C.
Smith, Van
Schartle, John W.
Tweed, Chapel W.
Toms, Charles F.
Vance, Robert B.
Wills, A. J., P. E. C.
Weeks, Francis M.
Whittaker, Chas. R.
Williams, John H.

PIEDMONT COMMANDERY No. 6—WINSTON.

Time of Stated Conclave: Fourth Monday in each month.

OFFICERS.

Robert H. Jones . . . . Eminent Commander.
James K. Norfleet . . . . Generalissimo.
Rufus W. Nading . . . . Captain General.
Robert E. Caldwell . . . . Prelate.
Fred. G. Schaum . . . . Treasurer.
Daniel P. Mast . . . . Recorder.
James H. Foote . . . . Senior Warden.
William C. Brown . . . . Junior Warden.

Eugene A. Ebert . . . . Standard Bearer.
William T. Brown . . . . Sword Bearer.
Thomas L. Farrow . . . . Warder.
Peter W. Dalton . . . . Sentinel.

SIR KNIGHTS.

Allen, S. E.	Griffith, J. W.	Smith, S. H., P. E. C.
Alspaugh, J. W.	Hanes, P. H.	Spach, E.
Bahnson, H. T., P. E. C.	Hauser, A. J.	Summerell, W. H.
Bahnson, W. G.	Hunter, J. W., P. E. C.	Transon, R. E.
Bailey, M. D., P. E. C.	Jones, E. L.	Thomas, DeLos
Bessent, J. C.	Johnston, R. D.	White, J. A.
DeVane, D. L.	McArthur, R. M.	Wilson, N. S.
Dalton, R. E., P. E. C.	Norfleet, R. C.	Wilson, P. A., P. E. C.
Dalton, R. I.	Quincy, G. R.	Whitaker, C. L.
Dalton, W. E. L.	Rich, E. D.	Yerex, J. W.
Franklin, W. E.	Ruffin, J. R.	

MT. LEBANON COMMANDERY No. 7—WILSON.

Time of Stated Conclave : Fourth Monday in each month.

OFFICERS.

W. J. Boykin . . . . Eminent Commander.
David Woodard . . . . Generalissimo.
Lat. Williams . . . . Captain General.
F. M. Moye, P. G. C. . . . . Prelate.
B. F. Briggs, P. C. . . . . Treasurer.
J. D. Bullock, P C. . . . . Recorder.
C. E. Moore . . . . S. Warden.
S. C. Wells, P. C. . . . . Junior Warden.
T. B. Sugg . . . . Standard Bearer.
R. S. Barnes, P. C. . . . . Sword Bearer.
J. W. Hays . . . . Warder.
W. P. Snakenberg . . . . Sentinel.

SIR KNIGHTS.

W. H. Applewhite, P. C.	W. J. Harriss,	W. M. Ward,
Jas. T. Cobb,	Jas. Lipscomb,	J. M. Ward,
R. G. Briggs,	J. K. Peacock,	R. J. Noble,
E. C. Exum,	W. W. Richardson,	Thos. Bell.
Wiley Farmer,		

IVANHOE COMMANDERY No. 8—GREENSBORO.

Time of Stated Conclave : First Thursday of each month.

OFFICERS.

Geo. W. Whitsett . . . . Eminent Commander.
John J. Thornton . . . . Generalissimo.
James D. Glenn, P. C. . . . . Captain General.
James D. Miller . . . . Prelate.
H. H. Cartland . . . . Treasurer.
William T. Gayle . . . . Recorder.
Clayton A. Bray . . . . Senior Warden.
Samuel Browne . . . . Junior Warden.
Cornelius M. Vanstory . . . . Standard Bearer.
George Woodroffe . . . . Sword Bearer.
Albert H. Alderman, P. C. . . . . Warder.
Wm. G. Crutchfield . . . . Sentinel.

SIR KNIGHTS.

Alderman, Sidney L. P. C.   Hall Nathaniel L., P. C.   Jones, Burgess E.
Berger, Henry C.   Hackett, Chas. M.   Kantner, Jacob E.
Carr, Obed W.   Hennessee, Wm. A.   Lindley, Jno Van Morris
Dodson, Silas C.   Hill, Wm. B.   Marsh, Myron
Eckle. Eugene   Holt, Jas. II., Jr.   Newell, Dwight W.
French, Wm. C.   Holt, Edwin C.   Richardson, Wm. R.
Frost. Wm. S.   Ireland, Chas. H.   Stevens, Jesse F.
Groome, Pinckney L.   Johnson, Calvin C.   Williams, Joseph M.
Hales, Wm. S.

ST. JOHNS COMMANDERY No. 10—NEW BERNE.

Time of Stated Conclave : First and third Friday of each month.

OFFICERS.

T. W Dewey . . . . Eminent Commander.
James Redmond . . . . Generalissimo.
T. G. Hyman . . . . Captain General.
T. F. McCarthy . . . . Prelate.
T. A. Green . . . . Treasurer.
R. S. Primrose . . . . Recorder.
W. A. McIntosh . . . . Senior Warden.
John C. Green . . . . Junior Warden.
L. J. Taylor . . . . Standard Bearer.
H. R. Bryan . . . . Sword Bearer.
O. H. Guion . . . . Warder.
W. R. Waters . . . . Sentinel.

SIR KNIGHTS.

Abbott, D. H.	Hackburn, E. B.	Rowe, E. F.
Bradham, C. D.	Henderson, George	Street, S. R,
Basnight, J. S.	Lovick, H. J.	Ulrich, F.
Daniels, Thomas	Neal, B. B.	Warren. J. E.
Hackburn. J. H.		

ST. ALDEMAR No. 12—ENFIELD.

Time of Stated Conclave : Third Friday in each month.

OFFICERS.

David Bell . . . . Eminent Commander.
J. J. Whitaker . . . . Generalissimo.
W. F. Parker . . . . Captain General.
F. L. Pippen . . . . Prelate.
J. H. Parker . . . . Treasurer.
John A. Collins . . . . Recorder.
C. E. McGwigan . . . . Senior Warden.
H. C. Atkinson . . . . Junior Warden.
H. S. Harrison . . . . Standard Bearer.
F. W. Gregory . . . . Sword Bearer.
M. J. Carr . . . . Warder.
Thomas H. Taylor . . . . Sentinel.

SIR KNIGHTS.

Pittman, W. D.   Williams, C. A.

Abstract Returns of Subordinate Commanderies.

COMMANDERIES.	Numbers.	LOCATION.	Members 1897.	Knighted.	Admitted.	Dimitted.	Suspended.	Expelled.	Died.	Members 1898.
Plantagenet	1	Wilmington	50	2	...	3	...	...	1	48
Charlotte	2	Charlotte	54	9	3	2	...	...	1	63
Durham	3	Durham	21	...	...	2	...	...	...	19
Raleigh	4	Raleigh	36	5	1	1	2	...	...	39
Cyrene	5	Asheville	41	4	2	...	1	...	...	46
Piedmont	6	Winston	45	...	...	1	...	...	...	44
Mt. Lebanon	7	Wilson	21	3	1	...	...	...	1	24
Ivanhoe	8	Greensboro	32	6	...	1	...	...	...	37
St. George	9	Tarboro	10	...	...	...	...	...	...	...
St. John	10	New Berne	25	1	...	...	...	...	1	25
St. Aldemar	12	Enfield	14	3	...	...	...	...	...	17
			349	33	7	10	3	...	3	362

Total Gain 13

Grand Officers of the Grand Commandery of North Carolina, From 1881 to 1897, Inclusive.

Yr.	Grand Commanders.	Deputy Grand Commanders.	Grand Generalissimos.	Grand Capt. Generals.	Grand Treasurers.	Grand Recorders.
1881	Horace H. Munson	Lee W. Battle	George H. King	*Samuel S. Everett	William Simpson	James C Munds
1882	Horace H. Munson	Lee W. Battle	George H. King	Julian S. Carr	William Simpson	James C. Munds
1883	†Eugene Grissom	George H. King	*Andrew J. Blair	Willinm R. Cox	William Simpson	James C. Munds
1884	†Eugene Grissom	*Andrew J. Blair	*George W. Blount	David G. Maxwell	William Simpson	James C. Munds
1885	*Donald W. Bain	George H. King	John A. Porter	William W. Allen	William Simpson	James C. Munds
1886	*Donald W. Bain	John A. Porter	William W. Allen	†Carl A. Woodruff	William Simpson	James C. Munds
1887	†Carl A. Woodruff	William W. Allen	*Francis H. Glover	*Carl A. Woodruff	William Simpson	Horace H. Munson
1888	John A. Porter	*Edward M. Nadal	*Francis H. Glover	*Edward M. Nadal	William Simpson	Horace H. Munson
1889	John A. Porter	William W. Allen	James Southgate	Alfred H Stubbs	William Simpson	Horace H. Munson
1890	William W. Allen	James Southgate	Eugene S. Martin	Eugene S. Martin	William Simpson	Horace H. Munson
1891	William W. Allen	James Southgate	Eugene S. Martin	Francis M. Moye	William Simpson	Horace H. Munson
1892	James Southgate	Eugene S. Martin	Francis M. Moye	Francis M. Moye	William Simpson	Horace H. Munson
1893	Francis M. Moye	Alphonso H. Cobb	Peter A. Wilson	Peter A. Wilson, Jr	William Simpson	Horace H. Munson
1894	Alphonso H. Cobb	John C. Chase	Walter S. Liddell	John C. Chase	William Simpson	Horace H. Munson
1895	Walter S. Liddell	Wm. A. Withers	Jos. H. Hackburn	Wm. A. Withers	William Simpson	Horace H. Munson
1896	Wm. A. Withers	Jos. H Hackburn	Munford D. Bailey	James D. Glenn	William Simpson	Horace H. Munson
1897	Jos. H. Hckburn	Munford D. Bailey	Walter E. Storm	Wm. F. Randolph	William Simpson	Horace H. Munson
1898	Munford D. Bailey	Walter E. Storm	Wm. F. Randolph	James D. Bullock	William Simpson	Horace H. Munson

*Deceased.   †Removed from Jurisdiction.

EMINENT COMMANDERS.

W. P. Toomer . . . . Plantagenet No. 1.
William H. Chadbourn . . . . Plantagenet No. 1.
William R. Kenan . . . . Plantagenet No. 1.
E. P. Bailey . . . . Plantagenet No. 1.
W. W. Allen . . . . Plantagenet No. 1.
E. S. Martin . . . . Plantagenet No. 1.
J. C. Chase . . . . Plantagenet No. 1.
W. E. Storm . . . . Plantagenet No. 1.
A. G. Brenizer . . . . Charlotte No. 2.
John H. McAden . . . . Charlotte No. 2.
William Anderson . . . . . Charlotte No. 2.
T. R. Robertson . . . . Charlotte No. 2.
Thomas S. Franklin . . . . . . Charlotte No. 2.
William L. Wall . . . . Durham No. 3.
J. S. Carr . . . . Durham No. 3.
J. Southgate . . . . Durham No. 3.
L. W. Battle . . . . Durham No. 3.
John C. Drewry . . . . Raleigh No. 4.
Michael Bowes . . . . Raleigh No. 4.
William Simpson . . . . Raleigh No. 4.
Z. P. Smith . . . . Raleigh No. 4.
D. S. Hamilton . . . . Raleigh No. 4.
John A. Nichols . . . . Cyrene No. 5.
F. L. Jacobs . . . . Cyrene No. 5.
William F. Randolph . . . . Cyrene No. 5.
Arthur J. Wills . . . . Cyrene No. 5.
John A. Wagner . . . . Cyrene No. 5.
Henry T. Bahnson . . . . Piedmont No. 6.
Daniel P. Mast . . . . Piedmont No. 6.
Samuel H. Smith . . . . Piedmont No. 6.
Robert E. Dalton . . . . Piedmont No. 6.
Robert H. Jones . . . . Piedmont No. 6.
Stephen C. Wells . . . . Mt. Lebanon No. 7.
James D. Bullock . . . . Mt. Lebanon No. 7.
Benjamin F. Briggs . . . . Mt. Lebanon No. 7.
W. H. Applewhite . . . . Mt. Lebanon No. 7.
John J. Thornton . . . . Ivanhoe No. 8.
Charles H. Ireland . . . . Ivanhoe No. 8.
Nathaniel N. S. Hall . . . . Ivanhoe No. 8.
Sidney L. Alderman . . . . Ivanhoe No. 8.
Albert H. Alderman . . . . Ivanhoe No. 8.
James D. Glenn . . . . Ivanhoe No. 8.

George W. Whitsett . . . . Ivanhoe No. 8.
John W. Cotten . . . . St. George No. 9.
George Howard, Jr. . . . . St. George No. 9.
J. R. Pender . . . . St. George No. 9.
H. J. Lovick . . . . St. John No. 10.
F. Ulrich . . . . St. John No. 10.
T. W. Dewey . . . . St. John No. 10.
William J. Boykin . . . . DeMolai No. 11.
Simeon H. Smith . . . . DeMolai No. 11.
B. S. Royster . . . . DeMolai No. 11.
David Bell . . . . St. Aldemar No. 12.

Subordinate Commanderies Working Under the Jurisdiction of the Grand Commandery of North Carolina.

COMMANDERIES.	NO.	LOCATION.	COUNTY.	DATE OF CHARTERS.	RECORDERS.
Plantagenet	1	Wilmington	New Hanover	May 11, 1881.	H. G. Smallbones.
Charlotte	2	Charlotte	Mecklenburg	May 11, 1881.	Geo. A. Page.
Durham	3	Durham	Durham	May 11, 1881.	C. C. Taylor.
Raleigh	4	Raleigh	Wake	Oct. 11, 1882.	Wm. A. Withers.
Cyrene	5	Asheville	Buncombe	Oct. 11, 1882.	M. W. Robertson.
Piedmont	6	Winston	Forsyth	Oct. 15, 1884.	Daniel P. Mast.
Mt. Lebanon	7	Wilson	Wilson	Oct. 15, 1884.	W. J. Boykin.
Ivanhoe	8	Greensboro	Guilford	Aug. 2, 1887.	Wm. T. Gayle.
St. George	9	Tarboro	Edgecombe	June —, 1892.	C. J. Austin.
St. John	10	Newbern	Craven	Feb'y 15, 1893.	R. S. Primrose.
St. Aldemar	12	Enfield	Halifax	May 9, 1894.	John A. Collins.

Grand Representatives Commissioned by the Grand Commandery of North Carolina.

GRAND COMMANDERIES.	FROM NORTH CAROLINA.	
	GRAND REPRESENTATIVE.	POSTOFFICE.
Arizona.	Fred. Gaston Brecht	Prescott.
Alabama.	John B. Porterfield	Tuscumbia.
Arkansas.	John L. Sumpter.	Hot Springs.
California	Reuben H. Lloyd	San Francisco.
Colorado	Wm. T. Bridwell	Canon City.
Connecticut	Jas. H. Welsh	Danbury.
District of Columbia	John H. Olcott	Washington.
Florida	Wm. H. Reynolds	Orlando.
Georgia	James L. Eleming	Augusta.
Illinois	Gilbert W. Barnard	Chicago.
Indiana	Nathan L. Agnew	Valpariso.
Indian Territory	James A. Scott	Muscogee.
Iowa	Alfred Wingate	Des Moines.
Kansas	Edward P. Allen	Independence.
Kentucky	Henry T. Jefferson	Louisville.
Louisiana	Wm. H. Chaffe	New Orleans.
Maine	Albert M. Spear	Gardiner.
Maryland	Joseph F. Hindes.	Baltimore.
Massachusetts and R. I.	Edward L. Freeman	Central Falls.
Minnesota.	John C. Munro	St. Cloud.
Mississippi	Ebenezer Thompson	Biloxi.
Missouri.	F. J. Tygard	Butler.
Montana	Henry E. Day	Glendine.
Nebraska	W. K. Williams	York.
New Hampshire	Don. H. Woodward	Keene.
New Jersey	Joseph D. Congdon	Paterson.
New York	William Brandreth	Sing Sing.
North Dakota	John D. Black	Valley City.
Ohio	William T. McLean	Sidney.
Oregon	William Preston	Eugene City.
Pennsylvania	William H. Dickson	Philadelphia.
South Dakota	Martin G. Carlyle	DeSmith.
Tennessee	W. C. Smith	Nashville.
Texas	Daniel S. Malvin	Austin.
Vermont	William H. Vinton	Battleboro.
Virginia	Elbert C. Walthall	Richmond.
West Virginia	S. B. Crandall	Huntington.
Wisconsin	George C. Teall	Eau Clare.
Washington	James P. DeMattos	NewWhatcom
Wyoming	Perry L. Smith	Rawlins.

Grand Representatives Commissioned to the Grand Commandery of North Carolina.

GRAND COMMANDERIES.	TO NORTH CAROLINA.	
	GRAND REPRESENTATIVE.	POSTOFFICE.
Arizona	Rev. Chas. L. Hoffman	Charlotte.
Alabama	Rev. Geo. H. Bell	Bell.
Arkansas	Alfred H. Alderman	Greensboro.
California	Samuel H. Smith	Winston.
Colorado	James D. Glenn	Greensboro.
Connecticut	M. D. Bailey	Winston.
District of Columbia	Thomas R. Robertson	Charlotte.
Florida	Geo. Howard	Tarboro.
Georgia	Benj. R. Lacy	Raleigh
Illinois	Julian S. Carr	Durham.
Indiana	James Southgate	Durham.
Indian Territory	John C. Drewry	Raleigh.
Iowa	Eugene S. Martin	Wilmington.
Kansas	William Simpson	Raleigh.
Kentucky	Wm. A. Slater	Durham.
Louisiana	Jacob E. Kantner	Greensboro.
Maine	John A. Porter	Asheville.
Maryland	William F. Randolph	Asheville.
Massachusetts and R. I.	George H. King	Charlotte.
Minnesota	Francis M. Moye	Wilson.
Mississippi	Martin S. Willard	Wilmington.
Missouri	P. A. Wilson	Winston.
Montana	A. J. Wills	Asheville.
Nebraska	Alphonso H. Cobb	Asheville.
New Hampshire	James C. Munds	Wilmington.
New Jersey	F. Ulrich	New Berne.
New York	Horace H. Munson	Wilmington.
North Dakota	Joseph H. Hackburn	New Berne.
Ohio	John J. Thornton	Greensboro.
Oregon	Walter S. Liddell	Charlotte.
Pensylvania	E. J. Parrish	Durham.
South Dakota	Charles J. Austin	Tarboro.
Tennessee	John W. Cotten	Tarboro.
Texas	Michael Bowes.	Raleigh.
Vermont	Walter E. Storm	Wilmington.
Virginia	Alfred H. Stubbs	Asheville.
West Virginia	Rev. Walter S. Creasy	Winston.
Wiscosin	James D. Bullock	Winston.
Washington	John C. Chase	Wilmington.
Wyoming	William A. Withers	Raleigh.

Address of Grand Recorders.

Arizona	Geo. J. Roskruge	Tucson.
Alabama	H. Clay Armstrong	Montgomery.
Arkansas	James A. Henry	Little Rock.
Australia	Charles Chapman	271 Collins St. Victoria.
California	Thomas H. Caswell	San Francisco.
Colorado	Edward C. Parmelee	Masonic Temple, Denver,
Connecticut	Eli C. Birdsey	Meriden.
Canada	Will H. Whyte G. Chan.	P. O. Box 1207, Montreal,
District of Columbia	Adolphas B Bennett	Washington.
England and Wales	C. F. Matier	Mark Mason's Hall, Lon.
Florida	William A. McLean	Jacksonville.
Georgia	Samuel P. Hamilton	Savannah.
Grand Encampment	William H. Mayo	Security Bld'g, St. L., Mo.
Illinois	Gilbert W. Barnard	1900 Mas. Tem., Chicago.
Indiana	William H. Smythe	Indianopolis.
Indian Territory	Leo E. Bennett	Muskogee.
Iowa	Alfred Wingate	Des Moines.
Ireland	John A. Baker	Dublin.
Kansas	Andrew M. Callahan	211 E. Ave., Topeka.
Kentucky	Lorenzo D. Croninger	Covington.
Louisiana	Richard Lambert	New Orleans.
Maine	Stephen Berry	Portland.
Maryland	John H. Miller	Baltimore, Brown's whf.
Massachusetts & R. I.,	Benjamin W. Rowell	Lynn.
Michigan	John J. Gerow	Detroit.
Minnesota	Thomas Montgomery	St. Paul.
Mississippi	John L. Power	Jackson.
Missouri	William H. Mayo	Security Bld'g, St. Louis.
Montana	Edward D. Neill	Helena.
Nebraska	William R. Bowen	Omaha.
New Hampshire	George P. Cleaves	Concord.
New Jersey	Charles Bechtel	Trenton.
New York	John F. Shafer	Albany.
North Carolina	Horace H. Munson	Wilmington.
North Dakota	Frank J. Thompson	Fargo.
Ohio	John N. Bell	Dayton.
Oregon	James F. Robinson	Eugene.
Oklahoma	Harper S. Cunningham	Guthrie.
Pennsylvania	William W. Allen	Masonic Temple, Phila.
South Dakota	George A. Pettigrew	Flandreau.
Scotland	Lindsay Mackersey	Edinburg.
Tennessee	Wilbur F. Foster	Nashville.
Texas	J. C. Kidd	Houston.
Vermont	Warren G. Reynolds	Burlington.
Virginia	James B. Blanks	Petersburg.
Victoria	J. C. Kennedy, Gr. Chan	36 Darlington St., So. Yara
Washington	Yancey C. Bullock	Walla Walla. [Melbourne
West Virginia	Robert C. Dunnington	Fairmont.
Wisconsin	John W. Laflin	Milwaukee.
Wyoming	John C. Baird	Cheyenne.

Distinguished Dead in Other Jurisdictions.

CANADA.

DANIEL SPRY, G. C. of S. G. P.,

Died August 13, 1897.

COLORADO.

THOMAS SPANGLER, P. G. C.,

Died December 12, 1897.

CONNECTICUT.

JAMES B. WILDMAN, P. G. C.,

Died June 27, 1897.

ILLINOIS.

VINCENT LOMBARD HURLBURT, P. G. M.,

Died July 24, 1896.

JEROME B. GORIN, P. G. C.,

Died September 1, 1897.

INDIANA.

THOMAS NEWBY, P. G. C.,

Died June 16, 1897.

ALEXANDER THOMAS, P. G. C.,

Died July 26, 1897.

LOUISIANA.

JOHN Q. A. FELLOWS, P. G. M.,

Died November 28, 1897.

MASSACHUSETTS.

BENJAMIN DEAN, P. G. M.,

Died April 9, 1897.

MICHIGAN.

EUGENE ROBINSON, P. G. C. G.,

Died October 28, 1897.

MINNESOTA.

LUTHER ZOAN ROGERS, P. G. C.,

Died April 27, 1897.

THOMAS SEWELL, P. G. C.,
Died February 28, 1898.

JOHN DWYER, Gr. Generalissimo,
Died May 7, 1897.

PENNSYLVANIA.

JOSEPH S. WRIGHT, P. G. C.,
Died May 26, 1897.

EUGENE STOCKER, P. G. C.,
Died May 23, 1897.

TENNESSEE.

WILLIAM MORGAN BROOKS, P. G. C.,
Died August 7, 1897.

TEXAS.

JOHN SAYLES, P. G. C. G.,
Died May 22, 1897.

WEST VIRGINIA.

ODELL SQUIER LONG, P. G. C.,
Died December 26, 1897.

We Mourn Our Dead.

PLANTAGENET No. 1—WILMINGTON.

JOHN C. MANN, P. E. C.,

Died Colorado, October 29, 1897.

CHARLOTTE No. 2—CHARLOTTE.

J. H. MORSE,

Died March 6, 1898.

MT. LEBANON No. 7—WILSON.

WILLIAM DANIEL.

Died September 25, 1897,

ST. JOHN No. 10—NEW BERNE.

JOHN B. CLARK,

Died October 20, 1897.

REPORT OF THE

Committee on Correspondence.

2

REPORT OF THE

COMMITTEE ON CORRESPONDENCE.

...

To the Grand Commandery of North Carolina:

Our Fourth Report on Correspondence is herewith presented for your consideration. As heretofore, the Proceedings have been reviewed in alphabetical order. The report is sent to the printer some weeks before the meeting of the Grand Commandery and at this writing several jurisdictions have not been heard from. Should they not appear in their proper place they may possibly be found at the rear of the procession, just in advance of the "Conclusion," if there be one.

ALABAMA.

THIRTY-SEVENTH ANNUAL CONCLAVE.   Birmingham, May 12th, 1897.
SIR ROBERT L. DOUGLASS. R. E. Grand Commander.

The Grand Commandery having been escorted by Cyrene Commandery to their Asylum were welcomed in a happy manner by Eminent Commander Polk. Grand Commander Douglass made a fitting response and after refreshments were served they got down to work.

Twelve Grand Officers were present and nine Commanderies represented. Seventeen Grand Representatives were in attendance, no one appearing for North Carolina, however.

The Grand Commander presents a detailed report of his official acts and announces the death of Sir Daniel Smith, Past Grand Commander and Sir John L. Rison, Grand Treasurer.

He says that the year has been a trying one, considered from a business standpoint and the returns do not show the desired growth, but they have taken no backward steps and are as ready as ever to rally to the defense of the principles of the Order.

An even dozen of dispensations were issued, three-fourths of them relating to the ballot.

The Christmas Observance does not seem to flourish in this jurisdiction, as he says that only one Commandery participated.

The several Grand Officers present reports of their visitations, which traverse the usual ground. One reports of a certain Commandery, that the,

"Membership is scattered to the four quarters of the earth, with a roll of 129 names, some of whom love gold and others love silver—none of whom have more than they wish."

From others we clip the following:

"There were two features of this banquet worthy of mention, to-wit: the presence of the ladies and a number of invited guests, and the absence of wine. The former is a source of enjoyment and pleasure to the Sir Knights and, no doubt, equally so to the visitors; the latter is in keeping with the high-toned morality which should characterize all Knights Templars who try to exemplify in their lives and conduct the teachings of Him whose doctrines are the Knights Templars' creed. Some of the most entertaining and decidedly the most learned, cultured and refined responses were made by the ladies."

The Grand Treasurer reports his cash balance as being $336.

A committee on Triennial was appointed and $400 appropriated for the Grand Commandery expenses on that occasion.

A unique ceremony was the presentation of the eight months' old son of the Grand Commander for adoption and dedication by the Grand Commandery, the presentation address being as follows:

"I have taken the liberty of presenting to you the first born of your Grand Commander. This boy comes of a Masonic ancestry; his great-grand fathers were prominent Masons, his grandfather is a Knight Templar and a thirty-second degree Scottish Rite Mason, and his father is your Grand Commander. When this baby was born, his mother, who is a Roman Catholic, foreseeing, perhaps, that he would probably desire to follow the example of his ancestors, gave him to me, and he was christened a Protestant Episcopalian that he might not be embarassed by the prohibition of the church when he reached his majority and desired to be initiated into our Order. As a man offers to what he loves best his dearest posessions, I dedicate to this Grand Commandery that which I hold most dear, this little curly haired boy, and promise, if the example of his father can incite in him a favorable opinion of our Order, I will so live that when he has grown to a man's estate, he will freely and voluntarily offer himself as a candidate for Masonry."

The Deputy Grand Commander made an appropriate response for the Grand Commandery, accepting and adopting the offering.

The evening was devoted to the Annual Oration by Sir and Rev. Owen P. Fitzsimmons, Grand Prelate, and an elegant banquet, in which the ladies participated.

The proceedings contain a portrait and biographical sketch of Grand Commander Douglass and it appears that he and the Grand Commandery are twins, at least they were born on the same day.

No Report on Correspondence appears, but a slip pasted into the volume and dated February 11th, 1898, reads as follows.

EXPLANATORY.

"As appears on page 38, Sir George F. Moore, Chairman of the Committee on Correspondence, made report, which was ordered printed with the Proceedings of the Grand Commandery. Soon after the report was handed the Grand Recorder, Sir Moore requested to be allowed to retain the manuscript for revision and correction, which request was granted and the manuscript has not been returned. A short time after the meeting of the Grand Commandery he was called to New York on business matters, and there became ill and has remained so until the present time; and inasmuch as it is not known when he will be able to return, it has been deemed proper to send out the Proceedings without the report."

Our sympathy and best wishes go out to Frater Moore in his affliction and we trust he will have a speedy recovery. We would suggest, however, that when they get another report they send it to the printer without waiting for a revision.

Ten Commanderies, 380 Knights; loss 2.

Sir Henry H. Matthews, Montgomery, Grand Commander.

Sir H. Clay Armstrong, Montgomery, Grand Recorder, (re-elected.)

Sir George F. Moore, Montgomery; Committee on Correspondence.

Next Conclave, Selma, May 11th, 1898.

ARIZONA.

Five Grand Officers failed to appear but every Commandery was represented. Eight Grand representatives were also in attendance, North Carolina's not being one of the number.

The Grand Commander presents a brief address and announces with pleasure that death has not invaded their ranks during the year.

The Christmas observance was celebrated by every Commandery, after which they attended religious services in full uniform.

" 'Phœnix' Commandery No. 3, was especially favored upon this occasion by being presented by Sir P. K. Hickey, with a case of wine from the vineyards of 'Patriarcat Latin of Jerusalem, Palestine.' The occasion is rare, indeed, when Sir Knights so far distant from the Holy City are permitted to drink the health of their Most Eminent Grand Master in pure and sparkling wine produced, perchance, from vines growing upon the very hills made holy by the footprints of our Lord and Savior."

He has some forcible words in regard to the necessity of proficiency in tactics, saying :

"It is as necessary, and should be considered by each Sir Knight, that he should be as familiar with the sword exercise and with the ordinary movements required in the conferring of the Orders, as the officers who do the principal part of the work. The absolute correctness of all military movements incident to the work is very important, and, unless properly executed, they detract very much from the beauties of the ceremony. When a Commandery appears on the street, it should at least be able to go through with ordinary precision the simple movements required for the street parade, otherwise they are liable to detract from the almost universally high opinion held of our Order and its military accomplishments."

The Grand Treasurer reports a gratifying increase in the funds in his hands during the year, they now amounting to $438.

The proceedings contain the following, which moves us to ask what the Grand Recorder did with the proceedings that he is supposed to have received? Perhaps they were "lost in transmission," to use a convenient expression invented by our

own Grand Recorder, to get a member of the Correspondence
Committee out of a cavity.

Sir Charles W. Johnstone, from the Committee on Correspondence, presented the following :

"Your Committee on Correspondence begs leave to report that no correspondence has been submitted to it."

On motion, the report was received.

The same Committee is continued for another year and we
hope that the proceedings now due will contain a report, "as
is a report."

Three Commanderies, 122 Knights; gain 8.

Sir John M. Ormsby, Tucson, Grand Commander.

Sir George J. Roskruge, Tucson, Grand Recorder, (re-
elected.)

Sir Archibald J. Sampson, Phœnix, Chairman of Committee on Correspondence.

Next Conclave, Bisbee, November 10th, 1897.

ARKANSAS.

TWENTY-FIFTH ANNUAL CONCLAVE.   Little Rock, April 20th, 1897.
   SIR GEORGE THORNBURGH, R. E. Grand Commander.

All of the Grand Officers were at their posts and nine of
the thirteen Commanderies represented. An even dozen of
Grand Representatives were also present but North Carolina's
was not among them.

The Grand Commander's address is quite brief when correspondence and orders are eliminated. One decision and two
dispensations are the sum total in their respective classes and
they arouse no adverse criticism.

Proposed official visitation had to be abandoned on account
of the serious and prolonged illness of his wife, whom we trust
by this time has been fully restored to health.

The Grand Commandery mourns the loss of Sir Knight
Frederick Kramer, Grand Treasurer, whose funeral called out
the largest assemblage of Sir Knights ever seen in the State.

The Grand Treasurer reports his cash balance as being $475, being practically the same amount the treasury contained at the beginning of the year. The failure of two Commanderies to make returns makes quite a shrinkage in their membership, and those reporting show that they have just barely held their own during the year.

The business of the Conclave was light and of local interest only.

Eminent Sir F. J. H. Rickon, Past Grand Generalissimo, and for several years Committee on Correspondence, having removed to California, the Grand Commandery adopted a very complimentary resolution commending him to the courtesy and hospitality of his new Templar associates. We have the most pleasant recollections of our reportorial associations with Frater Rickon and our best wishes follow him.

Sir Knight Oliver C. Gray, Committee on Foreign Correspondence, gives a list of the Grand Commandery proceedings he has received and placed on file, North Carolina for 1896 being included. We give a liberal quotation from his report, as follows:

"Hindered by causes not necessary to mention here we have not been able to prepare a review, but will, if possible, do so by the close of the next Templar year."

Basking in the light of this announcement we confidently look for the appearance of a double-header the coming year. Last year his name appeared in large type as Oliver *Cromwell;* this year it is *Crosby,* but no explanation is vouchsafed.

Thirteen Commanderies, 492 Knights; loss 42.

Sir George C. Latta, Hot Springs, Grand Commander.

Sir James A. Henry, Little Rock, Grand Recorder, (re-elected.)

Sir Oliver C. Gray, Little Rock, Committee on Foreign Correspondence.

Next Conclave, Fayetteville, April 19th, 1898.

CALIFORNIA.

THIRTY-NINTH ANNUAL CONCLAVE.   San Francisco, April 22d, 1897.
SIR TROWBRIDGE H. WARD, R. E. Grand Commander.

The Grand Officers were all present and thirty-four Commanderies represented. The representatives of 28 Grand Commanderies were also in attendance, North Carolina's being among the faithful.

The Grand Commander's address is a lengthy document as it includes his correspondence, orders and the reports of the inspecting officers. He reports the Order as being in good condition in spite of the financial condition of the country not being all that might be desired, also that peaceful relations universally prevail. A graceful tribute is paid to the memory of Past Grand Master, Benjamin Dean, who was at the head of the Grand Encampment when it convened in San Francisco in 1883. Ten dispensations were issued for a variety of purposes and he was called on for several decisions, all of which appear to be sound and were duly approved. He considers it fortunate that so few questions were asked as "our Templar law is in such a shape that it is a difficult matter to know just what it is."

Official visitation was indulged in to quite an extent, nearly one-half of the Commanderies having had an opportunity to welcome the Grand Commander. The only adverse comment he offers is, an excessive number of candidates on two occasions.

The Christmas Observance received due attention and he reports that the system of "Department Conclaves" had had its first trial and was "a success in every particular."

He does not believe in conferring the Order of the Red Cross upon more than two candidates at the same Conclave and Protests against the lavish expenditure by Commanderies for entertainment on such occasions, holding that a large majority of the members of the Order would prefer to have a portion or all of the large amount expended devoted to charitable purposes. If a majority are opposed to the present practice we do not see why the objectionable practice has not already been done away with.

He is a firm believer in their law requiring affiliation in Lodge and Chapter as a requisite to good standing in the Commandery and desires that their representatives to the next Grand Encampment use their efforts to have the conflicting laws of the Grand Encampment repealed. Without touching upon the merits of the question we think that the easiest and probably the only sure way to bring about an agreement in the conflicting laws would be to amend their own, for the Grand Encampment is a powerfully hard body to move. We quote as follows:

"If they were allowed, a large majority of the Sir Knights of this jurisdiction would have their dimits in their pocket and pay no dues and would affiliate with only our Commanderies; and I am afraid that if this practice is continued that some of our members will even take their dimits from our Commanderies and become members only of the Order known as the Mystic Shrine, of which order their connection with us as Knights only gives them the privilege of becoming members."

We can hardly believe that the case is as bad as he makes it out and trust that his fears are not well founded.

The Masonic Widows' and Orphans' home is heartily commended and he notes having assisted at the laying of the corner stone.

The reports of the Department Commanders and their Inspectors are very full and indicate a generally satisfactory state of affairs. Appended to the tabular report is a note that will interest Correspondents, which we quote.

"To the question, 'How many have read the report of the Committee on Correspondence?' of the twenty Commanderies answering there were forty who did."

An average of two to each Commandery, or practically two per cent. Well, all we can say is, that the others do not know what they missed, and can console ourself with the thought that Sodom and Gomorrah would have been saved if the same proportion of righteous men could have been found.

A portrait of Grand Commander Ward faces the title page.

The Grand Treasurer has $2,271, to his credit, which is a slight gain over the amount he had at the beginning of the year.

V. E. Sir Reuben Hedley Lloyd, Deputy Grand Master of

the Grand Encampment, was received with due honor and "responded in his usual happy and eloquent manner." North Carolina is proud to claim the distinguished frater as her representative near the Grand Commandery of California and if he should happen to be called upon to convene the Grand Encampment of 1901 in some city of our state we can assure him a "Tar Heel" welcome. We expect however that our delegation will be obliged to journey to larger and more prosperous jurisdictions for many a Triennial to come.

The business of the Conclave was generally of local interest only but we note the following resolution as showing one matter the Grand Encampment will have to wrestle with next year.

"Resolved, That it is the sense of this Grand Commandery that the organic law of the Grand Encampment ought to be modelled after that of the General Grand Chapter of Royal Arch Masons, and should embody the principle that the several Grand Commanderies are entitled to the sole government of their subordinates, subject only to the regulations of the Grand Encampment in the matter of the ritual, uniform, nomenclature, rank of officers and such matters as appertain exclusively to the general welfare of the Order, and leaving every matter and thing of local concern to the exclusive regulation of the Grand Commanderies"

Their Representatives near other Grand Commanderies are instructed to bring this matter to the attention of the bodies to whom they are commissioned.

We give a quotation from the report of the Committee on Reports of Grand Officers, which shows the hold that Frater Davies has on their affections.

"We also believe that the Committee on Correspondence should be maintained; that while the correspondence itself may not be read by a majority of the Templars of this jurisdiction, it is of great value to those who do read it, and should be placed in the hands of every Templar in this jurisdiction. The printing of such is the universal practice of all Templar Grand Jurisdictions."

Sir William A. Davies presents his fourth Report on Correspondence. He fills 126 pages with a genial review of the doings of 44 Templar Bodies, North Carolina for 1896 coming in for kindly mention and fair share of his space. Commenting on our note that the ladies joined in the Christmas Toast on one occasion in Michigan he says.

"We desire to go on record right here, as heartily favoring the innovation, and we believe that the general adoption of the custom would
quickly settle the vexed question of what beverage to use in the toast."

Of course we do not pretend to know the secret workings of
Frater Davies' mind, and do not wish to do him an injustice,
but it might naturally be inferred that he thought the function
would become a sort of a "high tea." There is a logical connection between *tea* and *toast*, but all the same he may have
"cold tea" in mind, that seductive beverage which achieved
such notoriety in legislative halls a few years ago.

We would like to tarry longer with Frater Davies but our
list is a long one and space limited and we shall have to part
company with the hope that next October will find us both in
Pittsburg.

Thirty-six Commanderies, 3,033 Knights; gain 92.

Sir George D. Metcalf, Oakland, Grand Commander.

Sir Thomas H. Caswell, San Francisco, Grand Recorder,
(re-elected.)

Sir William A Davies, Sacramento, Chairman of Committee
on Correspondence.

Next Conclave, San Francisco, April 21st, 1898.

CANADA.

FOURTEENTH ANNUAL ASSEMBLY.   Montreal, August 19th 1897.
SIR WILL H. WHYTE, Supreme Grand Master.

Only 17 of the 40 Grand Officers were in attendance and 10
of the 37 Preceptories were unrepresented.

The Grand Master presents a well prepared address. He
very properly regards the past year as an eventful one to the
British Empire on account of Her Majesty the Queen having
completed the longest reign in the history of Great Britain.
This event was recognized by the Senior and Past Officers of
Great Priory by sending her a congratulatory address illumi-
nated on Vellum and bound in a handsome Morocco covered
album.

A glowing account is given of his visitation to Detroit Commandery of Detroit, Michigan, honorary membership being conferred upon him and a handsome certificate and jewel of membership presented. Two Commanderies in Chicago were also visited and he says:

"The expressions of regard and good will that have been expressed during these international visits, I trust will long be remembered and help to bind more closely together in the bonds of harmony and good fellowship the fratres of the United States and Canada."

Two of his nine dispensations were to permit the making of "serving fratres." We presume that the majority of our brethren are as ignorant of the meaning of the term as we were ourself until we had perused the Report on Correspondence and will say right here that a "serving frater is one who has had the degrees conferred on him free of charge for the purpose of enabling him to 'serve' as Guard, (or Janitor.)"

A Preceptory asked for a dispensation to permit them to elect officers at a special meeting, having failed to hold their annual meeting. The dispensation not coming in time they proceeded without it and were brought up with a round turn by the Grand Master's refusal to confirm their action.

He well says:

"Preceptories should be careful to conform to our laws and regulations and not expect the Grand Master to condone illegal actions."

St. John Encampment, formerly an independent body, has come into the fold of Great Priory, but St. Stephen, the only remaining one, still holds aloof.

An affecting tribute is paid to the memory of Sir Knight Daniel Spry, Past Supreme Grand Master, and Grand Chancellor since 1876, who died the week before Great Priory convened.

He reports that the new ritual is ready for distribution, also that numerous objections had been made to the Baldric as a part of the uniform, to which he adds his own disapproval of it.

He strongly condems the custom of conferring the rank of Preceptor, (E. C. on our side of the line,) upon those who have never been elected and installed into the office and we consider his stand too sound to be questioned.

From one of his official circulars we take the following:

"Much, very much depends upon the presiding officer. As in the present month of December the elections of officers take place, I trust that only good and true men will be elected to this extremely important position.

"I deem it also a mistake to keep continually in office old members, no matter how competent they may be, if any of the younger members show any competency. It checks ambition in the younger fraters and deadens enthusiasm among those who might perhaps prove valuable members of the Order. I am in favor of giving the younger members an opportunity of proving themselves in office."

The various Provincial Priors submit full reports, which generally indicate a satisfactory state of affairs. A review of their reports by the Grand Council expresses the opinion that the adoption of a uniform by all of the Preceptories would lead to an increased membership and better attendance at the meetings; also that Provincial Priors should be selected who will faithfully visit the Preceptories under their charge, as it is unjust to some of those bodies who have been neglected year after year.

The Grand Treasurer reports his cash balance as being 2,223.00 there having been a slight increase during the year.

The Committee on Jurisprudence dealing with the question of conferring the honorary rank of Eminent Preceptor very sensibly say :

"We feel that we cannot advise Great Priory to confer honors alone for local benefits conferred, when in the usual order of affairs it lay within the powers of said Preceptories to confer such honors themselves, (by election to the office,) such vouched for recipients being willing to accept."

A pleasing feature of the occasion was the visit to Great Priory of two American Commanderies, Trinity No. 1 of Manchester, N. H. and Lewistown No. 7 of Lewistown, Me. Having been introduced they were received by the Supreme Grand Master with words of fraternal and Knightly welcome. Of course the American bird flapped his wings in response, E. Sir Heath of Trinity well saying that :

"Though Canadian and American Knights owed allegiance to different flags, they could all unite under one grand banner, the Beausant of the Temple."

The proceedings are embellished with portraits of the deceased Grand Chancellor, Sir Daniel Spry, and the new Supreme Grand Master, Sir Daniel F. McWatt.

Several pages of the proceedings are devoted to an account of the festivities incident to the visit of the American Sir Knights, consisting of a carriage ride, reception, parade and run through the Lachine Rapids.

"The sail up the Lachine canal was decidedly relieved by the thoroughly happy and entertaining spirit which seemed to permeate all. The time was not allowed to drag in the slightest degree. The presence of the bagpipes was a guarantee for that, for there was Scotch music galore, and the dancing of the Highland Fling, Ghillie Callum and Sailor's Hornpipe were greatly appreciated, especially by the American Visitors."

Report on Correspondence is again from the pen of Sir Henry Robertson, whom we regret to see retires from the corps. He has reviewed the proceedings of 36 Templar Bodies and the result fills 47 pages, net.

North Carolina for 1897 has brief space and her Correspondent gets courteous mention. As usual he is sparing of comment and we find no reason to dissent from the few opinions that have been allowed to break out. As there is no "conclusion" we shall look for his *vale* next year.

Thirty-seven Preceptories.   1,764 Knights; gain 216.

Sir Daniel F. McWatt, Barrie, Ont., Supreme Grand Master.

Sir Will H. Whyte, Montreal, Grand Chancellor.

Sir George J. Bennett, Toronto, Chairman of Committee on Fraternal Correspondence.

Next Assembly, Hamilton, Ont.   Time not fixed.

COLORADO.

TWENTY-SECOND ANNUAL CONLAVE.   Denver, June 1st, 1897.
    SIR EUGENE P. SHOVE, R. E. Grand Commander.

All of the Grand Officers were in attendance and only two of the Commanderies were without representation. We note that our Grand Representative was one of the 16 who shared the Grand Commander's welcome.

The Grand Commander announces peace and harmony as prevailing, the only discord which threatened having been amicably settled. We are inclined to think that it is well to have the monotony of eternal harmony suffer a slight fracture now and then. As Whittier says:

"Methinks the spirit's temper grows too soft in this still air;
The bark by tempest vainly tossed may founder in the calm,
And he who braved the polar frost faint by the isles of balm."

He announces the death of R. E. Sir Webster D. Anthony, the first Past Grand Commander they have been called upon to mourn and second oldest in point of rank. He was also Past Grand Master of the Grand Lodge of A. F. & A. M. The fraternal dead of sister jurisdictions are duly noticed.

Five dispensations were called for, one being for the formation of a new Commandery. Another permitted a Commandery to appear as escort at the funeral of the wife of one of the Sir Knights. The Committee on Jurisprudence considered it a bad precedent to establish and declined to give it their sanction.

Only three Commanderies basked in the refulgence of official visitation and we are not even told that he entered upon his term of office with the intention of visiting the whole number.

Ten Commanderies assembled on Christmas Day and 13 attended Divine service on Easter, which calls out the following.

"I urgently recommend that this day be observed by every Commandery 'Christ is risen' should be in every heart, and we of the Order of Christian Knighthood should assemble and render testimony to our faith."

The two decisions he reports were approved and we give one of them. The Eminent Commander and Captain General elect having refused to be installed he decides that,

"First—The Sir Knights had the right to refuse to be installed. Second —That there was no vacancy in either the office of Eminent Commander or Captain General, and that the old occupants of these offices held over respectively. Third—The election as to these offices may be declared void by the Commandery."

Their treasury has been depleted to a slight extent during the year, but they need not have any apprehensions of immediate want, as the Grand Treasurer reports $1,514, to his credit.

The Official Drill Master regrets that he cannot present a favorable report in regard to the advancement of the drill and work, and suggests some changes that he thinks would be productive of good results. The Jurisprudence Committee considered it best to give the present scheme another trial before making any changes, and their views prevailed.

A Triennial Committee was authorized, to have full charge of all arrangements.

The proposed change in the organic law of the Grand Encampment, which emanates from Past Commander Speed of Mississippi, did not commend itself to the Grand Commandery.

A charter was granted to a Commandery that had been working under a dispensation.

Sir Knight Harper M. Orahood comes to a present with his seventeenth Report on Correspondence. Forty-three Grand Jurisdictions have passed in review and his inspection fills 64 pages. As heretofore, extracts abound, but they are bonded with the cement of genial, if rather sparse criticism. He locates himself by saying, under Indiana:

"We come under the 'Extract' class, but try to cut out the greater part of what Brother Ruckle seems not to approve in our quotations. It is often more difficult to prune and cut down than to put it all in."

That last sentence is a solid nugget of truth.

North Carolina for 1896 is duly noticed and quoted from.

Under Connecticut we quote him on a live subject in many jurisdictions.

"We believe, as we have often stated, in voluntary membership Yet the other side of the question is to be considered, and we believe every Mason should help bear the burders as well, and that it is right, if he chooses to be a Knight Templar, that he should be required to keep up membership, under ordinary circumstances, in Lodge and Chapter."

Regarding the uniform question he says, in reviewing Maryland:

"The better way is to charge for the uniform with the fee for the Orders, and furnish it by the Commandery. It works in practice too."

We quote his concluding words, relating to the Triennial.

"Already the murmur of preparation for the next Triennial is heard. We commend to those who will compose the next body a careful con-

2

sideration of the many criticisms on past Conclaves for neglect of duty in failing to properly consider and dispose of needed legislation. As every society, organization or community reflects the general average standing, sentiment, feeling and morality of its members, we must conclude that the Triennial, with its attendant display and social features, is a fair index of the desires of the great body of the Order. If improvement and advancement are made, it must be by a general uplifting and improvement of our members."

Twenty-four Commanderies, 1,654 Knights; gain 3.

Sir George J. Dunbaugh, Pueblo, Grand Commander.

Sir Ed. C. Parmelee, Denver, Grand Recorder, (re-elected.)

Sir Harper M. Orahood, Denver, Chairman of Committee on Correspondence.

Next Conclave, Denver, June 7th, 1897.

CONNECTICUT.

SEVENTIETH ANNUAL CONCLAVE.　　　New Haven, March 16, 1897.
SIR LYMAN H. JOHNSON, R. E. Grand Commander.

The Grand Officers were all present and every Commandery represented. Twenty-nine Grand Representatives were also present but North Carolina's was among the missing.

The Grand Commander's address is not very long, but is a very complete account of his official acts. Two-thirds of his 28 dispensations permitted public appearance in uniform for various purposes, from which we infer that our Connecticut Sir Knights have solved the problem of keeping their plumes from becoming moth eaten. Official visitation was indulged in to a limited extent. No decisions were called for and "no complaints marring the peace and harmony of the body have arisen."

The funds in the Grand Treasurer's hands count up $593, a falling off of about a hundred dollars during the year.

The Grand Inspector presents a detailed report, having inspected ten of the eleven Commanderies, and we quote :

"It gives me great pleasure to be able to report that, as a whole, these bodies in the last two years have improved very much in the manner in which the orders are conferred, as well as in other particulars, and I am satisfied that they have received great benefit from the yearly inspections

ordered by this Grand Body, and, so long as the criticisms and suggestions of the Inspecting Officer are received in the spirit in which they are
made, the future will show greater improvement than has the past.''

Their inspection system has evidently come to stay, as we
note that Sir Knight Spencer, the present Inspector, was re-
elected for a term of five years.

The Committee on Testimonial to Past Grand Commander,
William R. Higby, who has rounded out his *thirtieth* year as
Grand Treasurer, reported that they had procured and placed
in his residence "an English hall clock with plate suitably inscribed thereon." We assume that it was *"English"* in name
only, for the idea of a Connecticut committee buying a clock of
foreign make is too absurd to be entertained for a moment. It
seems that the "good wife" of Brother Higby suggested the
procuring of a clock and we have no doubt that it is one that
will hold up its hands in horror if he stays too late at the
"Lodge;" certainly it can have no adjustment to deceive the
"good wife" as to the true time of his return.

The Committee on Accommodations at the Triennial reported that they had secured quarters at the same hotel at
which the Grand Encampment puts up.

It was voted that M. E. Grand Master Thomas be invited to
be present as the guest of the Grand Commandery at their next
Conclave.

V. E. Sir Henry W. Rugg, Grand Senior Warden of the
Grand Encampment, was present as the Representative of the
M. E. Grand Master and installed the newly elected officers.

A well written report is presented by the Committee on Necrology, in which the death of distinguished Fratres of sister
jurisdictions is announced in well chosen words, their own official circle having been spared any affliction during the year.

A reception and banquet given by New Haven Commandery
was the event of the evening preceding the Conclave. Among
the toasts we notice one to President McKinley: "The first
among his equals, the peer of kings, and a Sir Knight of Can-
ton Commandery, No. 38, of Ohio." As he has achieved no
prominence in Knighthood we are rather disposed to question
the propriety of such a toast at such a time, although we presume we are incurring the risk of an avalanche of reproaches

from some of our stalwart reviewers. We may probably miti-
gate somewhat the heinousness of our presumed crime by
heartily endorsing the following, the italics being ours :

"New Haven Commandery, Eminent Commander Hoadley and his as-
sistants, on this occasion, were deserving of great credit for their bound-
less hospitality, and *especially for limiting the after-dinner exercises to a
few*, and those few very excellent speeches, thus enabling the members of
the Grand Commandery to obtain the necessary rest for the labors of the
ensuing day, or rather the day that had already commenced."

The proceedings are embellished with steel-engraved portraits
of Grand Commander Johnson and Past Grand Commander,
John G. Root, the latter getting a biographical sketch in addition.

A special Conclave was held at Hartford on July 14th, for the
purpose of dedicating the Asylum of Washington Commandery,
and assisting in the celebration of the one hundreth anniversary of their organization. There was a large attendance
and a very successful and enjoyable occasion is reported.

The Report on Correspondence is the maiden effort of Past
Grand Commander Hugh Stirling, and he devotes 60 pages to
a genial review of the doings of 40 Grand Bodies. North Carolina for 1896 is courteously noticed. Commenting on the dispensations granted, he notes one permitting a Commandery
"to assist in the Story of the Reformation," and queries as to
its being a "Masonic Occasion." We give it up, and get out
of it by saying the proceedings of the following year will show
him that a repetition of the indulgence called out the censure
of the Committee on Jurisprudence. We are afraid that he
has missed the point about the printer being "set up" when he
printed the list of Past Commanders in their 1895 proceedings.
Apparently he has a leaning to the New York side of the question, as evidenced by the following :

"When we consider that the State of New York has over eleven thousand Templars upon its roll, and upon which it pays a per capita tax, and
its representation in the Grand Encampment is the same as that of a Grand
Commandery having only one hundred and fourteen members, we are
compelled in all fairness to admit the injustice of the plan."

A perusal of the Report of the Committee on Credentials at
the Grand Encampment will show that the large Grand Commanderies have about double the representation of the small

ones, on an average, so the present plan is not quite so inequitable as it appears.

Under Tennessee, commenting on their action relating to Knights Templar who are engaged in the sale of malt or spiritous liquors as a beverage, he says :

We don't like the following, for the simple reason that, as long as one does not violate the law, he should be at liberty to engage in any business he chooses ; and futher. we doubt if it will be the means of preventing the manufacture, sale or use of a single drop of spiritous liquors. The way to prevent Templars from following the liquor traffic is not to make such men Templars."

We are disposed to think that his reasoning is a little shaky, for what is to prevent a lapse from rectitude after becoming a Templar? Such things have happened. But this is Brother Foster's affair and we will drop out, for Brother Stirling continues as Correspondent and we do not care to risk a *spicy* (nutmeggy) rejoinder the coming year.

Eleven Commanderies, 2363 Knights ; gain 65.

Sir Samuel M. Bronson, Hartford, Grand Commander.

Sir Eli C. Birdsey, Meridan, Grand Recorder, (re-elected.)

Sir Hugh Stirling, Bridgeport, Committee on Correspondence.

Next Conclave, Hartford, March 15th, 1898.

1898.

SEVENTY-FIRST ANNUAL CONCLAVE.   Hartford, March 15th.

SIR SAMUEL M. BRONSON, R. E. Grand Commander.

Two Grand Officers were absent, but every Commandery was represented, with a large delegation of past officers and permanent members. Sir James H. Welsh, for North Carolina, was one of the 31 Grand Representatives in attendance.

M. E. Grand Master W. LaRue Thomas, V. E. Grand Recorder H. Wales Lines and V. E. Grand Warder Joseph A. Locke, of the Grand Encampment. were received with due honors and courteously welcomed.

The Grand Commander's address is a brief recital of his official acts. He reports with satisfaction that the year has been one of prosperity and the duties of office light. They have been called upon to mourn the death of Sir James B. Wildman,

Past Grand Commander, and Sir Henry Gardiner, the oldest Past Commander of their oldest Commandery.

Sixteen dispensations were issued, nine permitting public appearance in full Templar regalia of six Commanderies, and the other seven relating to the ballot. Official visitation was indulged in to limited extent. No decisions were called for.

He recommends that each Commandery observe Ascension Day by attending Divine service, also that they do honor to the M. E. Grand Master on Christmas Day by assembling at their Asylums at high 12, not forgetting on this occasion to make a voluntary offering for the Templar Hospital Fund for the sick at the Masonic Home. He also advises that each Commandery have a "Field Day" in each year, for social enjoyment. The several recommendations were endorsed by the Grand Commandery.

Their veteran Grand Treasurer, Sir William R. Higby, being absent for the first time in his official history, on account of sickness, a telegram of condolence was sent to him. His report shows a balance of $667 to the credit of the Grand Commandery.

The Grand Inspector presented a detailed report, which states that the Commanderies are following the ritual very closely and, with the exception of paraphernalia, appear to be in good condition.

Each of the first four officers that attend the Triennial Conclave are to have $50 each, and $350 was appropriated for Grand Commandery headquarters and entertainment on that occasion.

The Mississippi and Tennessee resolutions, which we have already mentioned, were considered by the Committee on Jurisprudence, who asked further time on the former, and considered that it was unwise for the Grand Commandery or Grand Encampment to attempt to legislate in regard to the latter. We do not find that any action was taken on the report.

An interesting and impressive incident of the Conclave was the presentation to the Grand Commandery of the Jewel belonging to Past Grand Commander John D. Patterson, of New Hampshire, who for many years held Connecticut's commission as Representative near his own Grand Body. Sir

Knight Patterson died last summer and, in accordance with his last wish, Past Grand Commander J. W. Fellows attended the Conclave and presented the Jewel with eloquent and impressive remarks.

The proceedings contain a fine steel-engraved portrait of Grand Commander Bronson.

The festivities of the occasion were a reception and banquet given by Washington Commandery No. 1, to the distinguished visitors. We are pleased to see that the ladies were included, and it goes without saying that it was a brilliant and successful affair.

The Report on Correspondence is the second from the pen of Sir Knight Hugh Stirling, Past Grand Commander. Eighty-six pages are filled with an entertaining review of the doings of 42 Templar Grand Bodies.

North Carolina for 1897 is accorded a page, mainly of quotation, and as no adverse comment appears, we are fain to believe that Brother Stirling is in general accord with what he may have read.

Under Kansas, noting that their regulations regarding the uniform permitted officers entitled to wear shoulder straps to dispense with the Baldric, he says, and we are fully in accord:

"It always seemed to us that the Baldric was out of place, covering almost entirely one of the straps."

The following sound utterance is found under Massachusetts:

"The main trouble is not in the doctrine of perpetual jurisdiction, but rather in the unlawful use of the black ballot. We maintain that one has no more right to cast a black ballot because of personal differences or business jealousies, or for any other cause that does not affect the moral character of the man, than he has to give his consent to the admission of one he knows is morally disqualified, but allows his acceptance because he is a 'good fellow.' We believe also that any modification of this doctrine will be a stepping stone for changes along other lines the existence of which has placed the Masonic Fraternity in the position it occupies, which is one no member thereof need to be ashamed."

We do not share his forebodings as to the dire results that would follow a well-considered modification of the present law in regard to perpetual jurisdiction.

Reviewing Ohio he was called upon to define his standing in relation to the Order of the Eastern Star, and we fancy Brother

Carson does not derive much satisfaction from the results of the cross-examination.

"If it were in our power, or the power of any man or body of men, we would prevent the use of the title Masonic in every instance where it is used other than in connection with bodies absolutely Masonic, but we fail to see how this can be accomplished, any more than the Christian Church can prevent the use and sometimes even the misuse of its honored title.

"The Eastern Star has its good qualities: it has in many instances, (known to us) ministered to the destitute and afflicted; in some of our jurisdictions it has rendered valuable aid in the maintenance and management of our Masonic Homes Knowing this we cannot feel that the title is degraded by the Order of the Eastern Star claiming to be 'Adoptive Masonry.' "

Eleven Commanderies; 2,506 Knights; gain 143.

Sir William E. Withey, New London, Grand Commander.

Sir Eli C. Birdsey, Meriden, Grand Commander, (re-elected.)

Sir Hugh Stirling, Bridgeport, Committee on Correspondence.

Next Conclave, New London, March 21st, 1899.

DISTRICT OF COLUMBIA.

SECOND ANNUAL CONCLAVE.   Washington, May 10th, 1897.
SIR FRANK H. THOMAS, R E Grand Commander.

Eleven Grand Officers were present and every Commandery represented. We do not see the name of North Carolina's representative among the 21 that were credited with being present.

Sir Warren La Rue Thomas, M. E. Grand Master of the Grand Encampment was announced and was received with the honors due his exalted station.

The Grand Commander presents a well written address. Their official ranks have been broken by the death of Eminent Sirs Robert E. Constant, Grand Standard Bearer and Joseph Brummett, Grand Sword Bearer, both being summoned in the brief period of eight days.

He is gratified to announce that no requests have been preferred for permission to ballot out of time. Six of the ten

dispensations related to public appearance in uniform and the
the balance granted permission to fill official vacancies. There
have been no disputes or decisions called for, the utmost
harmony and good feeling prevailing, and he says that their
"Eminent Commanders take pride in keeping informed on
Templar custom, practice and law."   He personally made an
official visit to each Commandery and they were also officially
visited by the Grand Officers, at another time, as required by
their Constitution. He reports the subordinate Commanderies
as being in a prosperous condition, although a less amount of
work has been done the past year on account of the unsatis-
factory condition of trade and the uncertain tenure of Government employees, which naturally follows a change of National Administration. We quote what he has to say in relation to suspensions, which have depleted their ranks to quite
an extent.

"The suspensions are, to me, an indication of that process of healthy
pruning our Templar bodies have so long needed. Prior to the formation
of this grand body some of our Commanderies paid no attention to the
status of a Sir Knight in Lodge and Chapter. A closer investigation dis-
closed the fact that many Sir Knights had been suspended from Lodge
or Chapter for nonpayment of dues. An observance of the law in that
particular has resulted in the temporary separation, at least, of quite a
number of Sir Knights from their Templar bodies.

When our subordinates were under the direct supervision of the Grand
Encampment, by reason of the five-cent per capita tax, presumably, but
few suspensions were made by Commanderies for non-payment of dues
and as a result, in each of the older Commanderies, at least, there were a
greater or less number of names borne upon the rolls of men who were
but Sir Knights in name, who contributed to the Order neither their presence, influence nor money; these dead weights have been removed.   I
am assured by those in authority that no Sir Knight whose circumstances
in life would not permit his contributing his just proportion toward the
expenses of the body has been oppressed, but where the willingness to
pay was manifest but the conditions would not warrant, appropriation
was always gladly made to square the account."

We are in full accord with his recommendation that no
Companion of the Red Cross should receive the Order of the
Temple until he has provided himself with a regulation uni-
form, and it is now the law with them.

He reports that all of the Commanderies joined in the Christmas Observance. He holds that the full form of opening

should be used in all cases, if possible, and that the minutes should show which form was used, for the information of the Grand Recorder, at the annual Grand Visitation, and a "standing resolution" to that effect was adopted.

The second annual Inspection and Review was carried out in an almost faultless manner, in the presence of thousands of spectators, and he holds that such inspections are very beneficial to the Sir Knights, which we fancy no one will venture to dispute.

Of course he is a strong believer in permanent headquarters for the Grand Encampment, at Washington, and we quote:

"Agitation of the subject of permanently locating the headquarters of the Grand Encampment in the city of Washington continues, and the idea is growing in favor the more the matter is discussed. I am in receipt of many letters from Grand Encampment warmly espousing the cause, and a number of able papers on this subject, both editorial and contributed, have appeared in various Masonic publications."

The coming century may see its accomplishment but we doubt if this one does.

The Grand Treasurer reports their funds as being $1,186., nearly seventy per cent. increase during the year.

No Report on Correspondence, but the plethoric condition of their treasury ought to insure one the coming year, if it cannot be had as a labor of love.

Five Commanderies, 1,534 Knights; *loss* 34.

Sir Rezin W. Darby, Washington, Grand Commander.

Sir A. B. Bennett, Grand Recorder and Chairman of Committee on Correspondence.

Next Conclave, uncertain, as the Conclave was "adjourned *sine die.*"

FLORIDA.

THIRD ANNUAL CONCLAVE.   Jacksonville, May 15th, 1897.
SIR WILBER P. WEBSTER, R. E. Grand Commander.

Eleven Grand Officers present and five of the six Commanderies represented.

Fourteen Grand Representatives were received in due form, but North Carolina was not "in it."

The Grand Commander reports that his official duties have been light and pleasant and that harmony prevails. No decisions called for and only three dispensations issued, each being for a different purpose.

The Grand Recorder being absent, on account of a prolonged and severe illness, tender resolutions of sympathy were adopted and ordered sent to him. We are pleased to note his complete recovery.

The Grand Treasurer reports $170 to his credit.

A goodly amount of business was transacted, but it was generally of a local interest solely. A committee was appointed to wrestle with the matter of representation and accommodations at the Triennial.

No Report on Correspondence, and we find no returns of the Commanderies given, for which the illness of the Grand Recorder is probably a valid excuse.

Six Commanderies.

Sir James W. Boyd, Bartow, Grand Commander.

Sir William A. McLean, Jacksonville, Grand Recorder, (re-elected) and Chairman of Committee on Correspondence.

Next Conclave, Jacksonville, May 12th, 1898.

GEORGIA.

THIRTY SIXTH ANNUAL CONCLAVE.   Rome, May 12th, 1897.
SIR WILLIAM H. FLEMING, R. E. Grand Commander.

The Grand Prelate was the only missing officer and every Commandery was represented. Sir James L. Fleming, Past Grand Commander, who holds North Carolina's commission, was one of the 23 Grand Representatives credited with being present and his portrait appears as a frontispiece.

The Grand Officers were escorted to the Asylum where they listened to a humorously eloquent address of welcome. After a genial response by Sir Roland B. Hall they were regaled with a luncheon, "which was much enjoyed by the participants," from which we infer that much talking makes the listeners hungry; if it is particularly "dry" they become thirsty.

The Grand Commander announces with thankfulness that there has been no break in their membership the past year. He began the year with an aspiration to visit officially every Commandery, but a loud call from his constituents to represent them in the halls of Congress allowed him to only half complete the task. He reports the work as being well done and the social attentions long to be remembered. He also has some impressive words in regard to conferring the orders in a proficient manner.

Of the eleven dispensations issued, eight permitted balloting out of time. The three decisions given called for no adverse criticism and were duly approved. We quote one point, merely saying that, in our opinion, if the party was tried and *acquitted* by one body the other would have the right to take the matter up.

"A Knight Templar who commits an offence against Masonry while on parade as a Knight Templar, may he tried either in the Blue Lodge or in the Commandery, preferably in the Commandery. But jurisdiction should be yielded to the authority first taking cognizance of his act by beginning an official trial."

Their funds have nearly doubled during the year, being now $858., but all they have gained will be needed a year hence, according to what follows.

By resolution the first four officers of the Grand Commandery were made a Committee of Arrangements to secure quarters at Pittsburgh. An appropriation of $500. was made with the proviso, that the sum should be for headquarters expenses alone and not to defray the personal expenses of any representatives of the Grand Commandery.

A crumb of comfort for ye hard-working and often poorly paid Correspondent is found, when we read that Brother Hall's report was accepted with thanks and that he was requested to continue in the great and glorious work of disseminating Templar information among the Sir Knights, and further on we note that an even hundred dollars was appropriated for his benefit. Truly the lot of some Correspondents is cast in pleasant places.   .

Impressive devotional exercises were held in the evening, the ritualistic services being conducted by Rev. R. B. Headden,

Grand Prelate. A fine musical programme was rendered and an instructive address given by Sir John P. Shannon.

"Knightly Hospitality" recounts the social features of the Conclave, in which rough habits and coarse fare cut no figure. Receptions at hospitable homes, the mazy dance and a barbecue among green hills were the pleasures whose recollections "linger with us as the glow of a summer's twilight." Selah.

The volume of proceedings is embellished with portraits of Past Grand Commanders James L. Fleming and Azariah G. Howard.

Out from his Maconian shore, as Poe came near saying, Sir Roland B. Hall sends his ninth Report on Correspondence, which is no whit behind his previous efforts in interest and value. One hundred and seven pages is its extent and 43 Grand Bodies have received careful and courteous attention, Indian Territory being the only absentee.

North Carolina for 1896 is accorded a due proportion of space and he notices with regret the death of Frater Blount.

We take it that he is not favorably disposed towards the "cuffs," for noticing that they have been restored as a part of our uniform he says :

"But why suffer discomfort unnecessarily? It has been generally conceded that cuffs are not proper unless for mounted Commanderies."

Give it up: we voted to get rid of the dog-goned things, but they seem to have "bobbed up serenely" when we happened to be absent.

He tackles Brer Munson on the Grand Representative question and we gladly give him space :

"We differ with the distinguished Frater in characterising the position of Grand Representative as 'an empty honor.' To some it may appear so. But if Representatives would sometimes visit the Grand Bodies which honor them with commissions, and show by their presence an appreciation of the compliment extended, this 'empty honor' idea would be exploded. Nothing in our experience as a Knight Templar gave us greater pleasure, or was more highly appreciated, than our reception by the Grand Commandery for New York at its Conclave at Saratoga in 1894, which State, then and now, we have the honor to represent."

As our "Horace" also represents New York we suggest that he do likewise, and he may meet with a change of heart.

. With a liberal quotation from his "Conclusion," which gives away his age, we part company with our genial brother, trusting that our orbits will cross each other another year. As both of our grandmothers bore his name we feel more like calling him *cousin* than any thing else.

"As usual we have endeavored to confine our report to a review of transactions, steering clear of controversy. But where occasion seemed to justify it, we have not hesitated to criticise This has been done always in a spirit of kindness and with no intention to wound the feelings of those whose acts it called forth. Another mile stone, which counts the passage of another year in life's journey, has been passed For us it bears the number 57. With the knowledge that but few more are ahead of us, we have no desire to make any man our enemy We rather court the friendship and love our fellow beings."

Ten Commanderies, 717 Knights; gain 27.

Sir Charles M. Wiley, Macon, Grand Commander.

Sir Samuel P. Hamilton, Savannah, Grand Recorder, (re-elected.)

Sir Roland B. Hall, Macon, Correspondent.

Next Conclave, Macon, April 20th, 1898.

ILLINOIS.

Twelve Grand Officers and the representatives of 62 Commanderies were in attendance. Thirty-six Grand Commanderies were also represented, North Carolina by Sir Gil W. Barnard.

The Grand Commander's address fills 51 pages being a full account of his official acts, with correspondence and orders. He states that the year has been a prosperous one. Heartfelt tributes are paid to the memory of Sir and Rev. James Miller, Grand Prelate, and Sir Jerome R. Gorin, Past Grand Commander. Other fraternal dead, of their own and sister jurisdictions, receive fitting mention.

The Christmas Toast was generally observed and 62 of their 67 Commanderies report Easter or Ascension day services.

Of the 19 dispensations issued, seven permitted balloting on petitions ahead of time and a like number sanctioned public appearance in uniform.

Several decisions are reported, which successfully run the gauntlet of the Jurisprudence Committee, but we discover nothing that calls for extended notice.

He reports that satisfactory headquarters at the coming Triennial have been secured for the Grand Commandery.

The unveiling of a statue to General John A. Logan was considered a "Masonic occasion" to the extent of allowing the Commanderies to participate and 18 availed themselves of the privilege. The parade was a gratifying success, over 1,100 Sir Knights being in line, and he says:

"The military demonstration represented the strong arm of the govern-ment, the elegant and costly trappings of the several governors repre-sented the pomp and splendor of position, while the white plumes of the Templars touched the heart of the people and called forth the loudest encomiums of praise and the wildest demonstrations of delight."

If any carping criticism should appear it will be met by saying that the distinguished general being a Knight Templar it was fitting that the Order should take part. We note that he declined to permit a Commandery to appear in uniform and "escort the Grand Army of the Republic on the occasion of the unveiling of the soldiers monument." Commanderies pre-ferring such requests would do well to ascertain if any Knight Templar is commemorated by the monument to be dedicated, in which case, if they do not go as escort to some non-masonic body, they will have as good grounds for receiving the desired permission as the Commanderies had for participating in the Logan demonstration.

He makes, what he presumes to be, an unprecedented state-ment to the effect that every Commandery has been inspected during the year.

The noble work of the Masonic Orphans' Home and the Masonic Home for the aged is highly commended.

The committee appointed at the last Conclave to purchase a flag have apparently attended to the duty assigned them, for he says:

"For the first time in the history of the Grand Commandery of Illinois we see standing side by side the flag of our country and the banner of our order."

The jurisdiction trouble with California is in a fair way to be settled if the world lasts long enough. The aggrieved Commandery is digesting an apology and,

"It is to be hoped that the action of the Grand Commandery of California will be satisfactory, and cordial relations between the two Grand Jurisdictions restored."

The other Grand Officers submit the usual reports of their visitations and it would appear that courtesy and hospitality were not "Lost Arts" if the drill and work did sometimes fail to attain the high standard desired.

The Grand Treasurer's holdings show a slight increase, being now $7,917.

Sir George M. Moulton, Grand Captain General and Sir William H. Mayo, Grand Recorder of the Grand Encampment were introduced and received a hearty welcome, to which they made fitting responses.

A well written report was presented by the committee on Templar Dead.

Sir Theodore S. Parvin, of Iowa, Past Grand Recorder of the Grand Encampment was introduced by the Grand Commander in a few well chosen words and the venerable Sir Knight made an affecting response.

A portrait of Past Grand Commander Jerome R. Gorin appears as a frontispiece.

The Report on Correspondence comes as heretofore from the genial John Corson Smith, who for the ninth time gives us the results of his labors in a 160 page review of the doings of 42 Templar Grand Bodies.

North Carolina for 1897 is pleasantly noticed, the correspondent's labors being honored with the greater portion of the space.

Referring to our suggestion that divorcing the parade and legislative sessions of the Grand Encampment might result in the transaction of more business he says:

"For ourself, we doubt if there would be any gain. We are all over-worked, and the triennials act as a safety valve and afford all in attendance a few days' recreation. The parade takes up but one day, brings thousands together, and all go home refreshed, determined to work more than ever for the interests of our glorious order. Let the triennials be as they are, and let the 'boys' parade."

In surveying the general field he finds three or four important questions which should receive the attention of the Grand Encampment at the coming Triennial. The first is "continuous membership in lodge and chapter " which he fully believes in, holding that it is just as essential that he should continue his membership as to possess it originally in order to become a Knight Templar. If he cannot afford to continue his membership in all of the bodies, let him demit from the higher ones. We are not fully in accord with him on this topic. If it was understood in the beginning that continuous membership must be maintained in the bodies subordinate to the Knights Templar it would probably deter some, if not a good many, from going beyond the Blue Lodge, as they would naturally hesitate about loading up with more than they could tote. At the same time it would savor of injustice to require a Sir Knight to cut loose from the body in which he found the most enjoyment if he found himself unable to maintain a membership in all three of the bodies.

The second question is that of "Perpetual Jurisdiction," which is a live one at the present time, but he holds that it will be a minor one to that of continuous membership before many years. He holds that "the claim over a rejected candidate is indefensible." We have already put ourself on record as believing that a statute of limitations would make a good running mate with the one on perpetual jurisdiction.

The other question is "what to do with the non-affiliate," and he advocates letting the brother, who wishes to retire, depart in peace, so long as "he came into the fraternity of his 'own free will and accord.' "

"Let them go as though they had dimitted, as though they had never been of us. Just say in so many words that voluntary or involuntary dismission for one year severs the member's connection with his Masonic body and all those upon which that membership rests, as does suspension or expulsion from the lodge."

We do not see anything in his course of reasoning that is exceptionable and fully concur in the following:

3

"But to a member being deprived of any Masonic right in lodge, chapter, or commandery without proper notice and the opportunity offered him of a fair hearing, we do most earnestly object."

Frater Smith's outing this year was a voyage to Jamaica and the Spanish Main, and 60 pages of the Report are filled with a profusely illustrated and entertaining account of his trip. As is the case with all Past Masters his experiences were "many and various," and it may safely be assumed that he saw all that there was to be seen, as witness the following.

"We were now down to the 9° north latitude, where a string of shell beads serves for full dress unless the dusky maiden is a stickler for fashion, and then she dresses in smiles only. Attended a ball one evening at the 'Gran Hotel,' where the music consisted of an accordeon, guitar and piano. The first was the principal instrument. Pierce and young Butler danced with the belles of Limon, while I constituted the audience. The Colonel being too modest remained on board ship."

It goes without saying that he did not take any of his family on this trip. We wonder towards what quarter "his wandering steps incline" next.

He thinks that Frater Carson has gone a little too far in his tilt against the Androgynal windmill and believes that there is more good than evil resulting from this association of the sexes. It would be a pretty serious reflection on the character of his brother Masons and their relatives of the other sex, if he believed or thought otherwise.

Space and time for this entertaining review are exhausted and we must say good-bye, much to our regret.

Sixty-six Commanderies, 9,506 Knights; *loss* 14.

Sir James P. Sherwin, Chicago, Grand Commander.

Sir Gilbert W. Barnard, Chicago, Grand Recorder, (re-elected.)

Sir John C. Smith, Chicago, Committee on Correspondence.

Next Conclave, Chicago, October 25th, 1898.

INDIANA.

FORTY-THIRD ANNUAL CONCLAVE.   Anderson, April 21th, 1897.
SIR WINFIELD T. DURBIN, R. E. Grand Commander.

After a parade through the principal streets the Grand Commandery was hospitably welcomed by the Mayor, who gave them the freedom of the city. We trust that no personal application was made of Past Grand Commander Ruckle's allusion to the "great gas belt" in his eloquent response.

All of the Grand Officers were present and all of the Commanderies represented, with delegates from two Commanderies that had been organized under dispensations. No less than 29 Grand Representatives are credited with being present and among the number we find the name of Sir Knight Agnew, who holds North Carolina's commission.

After the Conclave had been opened in ample form the floodgates of eloquence were again opened to let out a welcome from Anderson Commandery, from which we take a choice bit.

"We can show you the most beautiful women the world has ever seen, graceful, glorious in form, cultivated and refined in every thought and action, until it seems that every God has set his seal upon her brow, to give assurance of a perfect woman, and withal so lovely that were it possible even angels might ask for a day off that it might be spent in her society."

Past Grand Commander Adams, who responded for the Grand Commandery, very gracefully accepted everything that had been proffered but, having the fear of his own household in mind, had to enter a mild protest on the woman question.

"Your high praise of the women of Anderson, Sir Kittenger, is not a whit extravagant; they fully deserve the high encomiums you pronounce upon their loveliness of face, form and figure, and the graces of their minds and hearts—to all of this we agree, but I, as a loyal family man, who have four of the fair sex in my household, speaking for myself and the Templars around me, trust you will pardon me when I firmly but respectfully suggest that 'there are others.' "

The Grand Commander presents a well written address, announcing a peaceful year, with a gratifying gain in membership, in spite of the business depression.

The Grand Commandery has been afflicted in the death of Past Grand Commander Erville B. Bishop, whom he characterizes as :

"A lovable frater, earnest, positive, courteous, a student always in his endeavors to know and advance the best interests of the Order to which he had devoted years of unselfish labor. His advice and council I personally knew to be of a high order. Masonry in Indiana never lost a more valuable member than our good friend and frater, and though he has passed beyond, yet shall the memory of his wise council be fresh in still directing our labors."

Prominent fraternal dead of sister jurisdictions are noticed at length. Three dispensations were issued to form new Commanderies and 19 to appear in public on various proper occasions. Only one was issued permitting action on a petition before the statutory time had elapsed, and in declining to issue another of the same kind he says :

"They had already elected sixteen applicants and their desire being to increase the number for the occasion of the visitation by LaFayette, St. John, and Frankfort Commanderies, I could not see that an emergency existed. There is too often a rushing of candidates through the orders without exercising a due care to impress the valuable lessons taught. The Order of the Temple should never be conferred upon more than one candidate on the same evening, unless for the best of reasons."

His general reasoning is eminently correct, but with 16 candidates on hand we are inclined to think that almost any reason would be considered good enough to justify conferring the Orders on more than one the same evening. He is a believer in the Grand Representative system, but holds that the incumbents should be Past Commanders, instead of Past *Grand* Commanders, as is the custom in their jurisdictions, believing that all the honors should not be monopolized by those who have succeeded in obtaining the highest one in the gift of their body. He also believes in the three year term, saying :

"It is, I know, a debatable question whether there is more in pursuit than in possession. It is a fact that there is more alacrity and activity and interest displayed in looking forward to a reward or recognition than there is when we have attained the honor."

Three decisions are reported in one, regarding the reduction of fees to enable a Commandery to secure some new material, which would probably go to other Orders with smaller fees, and he well says :

"In reply I stated that a Commandery of Knights Templar was not a competitive organization, that the Orders were of too high a grade to be placed in competition with others furnished for much less money, and they were not to receive the appearence of being cheap by reason of the price of admission being reduced in order to attract those who are seeking admission into secret societies."

His good resolutions in regard to official visitation were kept to a limited extent only.

The Mississippi resolutions relative to a change in the organic law of the Grand Encampment are vigorously condemned and the Grand Commandery declined to take any action.

Their funds show a slight falling off during the year but there appears to be no occasion for feeling poor, as their treasury still contains $5,392.

The newly appointed Grand Representatives who were present received a Knightly greeting.

Charters were issued to two of the U. D. Commanderies and the other one was required to perform another year of pennance.

A resolution was offered permitting Commanderies to hold memorial services for deceased Sir Knights on Ascension Day, but it failed to pass.

The Triennial Committee reported progress in the matter of securing headquarters and the Grand Commandery appropriated $2,000 for "the use of the Committee," with the proviso that one-half of the sum should not be drawn from the treasury before May 1, 1898. Looks as though they were afraid that the Committee might get away with the funds, but why did they give them a chance at the last half so long before the time?

Portraits of Grand Commander Redmond and Past Grand Commander Bishop appear and the last named has a very eulogistic obituary notice.

Past Grand Commander Nicholas R. Ruckle presents an entertaining and instructive Report on Correspondence, in which 43 Templar Grand Bodies receive attention, the result filling CXXIII pages.

North Carolina for 1896 has full notice. He compliments our work, but complains that our opinions are not "put up in such chunks as to be conveniently portable." Well, our good Frater goes to the other extreme and his work is of such quality and quarried to such dimensions that we have to hold a tight grip on ourself in order to keep from loading up with more "chunks" than we can well tote.

We present the following as being his opinion on one topic.

"It has seemed to us that if certain Grands and Past Grands could be induced to go on excursions, picnics and trolley rides, that the business of the Grand Encampment would be greatly expedited. The born legislators who must be heard on every question are the persons who impede legislation. A Grand Encampment that would continue in session for two weeks would earn as loud and clamorous a condemnation as is visited on the usual legislature."

May be so, but these prolific talkers probably prevent no end of vicious legislating, which ought to be accounted in their favor. It certainly would be a good thing for the advocates of new measures if they could coax their opponents away on excursions, etc., for a short time, but we are rather doubtful about its being worked out in general practice. The same crowd of the classes he mentions are not always opposed to the same objects.

He is opposed to a permanent location for the Grand Encampment, and we quote :

"A permanent headquarters may not be desirable in any event, and more especially if located in a city that has no claim except the fact that it is the seat of government. A Conclave of the great Templar legislative body in Washington, the political storm center, is not an end which is worth struggling for. Nothing is to be gained by making the Federal Capital the post-office address of a Grand Recorder. It is better for the body, as a great national organization, that its Triennial Conclave shall remain a movable feast. Nothing will be gained by a separation of the legislative session from the great outpouring of Templars, which has become one of the great features of the nation."

The accumulation of a fund for the purpose of securing palatial quarters anywhere is also condemned and he holds that "the ownership of an estate is not one of the vital purposes of Templary."

We shall not join issue on the subject, although we see no objection to the Grand Recorder being permanently located at the Capital, provided that the offices are not too "palatial." We wait with interest to see what St. Louis has to say on the on the subject.

Thirty-nine Commanderies, 3,526 Knights ; gain 33.

Sir John E. Redmond, Logansport, Grand Commander.

Sir William H. Smythe, Indianapolis, Grand Recorder, (re-elected.)

Sir Nicholas R. Ruckle, Indianapolis, Chairman of Committee on Correspondence.

Next Conclave, Logansport, April 20th, 1898.

INDIAN TERRITORY.

SECOND ANNUAL CONCLAVE.   Muscogee, August 10th, 1896.
SIR ROBERT W. HILL, R. E. Grand Commander.

Nine Grand Officers present and every Commandery represented. We notice that the Grand Representatives present "were received and welcomed with appropriate expressions of Knightly regard," but their names do not appear.

The Grand Commander presents a high-toned and poetic address. He pays a heartfelt tribute to the memory of Grand Prelate William P. Paxson, who departed this life during his official term. Notes the appointment of a full list of Grand Representatives.

No dispensations called for and the only question asked was a query as to where a Sir Knight must affiliate. The answer returned was that he has the "right to select the Commandery for himself."

The selection of a manual for drill is advised in the interest of uniformity.

The Grand Recorder reports a net indebtedness of $79, the amount having been decreased somewhat during the year. Their annual per capita dues were doubled, being now one dollar.

A fine portrait of Grand Commander Hill appears as a frontispiece.

No Report on Correspondence. The names of the officers and their addresses do not appear on the back page of cover, as is customary, which is an inconvenience to those desiring that information, but we reckon that they will have it fixed up all right next time.

Three Commanderies, 125 Knights; gain 20.

Sir James E. Humphrey, Purcell, Grand Commander.

Sir Leo E. Bennett, Muscogee, Grand Recorder, (re-elected.)

Sir Robert W. Hill, Muscogee, Committee on Fraternal Correspondence. ·

Next Conclave, November 2d, 1897.

1897.

The third Annual Conclave was held at Purcell on November 2d.

Sir James E. Humphrey, R. E. Grand Commander.

Ten Grand Officers and the representatives of their four Commanderies were in attendance. Thirty Grand Jurisdictions were represented by 12 valiant Sir Knights who were introduced and cordially received.

"Their responses demonstrated the uniform comity and good feeling existing in Templarism throughout the United States."

The holder of North Carolina's commission was one of the participants.

The Grand Commander's address is a two-page account of his stewardship. He reports a quiet and harmonious year. A Commandery chartered at the last Conclave was duly constituted. Three dispensations and a like number of decisions were duly approved and call for no adverse comment. In recommending the Commanderies to assemble and observe the Christmas Toast he admonished them to "Remember the poor and widows and orphans."

The Grand Treasurer and Grand Recorder were both absent and no reports from them appear, except a communication from the former to the effect that no funds had passed through his hands during the year.

The Grand Commander was authorized to attend the Triennial Conclave and "draw on the Grand Treasurer for his actual traveling expenses." We trust the report of the Grand Treasurer at the next Conclave will show that there were funds to pass "through his hands" when the draft came.

The Grand Recorder was directed to see that a half-tone portrait of Grand Commander Humphrey adorned the first page of the volume of proceedings and it appears that he faithfully carried out his instructions.

A banquet was tendered the visiting Fratres and Companions "and the same was accepted and not only the delicious spread but the feast of reason and flow of soul was enjoyed by all."

No Report on Correspondence.

Four Commanderies, 145 Knights; gain 12.

Sir Edmond H. Doyle, South McAlester, Grand Commander.

Sir Joseph S. Murrow, Atoka, Grand Recorder.

Sir Robert W. Hill, Canadaigua, N. Y., Chairman of Committee on Correspondence.

Next Conclave, South McAlester, October 12th, 1898.

IOWA.

THIRTY-FOURTH ANNUAL CONCLAVE.   Templar Park, July 13th, 1897.

SIR THOMAS R. ERCANBRACK, R. E. Grand Commander.

Twelve Grand Officers and the representatives of 38 Commanderies reported for duty. Twenty Grand Representatives answered to their names at roll-call, Sir Alfred Wingate, who represents North Carolina, being on hand as usual. We notice that later on they were called on for reports, either verbal or written, and 13 responded, eight talking more or less. Apparently they propose to get value received for the honor in Iowa, and we commend the procedure.

The Grand Commander presents a well written address of 12 pages, all solid matter. He notes the passing of another quadrennial election and derives pleasure from the thought that a member of our Order is the Nation's Chief Magistrate. We are rather disposed to dissent from his view that the quietude of the general election was largely due to the spirit of fraternity inculcated by the various civic Orders now so widespread, but we will let it pass.

He pays affecting tributes to their fraternal dead, the most prominent being the venerable Father Schreiner who had been their Grand Sentinel since the organization of the Grand Commandery.

The gratifying announcement is made that the Order is increasing in proportion to the general advancement of their State, although disposed to believe the current opinion that the political and financial conditions are not conducive to the prosperity of social institutions. We trust by this time the expected "wave of prosperity" has reached them and that they are on top of it.

"Fuss and feathers" did not cut much of a figure during the past year, as only three dispensations were issued to permit public appearance in uniform. One of them permitted appearance at a "charity ball" under the sole direction of the Commandery. Although "the festivities were conducted with the utmost propriety, and a considerable sum was raised for the poor of the city," the Committee on Jurisprudence did not consider it a "Masonic occasion" and witheld their approval.

He considers it a cause for congratulation that harmony prevailed so generally that no decisions were called for and hopes that the Grand Encampment will adopt a new Constitution which will permit their adopting a new Code that has been prepared. The latter is supposed to be so "perfect in all its parts" that when any vexing questions are asked it will only be necessary to refer the anxious inquirer to Chapter and Section. Sounds well, but we are afraid that the Grand Commander has not "been brought to light," who will be the first to enjoy this labor saving device, at the present rate of progress with the Grand Encampment Constitution.

A new Commandery was formed under dispensation.

Congratulations are indulged in on the state of the Order, their Jurisdiction being the seventh in rank and unsurpassed, according to her population and material resources.

The Grand Treasurer has nearly doubled his holdings during the year, having now to his credit $801.

The Committee on "Invitations Extraordinary" reported that they did not deem it expedient for the Grand Commandery to accept an invitation to be present at the unveiling of a monument to General John A. Logan, but desired to put on record some recognition of this valiant and magnanimous Sir Knight as,

"A typical western ideal soldier, whose life was pre-eminently distinguished for devotion to duty, especially brightened by the practice of the Christian virtues, and blessed in its final ending by the promise of a future reward."

A Triennial Committee was appointed to make all necessary arrangements for taking in the coming Conclave.

No papers having been presented the Commandery U. D. so remains for another year.

Past Grand Commander Theodore S. Parvin presented a touching memorial tribute to the many virtues and graces of character of Father Schreiner. We regret that our space will only admit of a brief quotation.

"He was a Mason in whom there was no guile ; he loved the spirit rather than the forms of Masonry. It is the "letter that killeth, while the spirit giveth life.' Unlike the vast majority of his brethren, he considered, as a Mason should, the object of the ritualistic ceremony to be the discovery of the truth, the truth in Masonry and in the thought of the world. So, too, he felt the object and the aim of Masonry to be the knowledge and the practice of the truths discovered and revealed in and through the ritual and the exoteric ceremonies of the Order. In thus living daily up to his knowledge and opportunities, his was a good life.''

The proceedings are dumb regarding any festivities incident to the three days gathering, excepting that the ''wives, daughters and friends'' were admitted to the Asylum during the installation ceremonies. We are no less certain, however, that the arduous labors of the Conclave were lightened by seasons of jollity and mirth, as the ''Ladies Templar Club'' was on hand, and nothing more need be said.

The volume contains portraits of Grand Commander Ercanbrack and Father Schreiner and is further embellished (?) with a dozen or more memorial pages. Their design is an attractive one but its wholesale repetition has a depressing effect.

The Report on Correspondence is the fourth emanating from the pen of our good Brother, Rev. James C. W. Coxe, and he fills 76 pages with an entertaining account of what he has found of interest in the proceedings of 42 Templar Grand Jurisdictions, Georgia being the only one that failed to be ''in at the death.''

North Carolina for 1897 arrived just in time to prevent 1896, which was tardy last year, from being favored with a notice. However we have no cause for complaint and thank him for his genial and approving notice. He is rather astray in styling us ''Hawkeye'' and, while not objecting to the name, we do not acknowledge any lack of keenness in our vision or swiftness in the race if we are a ''Tar Heel.''

He commends the Committee on Jurisprudence for not approving the dispensation permitting public appearance in uniform to assist at the rendition of ''The Story of the Reformation,'' considering that it was in no sense a ''Masonic occasion.'' ''So say we all of us.''

There is much in this admirable review that we would like to quote but we are at a loss where to begin. His introduction contains some well chosen words on an important topic to the ''Corps.''

''Some of our fratres have doubted the wisdom of these reports on correspondence. The plea of economy is potent with some. 'To what purpose is all this waste?' We may not wisely forget who first asked this question, and may be pardoned if we shrink from his company. There are values higher than can be measured by either silver or gold. Life, love, honor, intelligence—these are not staples of barter, nor to be determined by yardstick or ledger. The man of large sympathies is the man of broad intelligence. The widest outlook is from the top of the loftiest towers. 'Masonry is a progressive science'—is it so? Then Masons should be progressive men, in close touch with to-day and with open vision for to-morrow. Reports on Correspondence have their place and value; they are indispensible to the alert and would-be intelligent man."

He puts on record his disapproval of wine drinking at the Christmas observance and several times voices his disagreement with the "other fellow's" views as to what is a "Masonic occasion," when he notes permission being given Commanderies to attend balls or picnics in uniform.

Under Montana, discussing the question of instructing a teller to cast the ballot of the meeting for some designated party, he expresses himself as follows, and we are fully in accord with his views.

"To us the justice of the case is clear, that where the law requires an election by ballot it means that each member shall have the right to cast his individual ballot for a candidate; and this right is invaded and denied when the tellers are instructed to cast the ballot for any specified candidate. This instruction is given *viva voce* or by show of hands—not by ballot; and a clear majority instructs. Were a case of this kind to come before us while in the chair, we should rule that instruction could be given only by unanimous consent; that one objection would be fatal; and were we on the floor when the motion to instruct was made, we should object, as a matter of principle."

From Vermont we cull the following in reference to what is considered a "Masonic occasion," although it is apparently rather a tender subject in that jurisdiction.

"Our frater thinks that the Triennial parade gave 'a most powerful impetus to Masonry in New England, especially so in Massachusetts,' and then asks: 'Would the effect have been the same, think you, my dear Frater, if they had paraded in plain citizens' dress?' To which we reply: The 'effect' would have been far less as a spectacular show; but — *that was a Masonic occasion.* That it may have induced more than 'one additional person' to knock at the door of a lodge-room or asylum is not improbable; but that would not prove the applicant worthy, nor that his admission would be a benefit to the body admitting him We place the emphasis on the character of the men composing the Order, and not on the parade of feathers, as an inducement to really worthy aspirants; and we honor ourselves most when we avoid display for its own sake, or as a cheap advertising medium. We revere the memory of our soldier dead ; we honor them no less when we decline to recognize as a 'Masonic' occasion a patriotic Memorial day."

It is nearly "low twelve" and the waning light of our lamp reminds us that it is time to close the labors of the day. We part company with Brother Coxe trusting that a few months hence we shall have the pleasure of greeting him in person.

Fifty-six Commanderies 4,434, Knights ; gain 90.

Sir Francis H. Loring, Waterloo, Grand Commander.

Sir Alfred Wingate, Des Moines, Grand Recorder, (re-elected.)

Sir Jas. C. W. Coxe, Washington, Committee on Correspondence.

Next Conclave, Templar Park, July 14, 1898.

KANSAS.

TWENTY-EIGHTH ANNUAL CONCLAVE.   Junction City. May 11th, 1897.

SIR WILLIAM C. HOLMES, R. E Grand Commander.

All of the Grand Officers were present and 36 Commanderies represented. Eighteen Grand Representatives were also in attendance but the name of the Sir Knight who holds the Tar Heel commission does not appear.

The Grand Commander's address is a brief recapitulation of his official acts. A fitting tribute is paid to the memory of Past Grand Commander Owen A. Bassett, who was called to his reward during the year. He announces with regret that their membership has decreased during the year, the net loss being the unlucky number of 13. The business and financial depression is credited with being the cause and he says :

"Unrest and uncertainty paralyzed the nerves of confidence and, whether one believed in the benefits of gold or silver, he felt the poverty of hard times. This, in a measure, accounts for the decrease in our membership during the past year."

Decisions and dispensations few and with one exception of little importance, and following we give the one in question :

"The petition of applicant for orders is read by Recorder and a motion is made and seconded that it be referred to the usual committee. Here objection was made and the whole matter withdrawn. The objector insists that the objection become part of the record."

"Answer. I decided that the withdrawal of the whole matter carried with it everything pertaining to it To show objection would necessitate showing what was objected to, and thus the matter would not be withdrawn."

We shall have to dissent from the above, even if the Committee on Jurisprudence did bolster it up with their approval. Title XLV, Section 10, of the Statutes of the Grand Encampment explicitly says:

"When a petition has been presented to a Commandery, it cannot be withdrawn unless it shall appear that the Commandery has not jurisdiction over the petitioner."

We may say further, although it is not needed to strengthen the case, that no officer or Commandery has the right to falsify the records by omitting or erasing any statement of what actually took place. Any motion to refer the petition to a committee seems to be uncalled for, and objection before a ballot is also out of place.

He reports that more than one-half of the Commanderies were officially visited but nothing more than the bare fact is chronicled.

Regarding the desirability of proficiency in the preceeding degrees before advancement he has the following sensible expression.

"Candidates will endeavor to learn what the initiated will defer. With the candidates, it is 'now is the time;' with the member it is 'any time,' and in many instances it is 'any time is no time.'"

Grand Recorder Callaham is favored with words of commendation, which we are sure he richly deserves.

The hard times do not seem to have shrunken their treasury, as the Grand Treasurer owns up to having $3,273., an increase during the year of practically thirty per cent.

The Grand Recorder's Report has a comforting statement of negative value. If they had not made an error of 17 last year in figuring their gain in membership they would show a net gain of 4 this year, instead of a loss of 13.   Figures should be handled with the utmost care and furthermore,

> " Of all sad words of tongue or pen,
> The saddest are these; 'It might have been ! ' "

A graceful report on Necrology was presented by Sir and Rev. Samuel E. Busser and we clip a bit of his sermonizing :

"It is to be taken for granted that relationships which have continued for so many thousands of years, are to remain as they are. If the future is the continuance of the present, we can assuredly say that we shall know one another in heaven. The death of my friend doesn't change my love and regard for him. If it destroys his love for me, it has annihilated him. If memory continues, and we can't conceive of existence without memory, it is certain that we shall renew our friendships in heaven, and the more we recount kindred experiences in the grerat battle of life, the closer will grow our intimacy."

. We are afraid that some of the controversial theologians may be disposed to differ from him in regard to the continuance of "relationships," particularly the marital.

A Charter was granted to a Commandery that had been working under dispensation.

The appointment of a Committee on the Triennial and an appropriation for expenses was deferred until the next annual Conclave.

A fine steel-engraved portrait of Grand Commander Holmes ornaments the volume and he is also honored with a biographical sketch.

The hilarity of the occasion comprised a competitive drill, the conferring of the Orders of the Temple and Malta in full costume and a banquet and ball; a pleasing feature of the latter being "the attendance of a large number of ladies accompanying the Sir Knights."   Frater Callaham must have been in clover.

The Report on Correspondence reviews the proceedings of 43 Templar Grand Bodies and fills 177 pages of fine type.   It is the third effort of our esteemed Frater Sir Andrew M. Callaham and in our humble opinion is one of the best that the members of the "Corps" have the pleasure of perusing.

North Carolina for 1896 has courteous mention to the extent of three pages and little is apparently found that he considers worthy of the ammunition necessary to bring it down. Noting that a dispensation permitted a commandery to assist in the rendition of the Story of the Reformation he says, with a surprised air :

"We never knew before that that was a masonic occasion "

Well, they discovered the same thing at home the following year when the Jurisprudence Committee sat down on a dispensation of the same breed.

Referring to our remark that "one would look askance at seeing it (the National flag) displayed on a church," he says :

"We think a people whose religious service would be disturbed because the American flag floated from its church belfry, should send for a revivalist, and take in a little more religion."

May be so. It is not worrying us in the least, but we think that it will be a long time first before he will see the beginning of such a custom. The church and State are too thoroughly divorced in this country to make it at all probable that we shall see the service of the one conducted under the insignia of the other.

Thirty-six pages of the review are devoted to a "Topical Department," which is a towering monument to the patience and industry of the reviewer. No less than thirty-one topics are dwelt upon; "Non-affiliation," "Templarism," "Temperance," "Masonic Occasions," "Representation in the Grand Encampment," and "Order of the Eastern Star" being some of the most prominent ones. He does not favor us with his own views on every question, but it is plain to be seen that he does not train with Frater Carson when "Androgynal Freemasonry" has its field day, and no more do we.

Regretting that our space does not permit a longer tarry with our esteemed Frater we bid him adieu and, with scrip and bottle replenished, take up the line of march.

Forty-four Commanderies, 3,234 Knights; *loss* 13.

Sir Will C. Chaffee, Topeka, Grand Commander.

Sir A. M. Callaham, Topeka, Grand Recorder, (re-elected) and Correspondent.

Next Conclave; Topeka, May 10th, 1898.

KENTUCKY.

FIFTIETH ANNUAL CONCLAVE.   Hopkinsville, May 19th, 1897.
SIR REGINALD H. THOMPSON. R. E. Grand Commander.

The Grand Commandery was escorted to the Baptist Church where the Office of Public Worship was conducted by the Grand Prelate, Sir John G. Orndorff, who afterwards delivered an instructive sermon. A cordial address of welcome from the Mayor brought out an elegant response from the Grand Commander. The sermon and addresses appear in print.

When the Asylum was reached it was found that all of the Grand Officers were on hand and 23 Commanderies represented. Twenty-one Grand Representatives graced the occasion with their presence, North Carolina's contributing a share.

The M. E. Grand Master, Sir Warren LaRue Thomas, was in attendance and received the honor due his exalted rank.

The Grand Commander says the year has been one of unusual prosperity, peace and harmony have prevailed and their official circle has been undisturbed by the dread destroyer. Numerous dispensations have been granted for various purposes, but all applications have had cautious scrutiny. Although not quite sure in regard to its being a "Masonic occasion" he permitted a Commandery to appear in uniform on Mason's Day at the Chautauqua Celebration. The R. W. Grand Master having set the example he "did not think it of sufficient importance to make it a point of difference between the two bodies."

The financial stringency caused the omission of the customary official inspection of the Commanderies. The few official visits he was able to make were enjoyable seasons of delightful hospitality and courteous entertainment, and he has nothing but praise in regard to what he witnessed.

From his dissertation on "Some Evils" we cull the following.

"The custom of soliciting Masons to apply for the Orders of Knighthood, sometimes before they have taken the Third degree, and then rushing them through the Chapters, in order to get into the Commandery in the shortest possible time, is an evil greatly to be deprecated. It lowers the dignity of Knighthood and degrades the Templar Orders. It is grossly unjust to Capitular Masonry; and equally so to the unfortunate

4

victim of that zeal without knowledge, which hurries him through the whole system of Masonry—with no opportunity to learn its mysteries, or see its beauty, and with no end in view but the poor gratification of wearing a Templar charm dangling at his watch chain. It is a violation of the Ancient Landmark, which requires the postulant to come of his own free will and accord."

We are in full accord with his views, but have always supposed that the Ancient Landmark referred to only applied to Ancient Craft Masonry.

He notes that the observance of Christmas Day is growing in favor, notwithstanding the objection to the toast, and recommends the preparation of a Ritual on that day, and also one for Good Friday and Ascension Day, the proper observance of the two last named to be obligatory.

He also recommends that a law be enacted requiring all Companions of the Red Cross to procure a uniform before they can receive the Order of the Temple, also that the wearing of the uniform at all stated conclaves should be made obligatory.

A graceful tribute is paid to Frater Woodruff's Report on Fraternal Correspondence.

Their financial condition has improved during the year and the Grand Treasurer has now $116, to his credit.

A Committee on Entertainment at the coming Triennial was appointed and $1,500. appropriated for headquarters. The Grand Commandery extended an invitation to the Grand Encampment to hold the Conclave of 1901 in Louisville.

"Addenda" notes the festivities of the Conclave. The Grand Recorder apparently did not feel able to do the subject justice and fell back on the report in "The American Tyler." Parades and drills, receptions and refreshments appear to have been the salient features.

The veteran reviewer, Sir Charles R. Woodruff, presents his twenty-fourth Report on Correspondence, prefacing it with his portrait, which we are sure all of the "Corps" will be pleased to see. To use his own language, it presents "the handsome appearance of a mild-mannered and well behaved citizen," and we are free to say that personal intercourse does not disabuse one's mind of that impression. The sitting must have been an older vintage than the current year, however.

He gets right down to work without a word of introduction
and we almost seem to hear him ask:

> "I beg to inquire
> If the gun that I carry has ever missed fire?
> And which was the muster roll—mention but one—
> That missed your old comrade who carries the gun?
>
> It is rusty, some tell me; I heed not the scoff,
> It is battered and bruised, but it always goes off!
> Why, it scares me to fire, lest the pieces should fly,
> Like the cannons that burst on the Fourth of July!"

Forty-three Templar Grand Bodies pass in review and the
result of his inspection fills 109 pages.

North Carolina for 1896 has full and courteous mention and
he does not seem to find anything to condemn. The pleasure
of meeting Frater Woodruff for a short time will always be
cherished as a pleasant recollection of a visit to his city last
summer.

He does not take any stock in the "topical" form of report
and puts himself on record as favoring permanent headquarters for the Grand Encampment, but does not localize the spot
that would meet his approval. He also says:

"We have always been disposed to take a broad and elevated view of
the mission of the Order of the Temple, and are therefore apprehensive
of ill results when we see suggestions made, or actions taken, which have
a tendency to narrow and dwarf the scope of its influence. Templary
was never intended to be used as a vehicle for *isms*—denominational or
political."

To all of which we say, amen, and bid him farewell for
another year.

Twenty-five Commanderies, 2,020 Knights; gain 89.

Sir Eugene A. Robinson, Maysville, Grand Commander.

Sir Lorenzo D. Croninger, Covington, Grand Recorder, (re-
elected.)

Sir Charles R. Woodruff, Louisville, Chairman of Committee
on Fraternal Correspondence.

Next Conclave, Maysville, May 18th, 1898.

LOUISIANA.

THIRTY-FOURTH ANNUAL CONCLAVE.   New Orleans, Feb'y 12th, 1897.

SIR M. L. SCOVELL, R. E. Grand Commander.

Seven Grand Officers present and representatives from four Commanderies. Twenty-three Grand Commanderies were represented, North Carolina being one of the number.

The Grand Commander sent word that he was unavoidably detained and his address was read by the Grand Recorder. He notes the death of John G. McWilliams, Past Grand Commander, and Fred. Eyle, Grand Junior Warden.

Announces with regret that the Commanderies have not been prosperous the past year, there being a loss in membership, and says he is unable to account for the general lack of interest.

One Commandery was three times refused permission to ballot on petitions without waiting the statutory time and the following comment will apply to other jurisdictions as well.

"It seems that the Companions in the jurisdiction of Monroe Commandery are slow in making up their minds to apply to become Knights Templar, but, when they do, they want the orders quick."

A general participation in the Christmas Observance is reported.

The Grand Treasurer's cash balance is about one-fifth smaller than it was at the beginning of the year, being now $323.

The Committee on the Grand Commander's address says:

"His decisions on the subject of dispensations are to be highly commended. To grant such privileges upon insufficient grounds has a tendency to destroy good laws."

A ten page Report on Correspondence is submitted by a committee composed of Past Grand Master J. Q. A. Fellows and Past Grand Commander Richard Lambert. It is constructed on the topical plan, like its predecessors, Necrology, Non-Affiliation and the Grand Encampment being the only subjects dwelt upon.

Quoting from Sir Knight Berry of Maine the Committee comment as follows:

"Your committee would add one qualification to the remark on the supposition, 'if a Grand Lodge were to pass a law that all married men should cease to be Masons, and proceed to expel them, they would necessarily cease to be Templars.   It would be an absured law, but it would be law.'   But would it be *Masonic law?*   We hold that the Fraternity submitting to the acts of such a Grand Lodge would cease to be Masonic, as much so as the Masons of France under the Grand Orient.   There are certain things a Grand Lodge cannot do and bind the Masons of its jurisdiction or any other, and we hold that among them would be the case supposed by the Maine committee, and the expulsion of a Mason, without at least the *form* of a trial or for a *Masonic* offense; that it is legally impossible to pass a law of expulsion from the general rights of Masonry which *shall execute* itself or to declare one expelled, in certain contingency and without the form of trial."

On another question which has caused much discussion they say:

"It seems that our fraters in New York are persistent for a larger representative or voting capacity in the Grand Encampment than smaller jurisdictions, by reason of the large number of Templars in New York.

Our fraters in New York have mistaken the nature of the organization of Templarism in the United States.   All membership in the Grand Encampment, as well as in the Grand Commanderies, is individual and *not* representative.

"The constitution of the Grand Encampment fixes the *membership* of the Grand Commanderies, giving each member one vote and no more, and if the Grand Commandery of New York has adopted the feature of an additional voting capacity, it has violated the constitution of the Grand Encampment—we have not noticed this before.   It had better be repealed."

Regarding the failure of the Grand Encampment to accomplish more in the way of legislation they quote and endorse Sir Knight Orahood of Colorado, as follows :

"However, as we have said of former Triennials, the social feature is the predominant idea.   We seem to get along very well without much legislation, and the statement that the world is governed too much is, to an extent, true, and may be applicable to our order.   So we join with the majority and vote this Triennial a grand success socially, and will continue under the statutes and regulations as they stand.   They seem to answer the purpose, and if so, it may be well enough to adopt the adage: 'Let well enough alone.' "

The brevity of their report is laid upon the poor printer, who insisted upon having copy when the committee had not begun their labors in season to satisfy his demands in time.

Since the foregoing was written we have learned with deep regret of the death of Sir Knight Fellows, which sad event took place at his home in New Orleans on November 28th. He was for many years Chairman of the Committee on Correspondence and among the pleasant recollections the Triennial of 1895 is the personal meeting at the banquet of the "Mutuals."

With one exception he was the Senior Past Grand Master of the Grand Encampment, having been M. E. Grand Master in 1871-'74.

Four Commanderies, 320 Knights; *loss* 8.

Sir Robert Strong, New Orleans, Grand Commander.

Sir Richard Lambert, New Orleans, Grand Recorder, (re-elected.)

Sir J. Q. A. Fellows, New Orleans, Chairman of Committee on Foreign Correspondence.

Next Conclave, New Orleans, February, 11th, 1898.

1898.

THIRTY-FIFTH ANNUAL CONCLAVE.   New Orleans, February 18th.

SIR ROBERT STRONG, R. E. Grand Commander.

All of the Grand Officers were present and every Commandery represented. Thirteen Grand Representatives were also in attendance, Sir Wm. H. Chaffe appearing for North Carolina.

The Grand Commander's address is quite brief and apparently his official duties have been light, as no decision or dispensations are reported.

From his announcement of the death of M. E. Sir J. Q. A. Fellows, Past Grand Master, we quote :

"This Grand Commandery has sustained an irreparable loss in the death of our Past Grand Commander and beloved Sir Knight.

"One has passed out of the lines to answer the Grand Commander and Grand Master's call to the beautiful asylum above, who held more than an ordinary place in our conclaves and our affections. Great men rise and pass away and others take their places, but who shall take Brother Fellows' place is yet, and may be, an unanswered question.

"There was not an interest of Masonry where his worth and influence was not felt and appreciated; in the Masonic bodies of this city he was always a leading spirit; in the Grand Bodies of the State and Nation his presence and influence was supreme. Loved by his friends with an un-

tiring devotion, and respected by his enemies for the manliness of his
opposition, endowed with an intellect superior to most men, his opinions
were respected alike by friend and foe.

" Within this Grand Commandery will he be most keenly missed. In
its conclaves he was the peer of all surrounding, and the personification
of Templar law and usage. Even in the Councils of the Grand Encampment of the United States he was the oracle consulted by all.''

He reports the observance of the Christmas Libation and
Ascension Day by the New Orleans Commanderies, the services on the last-named occasion being conducted by the Grand
Prelate. Judging from the following the spiritual gain in the
observation of Ascension Day is of secondary importance :

"I would highly recommend that this beautiful custom be continued,
as it gives the Sir Knights an opportunity to perfect themselves in march-
ing and in drill, as well as to receive good and wholesome instruction by
celebrating the glorious Ascension.''

The Grand Treasurer's report shows a slight gain in their
funds during the year, they now amounting to $329.

. V. E. Sir Henry B. Stoddard, Grand Generalissimo of the
Grand Encampment, with a body guard of prominent Texan
Sir Knights paid an official visit and was received with due
honors.

A dispensation was granted to form a new Commandery.

No Report on Correspondence.

Four Commanderies, 324 Knights ; gain 4.

Sir Robert Stroug, New Orleans, Grand Commander.

Sir Richard Lambert, New Orleans, Grand Recorder, (re-
elected.)

Sir Samuel M. Todd, New Orleans, Chairman of Committee
on Foreign Correspondence.

Next Conclave, New Orleans, February 17th, 1899.

MAINE.

FORTY-SIXTH ANNUAL CONCLAVE.   Portland, May 6th, 1897.
SIR ALBRO E. CHASE, R. E. Grand Commander.

Only one Grand Officer failed to appear and one Commandery
was unrepresented. North Carolina was one of the 31 Grand
Jurisdictions having representatives present.

The Grand Commander presents a business-like address of 17 pages. Fraternal dead are noted at length, their own official circle mourning Past Grand Commander Arlington B. Marston and Past Grand Generalissimo Richard W. Black.

Sixteen of his 20 dispensations permitted public appearance in uniform on divers occasions, seven being divine service on Easter Sunday.

He indulged in official visitation to a limited extent and the results, both authoritative and social appear to have been very satisfactory.

The uniform question receives attention and he urges immediate action, as many Sir Knights desire to procure the proper costume. We judge that considerable latitude of choice has existed heretofore from the following :

"We are called a semi-military order, but seeing the members of the majority of our commanderies in attendance at the conclaves, one would decide that it was not semi military, but an assemblage of persons under the charge of guards, who in variegated costume were to watch lest any one escape : and when the Sovereign Master 'founds a new order,' he would have good reason to believe that it really was an order new to nearly every one present, and that many for the first time were being created and constituted companions of that new order."

He advocates placing the fees for the orders at a figure that will uniform the candidate at the time that he receives the Order of the Temple.

The recorders are touched up for their laxity in responding to official communications and we presume that his strictures would apply as well in some other jurisdictions.

"If I was to judge of the condition of Templar Masonry by the notices of conclaves sent me by the Recorders of the subordinate commanderies, I should decide that nearly one-third of the commanderies of this jurisdiction were dead, as no notice has been received. I cannot understand how it is that a recorder who receives from the Grand Recorder a circular requiring the Grand Commander to be notified of each and every conclave and council, can be so negligent of his duty "

Full reports of inspections are given by the other members of the "Line of Knights," in which more praise than blame is found, and Knightly courtesy and hospitality are highly commended.

The Grand Treasurer reports their funds as amounting to

$1,827., being practically the same amount they had at the beginning of the year.

A fair amount of business of a local nature came before the conclave.

Three hundred and twenty-five dollars was appropriated for the Grand Officers to use for entertainment purposes at the Triennial.

A fine portrait of Grand Commander Chase adorns the volume of proceedings.

We heartily commend the Grand Recorder for devoting three pages to a recapitulation and table of contents, which materially aids those in search of the information contain therein.

Sir Knight Stephen Berry comes forward bright and smiling with his twenty-second Report on Correspondence. Forty-three Grand Commanderies have passed in review and the result of his labors fills 69 pages.

As usual, his introduction is written "down by the sea." This time he is watching the drift-wood floating in and felicitating himself on the "rare open fire" he will enjoy later on. We will let him speak for himself :

"So we wonder what the drift-wood from the Templar Ocean will bring us that is rich and sparkling. What pleasant saying from Old Kentucky, what happy turn of anecdote from Wisconsin, what graphic story of the Orient from Illinois, what incisive thrust from Mississippi, what charming literary quotations from Iowa, what eloquent illustration from Massachusetts, what—but every bit of drift-wood brings some happy thought, even when it comes from our silent friend from New Jersey, who thinks that speech only offends, for like the dumb boatman from Astolat he brings a precious freight though he speaks not of it. A hundred answers have been given to the question, what makes the sea salt, but the true answer is that every little rill brings its contribution of salt to the river, and every river to the ocean, and the ocean sends the water back in vapor to bring more, but gives it not up again. So every writer sends his contribution to our ocean and so our drift-wood sparkles."

He gives North Carolina for 1896 a pleasant notice, reminding us that we are in the "sere and yellow leaf" by the time vegetation gets fairly green on the islands in Casco Bay. Frater Berry has a tender feeling for our State, as, .

"The same sweet south wind that blew in these North Carolina proceedings blew in our little North Carolina maid, who brings us handfuls of sweet white clover from the fields, 'because it smells like honeysuckles.' "

Under Georgia we find the following on the dispensation question :

"Perhaps the most satisfactory way is to require a fee to be paid into the Charity Fund for every dispensation granted. The Grand Chapter of Maine requires such a fee, and the result is that only 2 per cent. of the candidates ask to have their probation shortened, and then, generally, for the most satisfactory reasons."

If this idea was adopted we think that there would be a bountiful harvest for the "Charity Fund" just before each Triennial.

Under Kansas he has a sound utterance, which we quote, although not essentially a Templar issue.

"It is a very serious issue about Masonic homes. A fund of one hundred thousand dollars put into a Masonic home will only maintain from ten to twenty inmates, while the same income distributed judiciously will maintain one hundred among their kindred. In a small jurisdiction the wider distribution is better. In a large jurisdiction both methods may be employed. On the other hand a larger amount can be raised for a home than for direct charity : but that is attended with disadvantages "

He also voices his views in regard to Grand Encampment legislation.

"The Grand Encampment does so little legislation that it does but little harm. Most of the evils he (Callaham) wants corrected are things that have crept in by bad decisions, or been foisted upon us by committees who thought the ideas of their jurisdictions were the only truly good ideas. The code will continually grow worse instead of better if there is time for legislation. The less the Grand Encampment legislates, and the more freedom is left to the subordinate commanderies, the happier we shall be. We have stoutly maintained this since our very first writing of correspondence, and twenty years' consideration strongly confirms our opinion."

On the liquor question we find the following under Michigan.

"It is instructive to see what changes time brings. We have known brethren who sat at lodge tables when liquor was served every lodge night by the lodge itself. Now liquor sellers are barred out, and the craft is moving on the wealthy brewers and distillers. We shall probably know brethren who will see tobacco forbidden at our tables, tobacco sellers ostracised and cigar manufacturers attacked. That crusade is already commenced, and although it grinds slowly it will grind its whole grist."

We are inclined to think that he takes an entirely too optimistic view in relation to this latter reform. The use of the

"weed" is too general to expect that public opinion will ever be as strong against it, as it is now against the use of liquor.
Reviewing Oregon he presents his views in relation to affiliation.

"To limit the freedom of affiliation would lead to infinite trouble. The final result would be that when a man left our jurisdiction his membership would cease there, and commence in his new abode, without the frater having any choice or the commandery any voice in choosing its own members. It would result from a series of decisions, and we object to the abrogation of old customs by permitting any such entrance wedge"

Again we have to dissent, and do not see that the final result that he fears would necessarily follow the action that he premises.

If we do not draw further on Brother Berry it is not from lack of inclination, but with his "Conclusion" we will close, merely remarking that he has managed to get in a good deal of "between."

"In one of our Cumberland County conventions the slate was broken by a county delegate who introduced a new candidate with such an admirable speech that he carried him in triumphantly. When congratulated on his oratory, he said, 'a speech should have a good beginning, a good ending, and not much between!' A good ending is not easily found for these reports, but we remember the wise remark of the California uncle to the little boy who was writing a composition on the Unicorn. 'Uncle Bob,' said the boy, 'has the Unicorn a tassel on the end of his tail?' 'When you get to the end,' replied Uncle Bob, 'why don't you stop?'"

Nineteen Commanderies, 3,153 Knights; gain 86.
Sir Fritz H. Twitchell, Bath, Grand Commander.
Sir Stephen Berry, Portland, Grand Recorder, (re-elected) and Chairman of Committee on Correspondence.
Next Conclave, Portland, May 5th, 1898.

MARYLAND.

TWENTY-SEVENTH ANNUAL CONCLAVE.   Baltimore, November 23, 1897.
SIR GEORGE COOK, R. E. Grand Commander.

Only one of their 16 Grand Officers was absent and every Commandery was represented. Twenty-eight Grand Representatives, including North Carolina's, were also in attendance.

Sir Warren LaRue Thomas, M. E. Grand Master of the Grand Encampment, was received in due form and expressed his thanks for the uniform courtesy extended to him since he had taken up his residence in Baltimore.

The Grand Commander presented a full and well prepared account of his official acts, announcing that good will and fellowship universally prevailed. He says that the absence of a regulation requiring Sir Knights to procure uniforms is a great obstacle to their progress, also that apparently some make the lack of a uniform an excuse to shirk their duty on funeral occasions.

"While I agree with some that morally and theoretically a man may be just as good a Templar without as with a uniform, yet I cannot see how a Sir Knight can practically comply with the edicts and usages of the Order unless he is fully equipped to perform his part of the law."

No decisions were called for. Nineteen dispensations measure his labor in this line, the majority permitting public appearance in uniform on divers occasions.

Official visitation had full attention and he says :

"Your Grand Commander is pleased to report that the Subordinate Commanderies are governed by officers who are well able to perform every duty required of them, and are a credit to this Templar Jurisdiction, and your Grand Commander feels proud in having such an efficient corps of officers, in whose hands, it is safe to say, Templar Masonry will ever flourish like the Green Bay Tree."

A fitting tribute is paid to the memory of Sir Knight C. B. Kleibacker, Past Grand Commander, the Grand Commandery having been convened to attend the funeral. Other fraternal dead, of their own and sister jurisdictions, receive appropriate mention, our own Grand Warder being among the number.

The Christmas observance was held under the auspices of the Grand Commandery, more than 300 Sir Knights participating. This innovation is an excellent idea where the Commanderies are few and readily mobilized, but it would be a long time between toasts, as our Governor is often quoted, if it was attempted in this jurisdiction, for example.

The Grand Commander accepted an invitation from the Rector of one of the Baltimore churches to attend their Ascension Day service and the city Commanderies were *ordered* to

assemble for the purpose.   A large number of Sir Knights assembled and marched to the church and greatly enjoyed the
beautiful service which was rendered.

The Grand Commander enlarges on one topic and we quote
with approval :

"It is with chagrin that I have noted on a number of occasions when
speeches were made by some who are looked upon as exemplars of Masonic conduct and deportment, but who have attained the so-called
'higher' degrees of Masonry, that in their remarks they have referred to
the Masons of the 'higher' degrees in terms not at all edifying, and in language sarcastic to our noble Order.

"One might suppose that Templars are the arch enemies of the Masonic
Fraternity, but, my dear brethren, let me inform you that we are of your
brethren and kindred, and that we are deeply interested in all that interests you, and in addition we have assumed graver responsibilities than
those by which you are bound to the Masonic Fraternity.   We have at
heart all that is noble, good and true.

"I have never in my experience of a number of years of active service,
heard the least word derogatory to the Masons of the 'lower' degree
spoken by a Templar.   Such is a far too unexemplary vocation, and as
Templars, we are too busy inculcating the beautiful teachings of our noble Order to stop to engage in such work.   It is not square work, true
work, or such work as the Sublime Grand Overseer of the Universe would
have us do."

The officers-elect of the Baltimore Commanderies were installed at a special Conclave held on the evening of Easter Monday, several appropriate musical selections being rendered by
the Templar Choir.

The report of the Grand Inspector shows that only about
sixty per cent. of the Sir Knights are provided with uniforms.

The Grand Treasurer's report has $1,252 on the right side,
which is a substantial gain over the amount last reported to
their credit.

The Mississippi resolutions relating to a change in the Grand
Encampment laws were very fully considered by a Committee,
who recommended that they should not be endorsed and of
course the Grand Commandery concurred.

The installation of officers was a particularly elaborate affair
and took place at the Music Hall in the presence of a large audience of the Craft and their ladies, M. E. Grand Master Thomas
being present and assisting in the ceremonies.   After their con-

clusion the Sir Knights returned to the Asylum and "partook of a splendid lunch, by invitation of the newly installed Grand Commander," which doubtless was the most popular way of occupying the time he could have devised.

The smiling countenance of Grand Commander Cook adorns the proceedings.

Sir Knight Ferdinand J. S. Gorgas presents his twenty-fourth Report on Correspondence, which, we are exceedingly sorry to learn, is to be his last. The proceedings of 41 Grand Jurisdictions have been reviewed in his usual careful and courteous manner, and 88 pages measures the extent of his work.

North Carolina for 1897 has generous attention to the extent of three pages and we heartily reciprocate his kindly leave-taking. He notes that Sir Knight Martin's address is not to be found in the proceedings and has the following in reply to our suggestion :

"We have not as yet been blessed with the fair typewriter you recommend to us Sir Knight Chase, but will very seriously think over the matter, for no doubt such a one would make a change in the antics of the printer, and as you say, have an influence in our own environment. Good bye Sir Knight Chase, may you live long to write as good reports in the future as you have in the past."

As the immediate necessity seems to have vanished, we reckon that he will never know what he has missed in not being "blessed with the fair typewriter," and yet, the *fair* ones are not always an unmixed blessing.

With an assurance of our undying esteem we regretfully take our leave of Sir Knight Gorgas, cherishing the most pleasant recollections of our meeting in Boston, and, later on, in his own home. We quote his "Conclusion" in full and extend a cordial greeting to his successor.

"We have now completed our *twenty first* and *last* Report on Correspondence for the Grand Commandery of Maryland. This long service, with the addition of seven years as Chairman of the Committee on Correspondence for the Grand Lodge of Maryland, has given us an experience which we would not willingly have been deprived of, and it has always been a 'labor of love,' notwithstanding the fact that this work has invariably been performed in hours that are generally devoted to rest. But few of the Correspondents are now living who formed the Reportorial Corps when we entered its ranks ; but others from time to time sup-

plied the places of the absent ones, and friendships have been formed
which afford pleasing episodes in the routine of daily business cares   To
our co-laborers we return the sincere thanks of a heart which has ever
regarded all branches of Masonry as being far beyond personal aspirations,
for the kind and fraternal treatment we have invariably received at their
hands during the entire time we have performed the duties of a Correspondent ; and although we are deprived of the pleasure of communing
with them, we sincerely pray that every one of them may be so blessed
with health and strength as will enable him to perform for many years to
come the noble work which has so greatly enchanced the honor of their
respective Grand Commanderies, and brought these Grand Bodies into
closer and more fraternal relations with each other.

"For our successor, R. E. Sir Edward T. Schultz, a distinguished Tem-
lar who is most favorably known to the Order throughout the United
States, and who is now the Chairman of the Committees on Correspondence of the Grand Lodge and Grand Chapter and Grand Commandery of
Maryland, we respectfully request the same kind and courteous consideration which we have always received from the Correspondents during our
twenty-one years of service.   With good will for all, and enmity towards
none."

Sir Thomas J. Shryock, Baltimore, Grand Commander.

Sir John H. Miller, Baltimore, Grand Recorder, (re-elected.)

Sir E. T. Schultz, Baltimore, Chairman of Committee on
Correspondence.

Next Conclave, Baltimore, November 22, 1898.

MASSACHUSETTS AND RHODE ISLAND.

NINETY-FIRST ANNUAL CONCLAVE.   Boston, October 28th, 1897.
        SIR WILLIAM R. WALKER, R. E. Grand Commander.

All of the Grand Officers were present and only one of the
Commanderies was unrepresented.   Sir E. L. Freeman, who
holds North Carolina's commission, was one of the 33 Grand
Representatives who responded at roll-call and were welcomed
in the customary manner.

The Grand Commander's address is quite brief.   Seven of
the 16 pages give in detail the dispensations issued and permission given to Commanderies to visit in other jurisdictions;
a large majority permitting parades "in full Templar uniform
with music and banners."   Verily, the Bay State Sir Knights

are fond of a good time and the moth evidently has little chance of devastating their waving plumes. Long may they wave!

Fraternal dead are duly mentioned, prominent among them being Past Grand Master Benjamin Dean.

The constituting of a new Commandery is reported. No decisions called for.

He presents some sound objections to putting the names of the candidates on the notices of Conclaves. He also condemns the custom of having the candidate in waiting to receive the degree "if elected," and that before the petition has even been reported on, he having been notified by some Sir Knight to be on hand. He recommends that the Grand Commandery prohibit conferring the Order of Red Cross upon a candidate the same night he is elected, except by special dispensation, also that the candidate be notified in writing by the Recorder of the result of the ballot, no other Sir Knight being allowed to communicate the knowledge to him. We are in general accord with his views on this subject, but we are afraid that they will not find it an easy task to keep the Sir Knights from "leaking," judging from our own experience and observation in several orders. The matter was referred to a special committee, but they did not report at this Conclave.

Their funds in the Grand Treasurer's hands have increased nearly one-half during the year, being now $9,272. We do not find any disbursement for Report on Correspondence, which accounts in part for the large gain. Their "Grand Fund," a separate affair, now amounts to $22,317.

The Jurisprudence Committee report that apologies for conferring the Orders on candidates belonging to Maine and New Hampshire do not affect the case, except to show that the errors were unintentional, the fact remaining that the candidates did not legally receive the Orders and are entitled to no Templar rights.

The Mississippi memorial to the Grand Encampment, relating to a change in the organic law, was indefinitely postponed and the same fate overtook a series of resolutions, from Tennessee, concerning the use of the Maltese Cross by other orders and societies.

A Special Conclave was held in Boston on April 12th, 1897, to conduct the funeral services of the late Most Eminent Grand Master, Benjamin Dean.

"The beautiful home of the late Frater was filled with representatives of Masonic and Civic Societies who were there to show their love and respect for their departed associate. Many emblematic floral designs and rare flowers bore testimony of the loving regard in which our Frater was held by his Brethren and associates."

The 91st, Semi-annual Conclave was held in Providence on May 20th, 1897, all of the Grand Officers being present and 42 Commanderies represented.

The Grand Commander pays an affecting tribute to the late M. E. Grand Master, Benjamin Dean.

He reports that every Commandery, so far as known, observed the Christmas Toast.

He decides that valid objection can be made to a Sir Knight signing the By-laws, after election to membership, and the Committee on Jurisprudence sustained the decision.

The same Committee, after thoroughly considering the question of life membership, recommended that the fee be fixed at fifteen times the sum required as annual dues, the amount in no case to be less than $50. This sum, with one-tenth of the fee paid by each candidate elected to receive the Orders, shall be invested in a fund, of which the income only is to be used for any purpose, unless a two-thirds vote of the Commandery shall decide otherwise. The recommendations of the Committee were adopted. ·

A steel engraved portrait of Grand Commander Walker appears in the proceedings and they are further embellished with a two-page reproduction of the photographs of the representatives of their Grand Commandery near other Grand Commanderies. We regret to see that the space devoted to North Carolina is one of the three displaying the legend, "Photograph could not be obtained." It is a very unique and interesting display and worthy of imitation. We are confident that Grand Recorder Rowell will feel flattered if his example is followed.

The usual scholarly Report on Correspondence appears, bearing the marks of R. E. Sir Henry W. Rugg and E. Sir

5

Thomas E. St. John.   Forty-three Grand Jurisdictions have received careful and courteous attention and the result of their labors fills 109 pages.

In his introduction Brother Rugg enlarges upon the character and scope of a Correspondence Report and sums up as follows.

"We conclude, therefore, that both kinds of literature ought to be included in such a paper as that on which we are now engaged. Our purpose is to communicate information, to state facts worthy of a place in the mental catalogue of our readers; and, also to draw inferences, discuss principles, enforce moral lessons, so that this report may have a ministry to the heart and the soul, and thus exert its due measure of influence upon the formation of character and the regulation of conduct."

Our Brother is well equipped by education and training for the preparation of that kind of a report, but "there are others" who, unable to make a golden offering have to content themselves with one of silver, or of copper even.   Regarding the high aims of the Order he says:

"Templary is not a mere social and fraternal institution, for its very life is permeated by intellectual and spiritual elements; nevertheless, one of its chief functions is to bring men into the relations of pleasant companionship, helping them to realize that as friends and brothers they are workers together towards common ends. The complete life of our humanity is made possible in no other way. 'There is only one real want in life,' says a modern writer, 'and that is comradeship—comradeship with the Divine, and that we call religion; with the human, and that we call love."

Reviewing Illinois and referring to the resolution adopted, requesting each Commandery of the Jurisdiction "to procure a regulation United Statas flag, to represent their fidelity to the greatest government of history," he well says:

"It is well to have the United States flag displayed in the Asylum of Knights Templar and shown conspicuously in Templar parades; but the wording of this resolution is in doubtful taste. The carrying of the National flag ought not to be regarded as a test of their loyalty to the Government."

Under Maryland, noting that the "Christian Religion" had been defined by Grand Commander Neill of Montana as "a full belief in the Apostles' creed which we recite upon occasions of public worship," he says;

"For ourself we may remark that, accepting as we do the Apostles' creed, we doubt whether it is to be taken as a full definition of the Christian religion, and we also doubt the expediency of making this creed the formal test of a Templar profession."

North Carolina for 1897 has full and courteous mention from the pen of Brother St. John. He looks askance at the dispensations granted and apparently does not take much stock in shortening the statutory time that petitions must wait for the ballot. We shall not join issue with him on this topic. He notices that Brother Martin's "History of Freemasonry in connection with the city of Wilmington," does not appear in the proceedings, notwithstanding a resolution to that effect was passed at the Conclave, and says;

"How can we know how much the lovers of antiquity among the Craft have lost by this omission? It is always interesting to learn about the beginnings of any institution, and we regret that these researches were not printed in the book, as voted."

He notes, with approval, the omission of "memorial tablets" and queries if we have been doing some missionary work in that connection, to which we can only reply that we are not aware that we are entitled to any credit for the reform. We also quote another personal reference:

"He makes frequent references to Frater Carson s paper on 'Androgynal Freemasonry,' in the Ohio Proceedings for 1895. as he finds the matter commented on by the different correspondents, from which we gather the conclusion that he finds no fault with the innocent as well as beautiful ritual of the 'Order of the Eastern Star.'"

Our Brother is right in his assumption and he will doubtless find that the question has received further consideration in this report.

Under Vermont we find the following which we deem more than worthy of a place in the more than filled space allotted to the Bay State proceedings.

"When Templar Masonry fastens itself to a creed, its sublimest ideals will fade away and be forgotten. Brethren, give us freedom to formulate our own ideals of theology, and while accepting the divine principles of life as given us by the Master, let us think for ourselves about what the creeds may tell us."

We regret that Brother St. John retires from the "Corps" on account of having removed to another Jurisdiction. Our

best wishes go with him to his new field of labor and we trust
that even yet we may meet face to face.

On his motion the Grand Commandery voted that the
Committee on Correspondence should consist of but one
member, who should have the same compensation that the
two have been drawing, and Brother Rugg is now in full command.

Forty-six Commanderies, 12,313 Knights; gain 537.

Sir Walter Cutting, Pittsfield, Mass., Grand Commander.

Sir Benjamin W. Rowell, Lynn, Mass., Grand Recorder,
(re-elected.)

Sir Henry W. Rugg, Providence, R. I., Committee on
Foreign Correspondence.

Next Annual Conclave, Boston, October 27th, 1898.

MICHIGAN.

Forty-first Annual Conclave   Detroit, May 18, 1897.
Sir Edward D. Wheeler. R. E. Grand Commander.

The Grand Officers were at their posts with one exception
and 45 Commanderies represented.

The Grand Commander presents a very readable address.
They mourn the loss of four members of their Grand Body.
Sir Alexander McGregor, Grand Sentinel and Past Grand Com-
manders, Sir Heman N. Moore, Sir Hollis F. Knapp and Sir
Garra B. Noble.

The several decisions asked for were generally answered by
reference to Chapter and Section of their statutes covering the
point in question, which would indicate that the inquirers "seeking light" had saved themselves trouble at the expense of the
Grand Commander.

One of them, however, strikes us as being rather attenuated.
The petition of a Companion for the Orders was "laid on the
table for future consideration" and before it was acted upon
the petitioner removed to another jurisdiction. He now asks
the Commandery, within whose jurisdiction he resides, to waive
any claims they may have and the Grand Commander is asked

for light on the question.   He decides that "Neither Commandery can receive his petition without a waiver of jurisdiction on the part of the other."   We should say that he belonged to either one or the other, but a very obvious moral is, that such matters should not be left on the table too long.   We fancy that the Jurisprudenc Committee, had this case in mind when they recommended that the petition of an applicant for the Orders should not be held by a Commandery for a longer period than three months without balloting upon it.   They approved the decision, however, in a lump with the others.

He reports the constituting of a new Commandery which was chartered at the last Conclave.

A large number of dispensations were granted, of which a large majority permitted public appearance in uniform on a variety of occasions.

Fourteen Commanderies were officially visited and the unsparing criticism indulged in is refreshing to see, as there appears to be a general tendency to gloss over any deficiencies that are apparent.   We quote one criticism which will apply in other jurisdictions as well.

"The most serious criticism I had to make was the practice of electing a Sir Knight to an office simply because he was a 'good fellow,' and the Commandery desired to honor him; not taking into consideration his fitness or unfitness for the position."

Most Eminent Sir Elias T. Malone, Past Supreme Grand Master of the Great Priory of Canada was a distinguished visitor at the Conclave.

The Grand Treasurer's report shows that their funds have a little more than held their own during the year, being now $4,056.

Twenty-three pages are filled with a Memorial from the pen of Rev. Francis A. Blades, Grand Prelate, in which the many virtues of prominent Sir Knights of their own and sister jurisdictions are set forth in an affecting and poetic manner.

The Committee on Jurisprudence offered the following, which was adopted.

"Your committee courteously recommend that the rule be adopted, and that the same be taken as the sense of this Grand Body that no subordinate commandery be permitted to hold the petition of an applicant for the orders for a longer period than three months, but that on or before that time the same be finally disposed of by ballot."

The Triennial Committee reported that they had secured headquarters at Pittsburg, so we shall count on seeing a full delegation of our Wolverine brethren.

The "Entertainment" of the occasion was a grand banquet attended by over 600 Sir Knights, a prominent feature being the presentation of a marble bust of himself to M. E. Sir Hugh McCurdy Past Grand Master of the Grand Encampment. The presentation was made by Sir John C. Smith of Chicago and Sir Knight McCurdy's response was up to the high water mark of his previous efforts of this kind.

The volume of proceedings contains nearly 450 pages and is the usual sumptuous specimen of the printer's art. A portrait of Grand Commander Wheeler faces the title page. We note that their elaborate memorial tablet appears to be taking a vacation this year, a black border to the page being substituted, which is much more pleasing, to our way of thinking.

We now come to the *bonne-bouche*, which, of course, is the Report on Correspondence. Two hundred and eighty pages is its measure and it is the fourth that Sir John A. Gerow has sent out to edify and instruct his fratres. Forty-four Grand Jurisdictions receive attention, North Carolina for 1896 having a rather brief but commendatory notice and the Correspondent catching it as follows:

"Sir John stands strictly on the defensive, and is non-committal. He rests content with a clear and concise resume of what 'the other feller' said, and by that means leaves no vulnerable point by which we can have a pick at him. Come out of your shell, Sir John; we won't hurt you, and if you get a dent or two it will do you good. 'He laughs at scars who never felt a wound.' We have all 'caught it' more or less and thus have learned to respect and admire the courteous foeman worthy of our steel. Just give us a chance at you and see how much better you will feel after slapping some of us fellows over in the lists with your mace of opinion."

We do not credit our good Brother with any ill will towards us, but he apparently desires to get us into trouble. When he gets to the current proceedings of Ohio he will find that we already have a "dent," which, however, we hope to be able to hammer out.

He voices his sentimants on the liquor question several times with no uncertain sound and we cull a few lines from his notice of Connecticut.

"We are safe in saying that nine-tenths of the hotel keepers of this or any other country are masons because it will further their business. This is a sweeping assertion we admit, but we cheerfully submit the fact for analysis to any unprejudiced mason to-day and he will sustain us in the allegation. We seek not to be understood as blindly fanatical, and are willing to concede that liquor is good in its place and legal as a business, but that place is not a Templar Asylum nor that legality incumbent upon a vowed soldier of the Cross of Jesus Christ."

We are inclined to think that his first assertion is rather wild, but otherwise are in accord with him.

Discussing the New Hampshire ruling in regard to the use of the title "Sir Knight" for "Sir," he says:

"We fear we have to plead guilty to an infraction of this ruling, which we believe right, but we use them all, like the implements of a M. M. indiscriminately, something like the dying Irishman, when the priest asked him if he knew where he was going, replied, it did not make much difference, as he had friends in both places."

He is carried away with the New York idea of having representation based on membership, saying:

"Why should a Commandery with 50 members have as much voting power as one with 500? Or why should 150 Sir Knights be practically disfranchised because of a method of representation which obtained without any conflict, when the strength of Masonry was but small in the subordinates? We side with Sir Jesse in toto."

Sorry we can not offer something more consoling, but we are afraid that they will have to put up with the old order of things for many a year yet.

Trusting that the "brown October" will bring a meeting in Pittsburg, we check off Brother Gerow's jurisdiction and pass to the next.

Forty-five Commanderies, 5,523 Knights; gain 66.

Sir Albert Stiles, Jackson, Grand Commander.

Sir John A. Gerow, Detroit, Grand Recorder, (re-elected,) and Chairman of Committee on Correspondence.

Next Conclave, Port Huron, May 17th, 1898.

MINNESOTA.

THIRTY-SECOND ANNUAL CONCLAVE.   Minneapolis, June 24th, 1897.

SIR JOHN H. RANDALL, R. E. Grand Commander.

Eleven Grand Officers were present and 21 of their 25 Commanderies represented. Twenty-seven Grand Representatives were also in attendance. Sir John C. Munroe appearing for North Carolina.

The Grand Commander's address gives a detailed account of his official acts. Fraternal dead are duly noted, their own body mourning Sir Knights Luther Z. Rogers, Past Grand Commander and H. B. Smith, Past Grand Junior Warden. The general observance of the Christmas Toast is announced with gratification. Dispensation business was rather light, a good proportion of those asked for being refused. He is strongly opposed to shortening the time on petitions and greatly deplores the fact that such requests are often made when no real necessity exists. He decided that a Companion who had lost his left arm could not receive the orders.

Every Commandery but two was officially visited. Although finding cause for criticism he is able to report that the work witnessed was uniformly of a high order and the opening ceremonies generally satisfactory. The Commanderies are in a sound financial condition and the future outlook is bright and promising. We note that several of the banquets he participated in were graced by the presence of the ladies and on one occasion "the ladies of the Eastern Star" were the providers.

The Grand Treasurer's Report indicates financial prosperity, their funds having made a gratifying increase during the year and now amounting to $2,414.

The Grand Recorder read a letter from our Grand Commander Hackburn to Sir J. C. Munro, our representative near their Grand Commandery, which conveyed to the Grand Commander of Minnesota assurance of his knightly regard and approval of Sir Knight Munro's conception of the duties of his position. Sir Knight Munro was requested to convey the regards of their Grand Commander to the Grand Commandery of North Carolina, with thanks for the sentiments expressed in the letter from R. E. Sir Knight Hackburn.

A committee was appointed to secure quarters at Pittsburg and $200. placed at their dsssposal.

The volume of proceedings is embellished with portraits of Grand Commander Randall and Past Grand Commander Thomas Montgomery, who has been Grand Recorder for several years. Brother Montgomery is also Chairman of the Committee on Correspondence and this year sent out the eighth report he has fathered, which fills 93 pages and reviews the proceedings of 43 Templar Grand Bodies in his usual courteous and dignified manner.

North Carolina for 1897 is accorded a fair amount of space and no adverse criticism.

Noting that the Maryland Commanderies were *"ordered"* to attend divine service on Ascension Day, he says :

"This matter of attending service and observing so-called holy days, and even the Christmas greeting to the Grand Master, should be left wholly optional with commanderies and with individual members in their commanderies."

We are naturally pleased to see that he does not endorse Brother Carson's views on the Eastern Star question, and what he says has all the more weight from the fact that he is not a member of the much abused Order:

" We believe he is altogether too severe on thousands of worthy Brothers who differ with him on this subject, and yet we have seen some excuse for criticism, caused by jealousies and a factional spirit here and there. This, however, is not confined to the Eastern Star alone. ' By their fruits ye shall know them ' Surely nothing so scandalous as he portrayed as existing in France during a dissolute period has been laid at the door of the ' wives, mothers, sisters, and daughters' of American Masons. God bless them ! We write this unprejudiced, for we do not belong to any Chapter of the Order, and never did, although in possession of the degree, from its author, Rob. Morris."

We gather in a fragmentary way, that our Brother is sound on the flag question; favors the prompt collection of yearly dues; does not believe in the general use of the summons for securing the attendance of members, and is opposed to the dogma of perpetual jurisdiction.

Twenty-five commanderies, 2448 Knights; gain 37.

Sir Benjamin F. Farmer, Spring Valley, Grand Commander.

Sir Thomas Montgomery, St. Paul, Grand Recorder, (re-elected,) and Chairman of Committee on Correspondence.

Next Conclave, Faribault, June 24th, 1898.

MISSISSIPPI.

THIRTY-SEVENTH ANNUAL CONCLAVE.   Biloxi, February 9th, 1897.

SIR J. M. BUCHANAN, R. E. Grand Commander.

The proceedings were not received until April 7th, 1898, and then only through the courtesy of Brother DeLap, who promptly responded to a personal appeal.

Only one Grand Officer failed to appear and every Commandery was represented. Twelve Grand Representatives were in attendance. North Carolina's not being one of the number.

The Grand Commander's address is a rather brief document. He returns thanks that peace and prosperity abound and that their Grand Commandery has been spared affliction by death during the year. He notes the death of Grand Recorder Brewster of Texas and pays a glowing tribute to their own Grand Recorder, Sir J. L. Power, who is now the oldest Grand Recorder in the world, in years of service.

He reports with great pleasure that the Order has prospered, a dormant Commandery having been revived and a new one organized under dispensation.

The four dispensations issued permitted balloting on petitions before the prescribed time. No decisions are reported.

The Offices of Devotion were celebrated in the evening at the Methodist Church, in the presence of a large audience, the Grand Prelate afterwards delivering an elevating discourse. The claims of the Orphan Asylum were presented by Sir Knights Speed and Power and the collection lifted for this worthy cause amounted to $55.

The Grand Recorder reports that the Orphan Asylum was never in better condition, many improvements having been made, looking to the comfort and health of the children.

The funds in the Grand Treasurer's hands show a slight increase during the year, being now $369.

A Triennial Committee was appointed and $250 appropriated for the expenses of the Grand Commandery on that occasion. We are also pleased to note the following, and tender our congratulations to Brother DeLap, with the wish that the lightning may strike again in the same place.

"On motion, the 'honorarium' of Correspondence Reporter was increased from $50.00 to $75 00, to take effect with the present Conclave."

The Grand Commandery adopted a preamble and resolutions, expressing their belief that the organic law of the Grand Encampment should be changed, so that the several Grand Commanderies should have sole control of their subordinates on all local matters, leaving to the Grand Encampment only such matters as relate to the general welfare. The sister Grand Commanderies are asked to take action on the resolutions and instruct their representatives to the next Triennial accordingly.

The Grand Prelate was promoted to Grand Captain General, which we suppose accounts for the following, which strikes us as a little queer:

"On motion, it was ordered that the Grand Commander elect may appoint a Grand Captain General from the Commandery stationed at the place of the next Grand Conclave."

The volume of proceedings contains a portrait of Past Grand Commander Giles M. Hillyer, with an interesting memoir from the facile pen of Sir Frederic Speed.

Sir E. George DeLap presents his seventeenth Report on Correspondence, which devotes 132 pages to a pungent review of the proceedings of 39 Templar Grand Bodies. North Carolina for 1896 has full and courteous attention. The Grand Commander's address is styled "a business document, well-written and to the point," and the Correspondent's work is commended, for which we extend our thanks.

Brother DeLap's love for the Grand Encampment does not increase as the years go by and various allusions to it by the other Correspondents draw out some of his most caustic utterances. The liquor question in its various phases as related to Templar affairs is touched upon from time to time and with no uncertain sound. He believes in a modified perpetual jurisdiction, a limit of three years being about his figure, and we shall not differ seriously on that issue.

Under Kentucky we find the following, which we are not ready to endorse, but shall not lie awake worrying about it.

" We dissent from his assertion (Grand Commander Stone's.) that the law requiring petitions to lie over for 30 days is certainly a good one, as, in our judgment, such matters as these should be left to the good judgment of the Subordinate Commanderies, where it belongs. The rule is all right in the Blue Lodge, but when a man is made a Master or Royal Arch Mason, he is no longer a ' Profane,' and is entitled to that measure of consideration usually accorded to members of the same family by each other."

Under Michigan we find the following, which is sound sense:

" We are not disposed to agree to the proposition that a Commandery can accept the petition of a Companion, and take no further action thereon, and thus acquire perpetual jurisdiction, neither electing or rejecting him itself or allowing another Commander to do so. In other words, perpetual jurisdiction results only from rejection, or election coupled with the conferring of one degree."

Referring to a decision of Grand Master McCurdy, reported at the Boston Triennial, we find the following, under Minnesota ;

"That the decision is arbitrary and without the leaven of sound sense is apparent to any one who takes the trouble to use his brains a little. There are several contingencies under which it would be perfectly right and proper for a Commandery to allow the withdrawal of a petition, and it is a right and a privilege that the Commanderies of this bailiwick will continue to exercise in the future as though the Central Excrescense had not neggected its legitimate functions for the purpose of nosing around among the domestic concerns of the Subordinate Commanderies."

Come up to the Triennial next fall Brother DeLap and meet your brother Correspondents. They will be more than glad to see you, and if you do not want to attend the sessions of the " Excrescence " we will go a-fishing in the opaque waters that flow by the " Smoky City " and you will find that the trip will not harm you " one little bit "; and who knows but what it would be the death blow to the arch fiend dyspepsia which has tormented you for so long. We are pleased to learn of the improvement in your health and trust that your reports may wax more and more " sunny" as the years go by. *Pax vobiscum !*

Fourteen Commanderies, 478 Knights ; gain 37.

Sir James T. Harrison, Columbus, Grand Commander.

Sir J. L. Power, Jackson, Grand Recorder, (re-elected.)

Sir E. George DeLap, Natchez, Committee on Fraternal Correspondence.

Next Conclave, Water Valley, February 8th, 1898.

MISSOURI.

THIRTY-SIXTH ANNUAL CONCLAVE.   St. Louis, April 20th 1897.

SIR IRA V. McMILLAN, R. E. Grand Commander.

Only one Grand Officer absent and two Commanderies un-represented. Thirty-one Grand Representatives were on hand, North Carolina's being one of the number.

The Grand Commander presents a well prepared address. Official visitation was indulged in to a limited extent only, it being made the duty of the other Grand Officers, who were placed in charge of the several districts created by the law enacted at a previous conclave. The reports received from the Commanderies, in compliance with another law, show a generally satisfactory condition as regards their property and the manner in which they conduct their local affairs.

He has a mild complaint to the effect that failure to peruse the laws required his answering many questions that need not have been asked, if the questioners had investigated a little for themselves.

Apparently the Commanderies of this jurisdiction consider it of little use to ask for dispensation to shorten the time that petitions must lie over for the ballot, as only one of those granted was for that purpose. He refused a dispensation to permit a Commandery to receive the petition of an officer of the regular army, who was not a resident of the State and claimed to be a resident of the United States only. He recommends the adoption of a law to cover such cases, providing that :

" One who is regularly engaged in the military or naval service of the United States, and who has no fixed home or place of abode, by reason of such occupation, if otherwise qualified, may petition the Commandery near which he is stationed for the Orders, which said Commandery shall certify the facts to the Grand Commander., who shall be authorized to grant a dispensation to said Commandery, permitting it to act upon said petition and confer the Orders."

We do not find that any action was taken in the matter.

The by-laws of a certain Commandery provided that its members after paying $75 in dues to that or any other Commandery should become life members, and he decided that the by-law complied with the law of the Grand Encampment requiring the payment of a fixed sum, but the Committee on Jurisprudence very properly reversed his decision. Replying to the question if a candidate " badly club-footed" was eligible for the Orders, he cites the law covering such cases, as follows :

"If the candidate can give all the signs and go through all the ceremonies, he is eligible, and not otherwise ; and the Eminent Commander and members of the Commandery are the judges of his eligibility under this rule."

He further says :

" I am not in harmony with those who contend for absolute *perfect* physical qualifications in Masonry. If the capacity to endure pilgrimage and warfare are the requisites absolute in modern Knighthood, then I should contend that there should be a provision for retiring aged and superannuated Sir Knights."

Several Commanderies reported that they had observed the Christmas Toast and he hopes that the beautiful custom will become general.

Their funds show a slight decrease during the year, but destitution is not imminent, as they still have $4,983 to their credit.

A goodly amount of business was transacted, but we find nothing of general interest.

Portraits of Grand Commander McMillan and Past Grand Commander George F. Gouley embellish the volume. The last named, who died in 1877, has a touching biographical memoir from the pen of Sir William H. Mayo, Grand Recorder, and the Grand Commander is likewise written up.

For the twentieth time Sir William H. Mayo presents the

Report on Correspondence, and 91 pages are filled with an
excellent review of the proceedings of 42 Grand Jurisdictions,
North Carolina for 1896 receiving courteous mention.   Under
Tennessee we find some cheering words for our Brother Foster,
which may also be a solace to other members of the "Corps."

"Now, Sir Wilber, just tell your friend that he is away off, that there
are several hundred bright intelligent Templars in this country who are
searching for light, and read with pleasure and profit every word of the
reviews that have cost the members of the guild so many hours of labor ;
of course there are some who never read anything, except, perhaps a
political speech, and appreciate nothing that comes their way except a
banquet."

The above was drawn forth by Sir Knight Foster's saying
that on his complaining that his work as reviewer was not satisfactory to himself, a cynical friend had consoled him by saying, "O don't bother ! nobody will read it, anyhow !"

Fifty-seven Commanderies, 4,237 Knights ; gain 3.

Sir John Gillies, Monett, Grand Commander.

Sir William H. Mayo, St. Louis, Grand Recorder, (re-
elected,) and Correspondent.

Next Conclave, St. Louis, April 26th, 1898.

MONTANA.

TENTH ANNUAL CONCLAVE.   Helena, September 13th, 1897.
SIR CORNELIUS HEDGES, R. E. Grand Commander.

The Grand Commandery inaugurated a new custom, to
them, by attending divine worship the night before the Conclave, at St. Peter's Episcopal Church, where the usual devotional services of the Order were conducted, accompanied by
fine music and followed by an impressive discourse by Sir and
Rev. John F. Pritchard.

Four Grand Officers were absent from their posts, but all of
the Commanderies were represented.   Grand Representatives
were conspicuous by their rarity, as only ten were present and
North Carolina's was not one of the number.

The lines being formed, the Grand Recorder read a communication from M. E. Grand Master Thomas, announcing

the death of Past Grand Masters Vincent L. Hurlburt and Benjamin Dean.

The Grand Commander presents a high-toned address, which is no more than was to be expected from the distinguished Frater who is the Alpha and Omega of this year's proceedings. In the poetical language of the Orient, towards which his thoughts so often turn, we say with all sincerity, "May his shadow never be less!"

He announces the death of Sir Ranald McDougall, Grand Standard Bearer. Says that little has occurred worthy of mention in the way of official acts, and that it has not been a year favorable to growth and activity, but one "well adapted to the cultivation of the virtues of patience, perseverence, courage, and constancy."

Only three dispensations were issued, one permitting balloting on a petition without waiting the statutory time, in order to secure a Prelate to officiate at Ascension Day services. The end certainly justified the means in this case. He felt obliged to decline the request of a Commandery for permission to go to another place with their equipments and confer the Orders on several petitioners, who were railroad employees and could not leave their posts.

They evidently do not consider the Grand Representative system an unmixed evil, for their exchange list has been increased to quite an extent.

He paid official visits to all of the Commanderies except his own. The pilgrimage took about sixteen days and he rather apologetically says, "it is hardly necessary to add, consumed the entire appropriation," of $100. While his journey may have been rough and at times perilous, a sixty-mile stage ride being one of the incidents, there is nothing in his account to indicate that he was confined to a rough diet and coarse fare. He thinks, however, that it is too much of an undertaking to be repeated every year, but that once in three would be about right.

The Christmas Toast was observed to a limited extent, the hour in their longitude not being favorable for a general response. He makes the sensible suggestion that the idea of making it simultaneous, all over the country, be abandoned

and allow the Sir Knights with ladies and their families, perhaps, to meet at their Asylums at the most convenient hour
on Christmas Day. They might meet at "high twelve" of
their meridian, which would enable the M. E. Grand Master
to respond at four different times. As to the effect of the
continued libations on the Most Eminent, "that is another
story," as Kipling says.

Referring to a prospective report from a committee appointed
to consider Past Grand Commander Neill's definition of the
"Christian Religion," he says,

"Without attempting to anticipate the report of the Committee on the
action of the Grand Commandery, we desire to remind the members that
this is no forum for the discussion of theological questions, and it seems
very clear to us that a profession of belief in the Christian Religion
was preliminary to admission to our Order; and that must be the religion of the only Christ known in Scripture and history. If there has been
anything omitted from the Apostles' Creed it should be inserted, but we
do not pretend to know more than the Apostles, and we earnestly advise
you to let the matter rest where the committee left it."

Calling to mind their "tiresome, hungry and inglorious position in the last division" at the Boston Triennial and considering the small number from their jurisdiction who will be
likely to go to Pittsburg, he is constrained to disapprove their
attempting to maintain headquarters, but suggests that they
"concentrate our strength for service after the parade is over."
Reading between the lines we opine that this means parlia-
mentary warfare against the "unspeakable Turk."

The purchase of a "fine national flag" is advocated, which
is to be borne by the Commandery making the best showing
in drill and evolution at a suggested general meeting of their
Commanderies.

Their funds are in practically the same condition as at the
beginning of the year, the Grand Treasurer reporting $528 to
his credit.

The report of a committee on Forms was adopted and it
would seem that they had provided for every conceivable case,
as their report fills sixteen pages of the proceedings.

The work of the Order of the Temple was exemplified by
Helena Commandery at the evening session. Triennial arrangements were left in the hands of a committee, as was the

6

purchase of a flag. A portrait of Grand Commander Hedges faces the title page.

Eighty-three pages is the extent of the Correspondence Report, in which Sir Cornelius Hedges reviews the proceedings of 41 Templar Grand Bodies in his happiest vein. As heretofore, the redemption of Palestine is a live question and the pages are few that do not contain some allusion to the subject.

Under Ohio he has some vigorous words in reply to Sir Knight Carson's strictures on the Order of the Eastern Star and it also strikes him as a new idea that a Grand Commander may not "order," but must only request a Commandery to assemble for any purpose.

North Carolina for 1897 has a particularly genial notice, the correspondent's offorts receiving flattering mention. Referring to our assertion that a dispensation was necessary to permit church attendance in uniform by Commanderies on Easter and Ascension Day, he says :

"If it is not a Templar duty to turn out in full ranks to honor these occasions and make public profession of our belief in a risen and ascended Saviour. it ought to be, and we covered the doubt in our jurisdiction by a general dispensation."

May be so, but we do not so construe the Grand Encampment law in this jurisdiction; we have a standing resolution that permits the Grand Commander to issue an "omnibus" dispensation permitting public appearance in uniform on all the so-called Christian Days.

We regret that we cannot linger longer with this entertaining Frater, but assuring him that we shall be certain to search out the prospective " Montana headquarters on a flatboat," if we are privileged to be in Pittsburg next fall, we tick off Montana and pass to the next in line.

Eight Commanderies, 366 Knights ; gain 18.

Sir William E. Chamberlain, Great Falls, Grand Commander.

Sir Edward D. Neill, Helena, Grand Recorder, (re-elected.)

Sir Cornelius Hedges, Helena. Committee on Correspondence.

Next Conclave, Helena, September 19th, 1898.

NEBRASKA.

TWENTY-FIFTH ANNUAL CONCLAVE.   Lincoln, April 29th, 1897.
SIR RICHARD P. R. MILLER, R. E Grand Commander.

Twelve Grand Officers present and 19 Commanderies represented. Twenty Grand Representatives were also in attendance, Sir Wilton K. Williams appearing for North Carolina.

The Grand Commandery was welcomed by the Eminent Commander of the home Commandery in a few well chosen words, to which the Grand Commander made a fitting response, and R. E. Sir Edgar S. Dudley, Grand Sword Bearer of the Grand Encampment having been received and welcomed they got down to business.

The Grand Commander laments that the year has not been a prosperous one following, as it has, in the wake of three years of crop failure, but the bountiful harvest of the present year gives promise of prosperity and he hopes that the orde will feel the results thereof.

They have been called upon to mourn the death of Sir Joseph K. Marley, Past Grand Commander, and other fraternal dead are duly noticed.

Among his eight decisions we find one saying that charges could not be preferred against two Sir Knights, who failed to obey a summons to appear and show cause why they should not be suspended for non-payment of dues. They were duly suspended and later on it was decided to discipline them for disobeying the summons. He held that it would virtually be punishing them twice for the same offense, but the Committee on Jurisprudence did not take that view of the case and disapproved the decision. We think the Grand Commander was in the right.

He approved the By-Law of a Commandery, which provided that any member, who had paid dues for 21 years and was square on the books, should be exempt from further dues upon the payment of $5. We suppose that this will clear the Grand Encampment Law on the subject, but it is pretty close to an evasion of it, certainly so far as the intent is concerned. For a dispensation to act on a petition without waiting the statutory time and confer the Orders if the candidate was elected, he collected the required fee of $10 for the benefit of their treasury.

The Grand Treasurer's report shows $973. to their credit, but their indebtedness slightly exceeds that amount.

A Committee on Triennial was appointed, to make all necessary arrangements for their pilgrimage to Pittsburg, where we hope to have the pleasure of greeting the Chairman of the Correspondence Committee. He fails to report this year, but it cannot be for lack of space in the proceedings, as there are several blank pages, which would indicate that the printer was expecting to hear from him. A fine steel-engraved portrait of Grand Commander Miller appears as a frontispiece.

Twenty-three Commanderies, 1,679 Knights; *loss* 33.

Sir Edwin C. Webster, Hastings, Grand Commander.

Sir William R. Bowen, Grand Recorder, (re-elected,) and Chairman of Committee on Foreign Correspondence.

Next Conclave, Omaha, April 21st, 1898.

NEW HAMPSHIRE.

THIRTY-EIGHTH ANNUAL CONCLAVE.   Concord, Sepember 28th, 1897.
SIR JOHN HATCH, R. E. Grand Commander.

Twelve Grand Officers, Representatives from seven of their eleven Commanderies and a goodly number of past officers and permanent members were in attendance. Twenty-two Grand Jurisdictions were also represented, but North Carolina was not one of the number.

We are obliged to infer that the annual Conclaves are not considered one of the events of the year, considering that so many Commanderies are unrepresented in a jurisdiction of such small territorial limits, comparatively speaking.

The Grand Commander presented a well-written and interesting address of thirty pages. He announces with gratification that they have been blessed with prosperity, a very steady increase in membership being reported.

Only two Commanderies failed to receive an official visit and he found nothing calling for extended criticism or admonition.

The practice of having an official count of those in attendance at the visitation has incited exertions to secure a good turnout and the statistics given show a decided gain over the number reported the preceeding year.

The sixteen dispensations reported permitted public appearance in uniform, only four being for the purpose of attending divine service. He favors frequent interchange of friendly visitations among the Commanderies, as designed to promote the best interests of the Order.

The announcement of the Christmas Toast afforded opportunity for an admonition against general conviviality.

On the question of personal deformity in a candidate he decides that the Eminent Commander and Commandery are the judges of the petitioner's eligibility. He counsels impartial and faithful scrutiny, however harsh and unkind it may seem, to see that the candidate is capable of properly taking part in the ceremonies of the Order. He also says :

"In reply to the second question, notwithstanding the ordinary rule of. Templar law, that a petition presented to a Commandery cannot be withdrawn, and that an unfavorable report does not dispense with the necessity of a ballot, in the case under consideration, should the Commandery find as a matter of .fact that the petitioner was incapable of giving the signs or of passing through all the ceremonies of the Order, or that his presence would mar the symmetry of a parade, the petition should not be further acted upon. While the statute in question does not expressly provide that the petition in such a case may be dismissed, there are certain contingencies where the formality of a ballot would seem to be useless.—'The reason and spirit of the cases make law, not the letter of particular precedents,' said Chief Justice Mansfield —this among the number. For instance, should it appear from the investigation of the committee that the petitioner was not a believer in the Christian religion; or where the report of the committee shows the petitioner has been rejected on a former petition within six months; or that the Commandery has no jurisdiction over the petitioner, a ballot would be futile."

Another novel question was in relation to the reception of petitions for the Orders from foreign born residents who had not become citizens of the United States. He considers the question in its various bearings and decides to the contrary, but suggests that the Committee on Jurisprudence wrestle with the question. They deemed it of suffcient importance to require a year's time for its consideration and the next annual Conclave is expected to receive the result of their labors.

The Grand Commandery has been called upon to mourn the death of four of its members: Sir Knights Joseph Shattuck, Grand Senior Warden, John D. Patterson and Andrew Bunton, Past Grand Commanders, being of the number. Very complete and fitting memorial notices appear, accompanied by portraits of Sir Knights Patterson and Bunton. It was our good fortune to enjoy the personal acquaintance of the two last-named for a period of nearly thirty years and their death brings a deep sense of personal loss.

The Grand Treasurer reports $1,063. to his credit. Finding that their ordinary expenses for the past few years have exceeded their income the per capita and candidate tax is to be increased for the next two years.

Considering the Tennessee resolutions in regard to the general use of the Maltese Cross, the Jurisprudence Committee signify their approval of the sentiments expressed and deprecate the practice, but do not see clearly how it is to be prevented. They believe that any attempt to interfere with the practices of other societies might produce the opposite effect from the desired one.

Five hundred dollars was appropriated for the expenses of the Grand Commandery at the coming Triennial.

The Report on Correspondence is from the cultured pen of Sir Albert S. Wait, who for the eighth time enlightens and edifies his readers with a 113 page review of the doings of 40 Templar Grand Bodies.

North Carolina for 1897 is accorded a good proportion of space with courteous and approving comment.

Replying to Sir Knight Cox's criticism on "Masonic sociables;" he says :

"We have no great predilection for the fuss and feathers, but are much of the opinion that when the Templar Orders, if they ever do, get out of touch with the social tendencies of the world, they will have lost the influence which they are now so manifestly exerting upon society. If this is ever the case the spirit of Knight Templary will have gone out of them and their value for any purpose will have departed."

Under Michigan, commenting on a decision, which we have also noticed, he says :

"We should think it a better, as well as a more just rule, that a Commandery laying an application for the Orders upon the table until the candidate has removed from the jurisdiction, should be held to have surrendered its jurisdiction over him, restoring to him the privilege of applying to the body of his newly acquired residence.

It seems to us, moreover, that there is something of incongruousness, not to say absurdity, in holding that two Masonic bodies can at the same time have exclusive jurisdiction over the same candidate. It seems to our comprehension that to assume that any one body has exclusive jurisdiction over a candidate implies that no other has any such."

He disagrees with the ruling of the Nebraska Committee on Jurisprudence, to the effect that some Sir Knights could be tried for failure to obey a summons to appear and show cause why they should not be suspended for non-payment of dues, they having been duly suspended for the original offence. We quote at length with approval :

"We query as to the views of the committee. The offence was not one against the general law of masonry or the Knightly Orders, but was for contempt in disobeying an order of the Commandery. It was for an offence in which the Commandery alone, and not the Order at large, had any interest. We query, whether, in such a case, when the Commandery suspended the Sir Knight, it did not lose jurisdiction over him, for an offence against its mere authority.

"We question the view of the committee, moreover, on the merits of the case. The sole object of the summons was to give the Sir Knights an opportunity to show cause why they should not be suspended. Their non-appearance was an admission that they could show no such cause, and thus authorize the Commandery to proceed *ex parte*. It was equivalent to a default in a civil court. No court ever held a failure to appear in obedience to such summons to be a contempt of their authority. It simply proceeds to judgment without the party. . . . If summoned to appear for some purpose which could not be accomplished without their personal presence, for instance, to give evidence on a trial, or to furnish aid in any other matter in hand, the refusal or neglect, without a valid excuse, would doubtless be a contempt for which a Sir Knight would be punishable. The two cases are in principle radically different, and we doubt the correctness of the conclusion of the committee."

He is a non-believer in the New York idea of increased representation of the large Grand Commanderies in the Grand Encampment and deals with the subject at length. We regret that the limitations of our space prevent giving his discussion of the subject in full, as well as quoting his entertaining and instructive views on other subjects, but must make our adieu and hasten on.

Eleven Commanderies, 2,115 Knights; gain 55.

Sir John Hatch, Concord, Grand Commander, (re-elected.)

Sir George P. Cleaves, Concord, Grand Recorder, (re-elected.)

Sir Albert S. Wait, Newport, Chairman of Committee on Correspondence.

Next Conclave, Concord, September 27th, 1898.

NEW JERSEY.

THIRTY-NINTH ANNUAL CONCLAVE.   Trenton, May 11th, 1897.

SIR JOHN E. ROWE, V. E. Deputy Grand Commander.

Twelve Grand Officers present and 15 Commanderies represented. Twenty-six Grand Representatives were introduced and welcomed in a hearty manner, but the Sir Knight who holds North Carolina's commission was not among the number.

The Grand Commandery mourns the death of R. E. Sir Robert Dingwell, Grand Commander, who was called to his reward in less than three months after his installation.

Sir Knight Rowe, the Acting Grand Commander, presented a detailed account of his official acts. Only one dispensation was called for and but one decision is reported.

The "Field Day" was held in October, nine Commanderies being present. He says that the Sir Knights attending never appeared to better advantage or reflected more credit on the Order by their conduct.

Official visitation showed a general improvement in Asylum tactics and satisfactory financial conditions.

A heartfelt tribute is paid to the memory of the deceased Grand Commander, and the death is also noted of Past Grand Commander, Sir Jerome B. Borden, who was Grand Warder of the Grand Encampment in 1880.

The Grand Treasurer reports the funds in his hands as being $1,569, a slight increase during the year.

The Triennial Committee reported that they had secured headquarters for the Grand Commandery at the coming Triennial.

A portrait of Grand Commander Dingwell, heavily bordered with black, faces the title page, and each page of the proceedings is bordered with heavy black rules.

Sir Peter McGill, for the committee, presents a 74-page Report on Correspondence, in which the proceedings of 40 Templar Grand Jurisdictions have been courteously reviewed.

North Carolina for 1896 is duly noticed and referring to the Report on Correspondence he says :

"The pleasure of reading his previous reports has not been ours, but we know that his work improves with experience."

We are curious to learn if his assertion is the result of belief in the general law, or of intuition in this particular case.

He quotes, with approval, Grand Commander Liddell's recommendation that the Sir Knights contribute to the Oxford Asylum fund, which would show fidelity to Masonry far better "than by flowery speeches or nicely worded resolutions."

Under Ohio, we find that he considers Good Friday, Easter Sunday and Ascension Day as "Masonic occasions," in a "Templar sense," and, we infer, believes that the Grand Commandery could so declare and let the Commanderies appear in uniform, without asking the consent of the Grand Commander. If the Grand Encampment would only settle the question as to what *are* "Masonic occasions," it would be time well spent.

Like others of the "Corps," he "lays down his pen with a feeling of relief," but we hope to see him in print, again and in person as well the coming October.

Sixteen Commanderies, 1,779 Knights ; gain 43.

Sir John E. Rowe, Newark, Grand Commander.

Sir Charles Bechtel, Trenton, Grand Recorder, (re-elected,) and Chairman of Committee on Correspondence.

Next Conclave, Trenton, May 10th, 1898.

NEW YORK.

EIGHTY-FOURTH ANNUAL CONCLAVE   Jamestown, Sept. 14th, 1897.

SIR JAMES A. MAPES, R. E. Grand Commander.

All of the Grand Officers were at their stations and 56 Commanderies represented. North Carolina was not one of the twenty Grand Jurisdictions whose representatives were introduced and welcomed.

Eloquent addresses of welcome were made by the Mayor and Sir and Rev. Charles C. Albertson of Jamestown Commandery, to which the Grand Commander made happy responses.

The Grand Commander's address is a well prepared and interesting production, with correspondence, orders, etc., relegated to an appendix.

Fraternal dead receive extended mention, their own body mourning Sir Robert Black, past Grand Commander.

The utmost harmony is announced as prevailing and the year has been a prosperous one. Only three decisions are reported, one of which we give in full.

" Q. A Sir Knight, who had been dropped from the roll of his Commandery for non-payment of dues, afterwards paid up his indebtedness, and asked for a receipt in full, which was given him under seal of the Commandery. He now asks for a demit, that he may join another Commandery. Can it be given him?

" A His payment of the arrearages of the dues merely discharged his indebtedness to the Commandery. It did not restore him to membership. That can only be effected by a majority vote. Dimits can properly be granted only to members. He is entitled, however, upon his application therefor to a vote upon the question of restoration. Should that vote be adverse, the Commandery should give him a certificate under seal, stating that he had been a member; that his name had been dropped from the roll for non-payment of dues only, and that thereafter such dues had been fully paid by him ; but that he had not been fully restored to membership. Such a certificate would be equivalent to a dimit."

While we are not disposed to except to the decision, which passed the square of the Jurisprudence Committee, we are inclined to think that a dimit of that kind would be likely to be regarded as a little off color.

Numerous dispensations are reported, the greater number

permitting public appearance in uniform on divers occasions, and we quote with approval what he has to say on two important points :

"When we consider the large number of our Commanderies who attended Divine service on Easter and Ascension Days, for which no dispensation was needed, it would appear that the practice of attending in a body the public services of our religion is growing among us. We may, I think, congratulate ourselves upon this fact, for certainly it is most fitting that we should thus publicly show the sincerity of our professions as Soldiers of the Cross.

"The dispensations to visit Orphan Asylums on New Year's Day need, I think, no apology from me. 'Helpless Orphans' are especially commended to our care and protection, while our Holy Religion enjoins us ' to visit the fatherless and the widows in their affliction.' As these visits not only bring great pleasure to the little ones, but are usually accompanied with substantial additions to their comforts, we may be pardoned for calling them ' Masonic Occasions,' and hope that they may be more frequent in the future."

Official visitation was indulged in to quite an extent and with gratifying results, so far as courtesy and hospitality were concerned.

He devotes considerable space to consideration of " The effect of unaffiliation for non-payment of dues in Lodge or Chapter," and is disposed to believe that their law on the subject is susceptible of some improvement. As it now stands, they are " inflicting *a penalty of our own* for failure to pay dues in other bodies, which penalty is to be enforced without even the semblance of a trial," and he very properly maintains that no Sir Knight should be deprived of any of his rights without due trial.

He is pleased to announce a gratifying increase in membership and well says :

"I am not unmindful of the fact that numbers alone are not the true test of success. One unworthy name added to our rolls will more than counterbalance the addition of ten worthy ones. I am, however, so familiar with the care which is being exercised by our Subordinate bodies in this respect, that I have no fear whatever that any desire for increased membership will induce any of them in the slightest degree to lower the standard of qualification for admission to the Order."

The Grand Recorder makes the gratifying statement that " Returns have been received from ALL the subordinate Commanderies."

The Grand Treasurer reports the funds in his hands as amounting to $10,101, some three hundred dollars less than he started the year with.

Sir and Rev. Cornelius L. Twing, Grand Prelate, presented a Report on Necrology, in which the many virtues of deceased Sir Knights are set forth in fitting terms.

"The positive assurance is ours, that they who are absent from the post of duty, were not faithless to trust, nor were they recreant, ingrate, or false. The designs made upon their trestle boards prove that they were workmen of whom we need not be ashamed. The enemy of all mortality met some of them at the South, some at the West, and some at the East gate. In whatever stage of life, the demand was made upon them, the answer to the great Assassin was the same. 'My life you may take, but my integrity never.' They have fallen, some crowned with honors and years, and some were only in the prime of manhood."

The Committee on Jurisprudence presents a lengthy report, in which full consideration is given to their present regulation relating to the standing of Sir Knights who have been suspended from Lodge or Chapter for non-payment of dues. The Committee are in accord with the Grand Commander on the subject and recommend that their regulation be amended to read as follows :

"Unaffiliation or suspension for non payment of dues by Lodge or Chapter—that fact having been duly certified to the Commandery under seal of such Lodge or Chapter—shall · after thirty days' notice, and the Sir Knight having failed to reinstate himself in those bodies—deprive a Knight of membership in the Commandery until such unaffiliation or suspension shall cease, or his dues be paid."

Their recommendation was adopted and the amendment lies over until the next annual conclave for action.

Fine steel engraved portraits of Grand Commander Mapes and Past Grand Commander Robert Black embellish the volume.

The Report on Correspondence fills 131 pages and reviews the proceedings of 43 Grand Commanderies in an instructive and entertaining manner. As heretofore, it emanates from a Committee, of which Sir Jesse B. Anthony is Chairman, and he admits our soft impeachment that he alone is to be credited with all its good points, and bad ones it has none. His line of action is outlined in his introduction and he has kept well within bounds.

" We have given the proceedings before us careful attention, and it has been our object and aim to embrace in the review such matters of importance as we deem to be of interest to the Fratres of this jurisdiction. Within the lines of fraternal courtesy we have made personal comments upon various points, and, wherein we have entertained a different opinion from others, have not hesitated to express our views. We trust that no one will take offense, as our design in any criticism has been for the common good."

North Carolina for 1897 is courteously noticed. He notes that Sir Knight Martin's "interesting address on the History of Freemasonry in connection with the city of Wilmington" was not printed and assumes that it was because the copy failed to materialize, which we suspect is the true explanation. We quote him on another point, and " Horace," who is the Representative of their Jurisdiction, will have to explain :

" They must have something new in this jurisdiction, judging from the following caption : 'The following Grand Representatives present were received in the usual *solemn* manner.' What was the name of the March ?"

He quotes in full our criticism upon the question of " Representation in the Grand Encampment." As the matter appears to be dormant at the present time, we have nothing further to say. Our Frater is called upon to answer the views in opposition of nearly every reviewer, which he does in a courteous and dignified manner and we are free to admit that some of his reasoning is not easily disproved.

Under Ohio we find the following, which was called out in Frater Carson's review of North Carolina :

" We beg to differ with our Frater in the general statement that ' a Grand Commander has no authority to order a Commandery to assemble for any purpose.' We would, however, question the propriety of any such order 'to meet on Christmas morning to join in the toast to the M. E. Grand Master.'"

The statistical tables appear as usual and are a credit to the industry of the compiler.

Sixty-four Commanderies, 11,376 Knights ; gain 339.

Sir Arthur McArthur, Troy, Grand Commander.

Sir John F. Shafer, Albany, Grand Recorder, (re-elected.)
Sir Jesse B. Anthony, Utica, Chairman of Committee on Correspondence.

Next Conclave, Geneva, October 25th, 1898.

NORTH DAKOTA.

EIGHTH ANNUAL CONCLAVE.   Devil's Lake, July, 1st, 1897.
SIR WILLIAM T. PERKINS, R. E. Grand Commander.

Ten Grand Officers and the representatives of seven Commanderies were in attendance, with the usual contingent of Past Officers and permanent members. Sir John D. Black, who holds North Carolina's commission, was one of the 12 Grand Representatives present.

The Grand Commander reports that he was necessarily absent from the State the greater part of the year and that the V. E. Deputy Grand Commander, Sir John D. Black, was placed in command.

Fraternal dead receive extended notice. The Christmas Toast was observed by every Commandery. Decisions and dispensations were few in number and of local interest only. Official inspection of the several Commanderies indicate harmony and general proficiency, and a fair degree of prosperity.

The Finance Committee report that the funds in the Grand Treasurer's hands amount to $530., being a slight increase over the amount last reported. As the Grand Treasurer happens to be the Governor of the state, he was unavoidably detained by official duties.

The Grand Recorder presents a detailed report, in which he makes a strong plea for earnest effort in building up the Order. The Membership Register is not yet complete, but fair progress is being made.

A Triennial Committee was appointed, also one to procure a Grand Commandery Banner. A portrait of Grand Commander Perkins adorns the volume.

There is no Report on Correspondence, nor do we find any mention of the subject, or the appointment of any committee.

Under the heading of "Episode" we find an account of the

hospitality the Grand Commandery enjoyed at the hands of the local Commandery. A visit to the Indian Reservation was a prominent feature and what they saw, and the result thereof, follows :

"The Grand Commandery had the pleasure of witnessing a Squaw Dance, the participants of which were not only matronly looking squaws, but the dusky belles of the aborigines of our country. And also witnessing what is known as the Grass Dance in which the braves, or as called in the West the 'bucks,' participated, a scene which to be appreciated must be witnessed; for no language can describe the grotesque, unique and bizarre costumes; and lack of costumes, which these dowdy red-men possessed, or did not possess. We shall not mention names, but a number of the members of our Grand Commandery are old frontier men, who had hunted the buffalo, and, no doubt, in the past have had many an Indian scalp dangling at their belts, were so vividly reminded of old times that they leaped into the arena and kept time to the beating of the tom-toms, and gave vent to such blood-curdling yells that not a few of the Indians were scared from the ring."

And this was near "Devil's Lake." It must have been about as exciting as the parade of the "Shriners" when our Grand Commandery met in Wilmington last May.

Seven Commanderies, 426 Knights. No change.

Sir John D. Black, Valley City, Grand Commander.

Sir Frank J. Thompson, Fargo, Grand Recorder, (re-elected.)

Next Conclave. To be announced.

OHIO.

Fifty-fifth Annual Conclave.   Toledo, September 8th, 1897.

Sir Barton Smith, R. E. Grand Commander.

Only one Grand Officer missing and 54 Commanderies represented. Twenty-seven Grand Representatives were in attendance, Sir W. T. McLean appearing for the "Old North State."

The Governor of the State, Mayor of the City and a representative of Toledo Commandery extended a hearty welcome to the Grand Commandery, the address of the Mayor calling out a response from Sir William B. Melish, Grand Junior Warden of the Grand Encampment.

The Grand Commander presented a well prepared address. Fraternal dead have appropriate and tender mention, their own body mourning the decease of Sir Thomas J. Melish, Grand Prelate, and Sir Robert Gwynn, Past Grand Junior Warden. A special Conclave of the Grand Commandery was held to conduct the funeral services of Sir Knight Melish and from the glowing tributes to his memory we quote :

"Few men have ever so closely endeared themselves to this Grand Commandery as Em. Sir Melish. He was the embodiment of knightly courtesy and Christian kindness. The sweet courtliness of his manner, his every-ready and genial welcome, his sterling honesty and unbounded generosity, stole like sunshine into our hearts, to open them with love and reverence for him.

"The influence of such a character can not die. Such a soul was not created to vanish into nothingness. Some time, some where, we shall again feel the helpful, loving charm of this wise and tender spirit, and our meeting with him then shall be to part no more forever,"

The Commandery which was granted a Charter at the last Conclave is reported as having been duly constituted.

The usual official circular in regard to the Chistmas Toast was issued, but he says that the responses were so meager that he is unable to say to what extent it was observed.

An inspecting officer was appointed for each Commandery and their reports show that the Commanderies are generally in a satisfactory and prosperous condition, and also show very clearly, to use his own words, that the inspection had come to be needed.

Forty dispensations appear in an appendix, and are about equally divided between balloting on petitions ahead of time and public appearance in uniform.

Few decisions were called for, which he credits to the clearness of their laws, and the three reported call for no adverse criticism.

In closing, the Grand Commander says that the year has been one one of peace and harmony, the Commanderies generally are thriving and prosperous, and the growth of the Order has been satisfactory.

One new Commandery was formed under dispensation and was granted a Charter at this Conclave.

Their funds show a gratifying increase of about twenty per cent. during the year and now amount to $8,758. according to the Grand Treasurer's peport.

A full report appears from the Superintendent of the Masonic Home, which shows that this noble charity is caring for 57 inmates, 18 being children, the average age of the adults being above 70 years. This magnificent benefaction has cost upwards of $200,000. and the annual expense of maintainance is about $13,000. It is a magnificent monument to the charitable impulses of the Craft, but is is an open question if more good could not be accomplished by local aid to the beneficiaries, instead of assembing them in such a palatial home. It is quite probable, however, that no such amount of money could have been raised for the purpose had there not been the object of a home in view. The foregoing is not to be taken as any criticism of the noble work of our Ohio Brethren, but as the enunciation of a general principle. The Grand Commandery has already given $6,000. to the Home and their donation at this Conclave was $1,500.

The Committee on Jurisprudence endorsed the Mississippi memorial to the Grand Encampment, in relation to a change in the organic law, and their recommendation was adopted.

The Triennial Committee reported that they had not been able to secure satisfactory quarters. They were authorized to continue their efforts and an appropriation of $1,500. was made forentertainment purposes.

Sir E. T. Carson sent a letter of regret announcing his inability to be present on account of illness, from which he had not fully recovered. A telegram of fraternal greeting and condolence was sent him with wishes for his speedy recovery.

A fine portrait of Grand Commander Smith adorns the proceedings.

"Præludiume gives a full account of the social features of the Conclave. Toledo Commandery celebrated its fiftieth anniversary in a fitting manner, and a grand parade, exhibition drill, reception, banquet and excursions were prominent features of the occasion.

Sir E. T. Carson presents his twenty-second Report on Correspondence, in which he reviews the proceedings of 39 Tem-

7

plar Grand Bodies, the result filling 156 pages. Although not
mentioned in the report, we regret to learn of his late and
severe illness and trust that he is by this time fully restored to
health.

North Carolina for 1897 is noticed to the extent of nearly
five pages, the correspondence part of the proceedings getting
the lion's share of space, and it ought to warm the cockles of
Sir Knight Gerow's heart to see the storm we have raised
about our devoted dead. However, we are not asking for
sympathy just yet.

Of course the main point of attack is the Eastern Star question and we quote a few of his utterances.

"Brother Chase, we look upon our brothers who have the Eastern Star
craze more in sorrow than in anger. We feel, as you express yourself,
that possibly we are leading a forlorn hope; for we appear to live in an
age when the human race is given to more than usual tom-foolery-witness
the craze of base-ball, prize fighting, and women riding bicycles in public
thoroughfares. We hope the time is not far distant when you will be
filled with disgust at the Eastern Star fad. To have any sympathy with
Androgynal Freemasonry we regard as a case of Masonic seasickness   It
is very interesting while it lasts."

Now we are not carried away with the Masonic connection
that is assumed by the Order in question, nor do we feel particularly called upon to take up the cudgels in its defence, as
it is apparently not lacking for friends among the Corps, but we
cannot help reminding our good Brother that the strictures he
has indulged in from time to time are aspersions on the character of the wives, widows, mothers, daughters and sisters of
Masons, as well as the Brethren themselves, and we think that
he has no right to assume that the Order in this country practices in any way, shape, or manner the rites he very properly
condemned in his paper on Androgynal Freemasonry. Under
Iowa he enlarges the field by saying :

"Our objection is to any secret society that admits both males and
females. It may start as pure as the River Clyde, but there is danger
that it will end as does the River Clyde."

Again we have to disagree with him, but the discussion is a
profitless one and we will let it drop, merely saying that we
have some personal knowledge of the workings of some of
these much abused bodies and have never seen anything con-

nected with them that was reprehensible in the least. Perhaps we may have been particularly fortunate in our location and associates, however.

Brother Carson presents an admirable report and we regret that we cannot give it the space that it deserves. The following, from California, is a ray of sunshine through the clouds.

"We hope that the farcical proceedings of the Grand Encampment at Boston will not be repeated in Pittsburg, in fact, we feel fairly sure that they will not be."

Under Montana we find this refererence to his pet idea of a permanent home for the Order :

"Oh, no, Brother Hedges, you must give us some stronger arguments against the Temple, or your case will be lost and the Temple will be built, as we believe it will be. The popular tendency is in that direction. We do not expect to live to see it finished, but it will be all the same, and that before many years have passed."

We trust that he may be spared to see its completion and fully believe that its building up will be a far easier undertaking than the pulling down of the Order of the Eastern Star.

The conclusion of his report is an interesting personal and autobiographical sketch of 13 pages, which is a valuable historical contribution.

Fifty-five Commanderies, 8,263 Knights; gain 192.

Sir Robert V. Hampson, Salem, Grand Commander.

Sir John N. Bell, Dayton, Grand Recorder, (re-elected.)

Sir Enoch T. Carson, Cincinnati, Chairman of Committee on Foreign Correspondence.

Next Conclave, Springfield, September 7th, 1898.

OKLAHOMA.

SECOND ANNUAL CONCLAVE.   El Reno, February 1st, 1897.
SIR CASSIUS McD. BARNES, R. E. Grand Commander.

The Grand Officers were all present and every Commandery represented. No mention is made of Grand Representatives, they probably being one of the luxuries that a newly established household do not feel like affording.

The Grand Commander begins his very brief address by saying that if the wisdom and expediency of forming this Grand Commandery was ever in doubt, this Conclave had demonstrated that no further apprehensions need be entertained. For business details we are referred to the Grand Recorder's report, from which we learn that a new Commandery was formed under dispensation and that balloting on several petitions, without waiting the usual time, was authorized. A few Representatives were appointed near other Grand Commanderies.

The Grand Treasurer reports that their funds amount to $130.

The Commandery that had been working under dispensation was granted a Charter. A resolution was adopted requiring Eminent Commanders to report to the Grand Recorder the fact of the Christmas observance, with the nature and character of the ceremonies.

A committee was appointed to collect voluntary offerings for the purpose of defraying Triennial expenses. No report on Correspondence.

The proceedings contain a portrait of Grand Commander Leach.

Four Commanderies, 152 Knights ; gain 21.

Sir DeForest DeF. Leach, Oklahoma City, Grand Commander.

Sir Harper S. Cunningham, Guthrie, Grand Recorder, (reelected,) and Chairman of Committee on Fraternal Correspondence.

Next Conclave, Oklahoma City, May 10th, 1898.

OREGON.

ELEVENTH ANNUAL CONCLAVE.   Eugene, October 14th, 1897.
SIR ROBERT S. BEAN, R. E. Grand Commander.

Only eight Grand Officers reported for duty, but every Commandery was represented, and in addition fourteen Representatives of sixteen Grand Jurisdictions graced the occasion, North Carolina's fraction being present.

The Grand Commander begins his address with the cheering announcement that peace and harmony prevail, and that the Order is stronger and rests upon a firmer foundation than ever before, although its growth has been retarded by the prevailing financial depression.

He announces the death of three distinguished Fratres of their Jurisdiction, but their own circle has not been invaded.

Two dispensations, one decision and a few Grand Representatives commissioned make the sum of his official acts. He urges action in relation to their being represented at the Triennial.

The Grand Treasurer reports that he has $462 to his credit, having disbursed a few dollars more than he received.

The business of the Conclave was not extensive, nor of general interest. We do not find any mention of a Triennial Committee and fear that our Oregon Fratres do not propose to be in evidence at Pittsburg.

The ladies of the Sir Knights were admitted to the installation ceremonies, which were followed by music and addresses. After a brief social time a banquet was served and those so disposed concluded the festivities by dancing. The following extract would indicate that the much abused Order of the Eastern Star should have unstinted credit for the good time:

"Masons never do anything without doing it thoroughly, and, when assisted by the Order of the Eastern Star, no one can ask for more. The banquet was a grand success, nearly everything known to the epicurean art being in evidence. In addition to the attractive fruits and other viands which adorned the tables the most delicate floral decorations acted as additional appetizers. Covers were laid for 225 Sir Knights and guests, and the master hand of the Eastern Star ladies was everywhere observed. A noticeable feature of all the addresses was the emphasis laid upon the co-operation of the Eastern Star workers."

Sir John M. Hodson presents his eighth Report on Correspondence, in which he has filled 76 pages with his usual keen and interesting review of the doings of 40 Templar Grand Bodies.

North Carolina for 1897 receives due and kindly mention and we heartily reciprocate his expressed hope of meeting at Pittsburg. Commenting on what we said about divorcing the parades and legislative sessions he says :

"We think, however, that he does conjecture, and truly, too, that while it would not die, not only its popularity but a great deal of its usefulness would be lost. In fact, the real good of the Order requires very little legislation ; a very few points might be profitably covered, but if the Grand Encampment was to have every member present and legislate for an entire month, the chances are that as much harm as good would be accomplished. We think that there is such a thing as being governed too much."

True enough, but the trouble is to get the desired legislation so palpably needed on the " few points."

Under Illinois we find him expressing his disapproval of any " life-member" plan.

On the non-affiliate question we quote as follows from Iowa, in reply to Frater Coxe's belief in letting " every tub stand on its own bottom."

"Exactly. The bottom of our tub is Ancient Craft Masonry. We have always stood upon it, and propose to continue to do so, and when we find a Frater who has used the fraternity to gratify his ambitions for feathers, and who now dishonors the path by which he reached the goal, by neglecting or refusing to stand upon that bottom, we propose that he shall know that we have no respect whatever for his Masonic position. And we are sure that Brother Coxe feels just as we do, only he allows his sense of justice to give way before his kind-heartedness."

Under Massachusetts we find the following chunk of wisdom :

"He is sound on the 'Old Glory' proposition. Let all display it who wish, but do not make it compulsory, nor reflect adversely upon the patriotism of those who do not display the flag in either their Asylums or on parade."

He voices, under Michigan, his opinion of what should be the Templar idea of the Christian Religion.

"We have frequently had occasion to speak and write against the proposals of certain correspondents to define the creed of a Templar, adding qualifications of 'belief' to what is now required, and, in common with many others, our esteemed Frater (Sir Knight Gerow) looks slightly askance upon our opinions thus expressed We think, and very earnestly, too, that a simple acknowledgement of firm belief in the Christian religion is all that ever should be required of any Companion seeking the orders. If this is not sufficient, who shall fix the standard? Let us rather continue to enjoy liberty in union rather than bind burdens grievous to be borne and lay them on men's consciences. The fathers who founded perchance were wiser than some of the sons who build after them."

On another question he speaks with no uncertain sound in his review of Mississippi:

> "We do not think the Christian Order of Knights Templar needs any saloon-keepers; and while we might not make a special law upon the subject, it should be emphatically so understood and acted up to."

Under Montana he refers to Frater Hedges' burning issue as follows, and we reckon that "there are others" who have the same sympathetic feeling:

> "He is as anxious for something to be done for the 'unspeakable Turk' as ever, and while we are fully in 'sympathy' with his 'sympathy' for the unfortunate victims of such monstrous cruelty, we have not been able to propose anything which we consider at all practicable or useful; hence we simply sit and sympathize."

Brother Jumper of South Dakota is brought up with a round turn and we trust will be made to see the error of his inclination:

> "He half inclines to sympathize with those who ridicule and oppose the innocent Order of the Eastern Star. Now, Frater, you had better keep off that train. There is not a member of that Order which we are not obligated to guard and protect, and don't you fear for a moment that the American wives, sisters and daughters of American Masons are ever to be found with their influence for evil. If the Christian gentlemen forming the magnanimous Order of Knights Templar will all be as faithful to the principles we profess as our wives, sisters and daughters who compose the membership of the Eastern Star, we will be better than we have been; yes, better than we are."

He has been having a little tilt with Brother Foster of Tennessee, on the powers of a Commandery U. D., and we quote his summing up:

> "The organization is complete as a Commandery U. D. It has the right to buy paraphernalia, rent an asylum, collect money, pay out money, have banquets, get into debt, attend church in uniform, bury its dead, receive and affiliate members, dismiss or dimit members, in fact, just as we have said, do any or all things proper to be done by a Commandery in accordance with the organic law authorizing its existence."

Well, there is plenty more that we would like to quote for the edification of our Fratres, but we must reserve some space for those who follow, and so bid him adieu.

Six Commanderies, 398 Knights; *loss* 16.

Sir L. C. Marshall, Albany, Grand Commander.

Sir James F. Robinson, Eugene, Grand Recorder, (re-elected.)

Sir John M. Hodson, Portland, Chairman of Committee on Correspondence.

Next Conclave, Salem, September 22d, 1898.

PENNSYLVANIA.

FORTY-FOURTH ANNUAL CONCLAVE.　　　　Easton, May 25th, 1897.

SIR SAMUEL S. YOHE, R. E. Grand Commander.

The Grand Officers were present with one exception and Representatives from 70 Commanderies. Grand Representatives were comparatively few in number, as only 14 reported, Sir William H. Dickson appearing for North Carolina.

The Mayor of Easton, who is a Sir Knight of the home Commandery, extended a cordial welcome to the Grand Commandery and Sir Lee S. Smith, Past Grand Commander, responded in a felicitous manner.

V. E. Sir and Rev. Cornelius S. Twing, Grand Prelate of the Grand Encampment and R. E. Sir John E. Rowe, Grand Commander of the Grand Commandery of New Jersey, with his staff, honored the Conclave with their presence and received a hearty welcome.

The annual report of the Grand Commander is a full and readable account of his official acts. He reports the Constitution of a new Commandery and having made sixteen official visits, and testifies to the correctness of the work and the kindness of his reception. Numerous dispensations were issued, principally to permit public appearance in uniform. He refused permission to two Commanderies to attend Divine Service in uniform on Sunday, but does not favor us with the reasons for his refusal. Among his decisions we notice the following :

"Q. Can the Generalissimo issue summons to attend a funeral in full Templar uniform ?

"A. Summons improper. Members cannot be compelled to attend a funeral."

The Grand Encampment Law says :

"A summons in a Subordinate Commandery should be used only in cases of urgent necessity."

This would seem to indicate that, if the necessity seemed to require it, members of a Commandery could be summoned to attend a funeral.

The Christmas Toast was generally observed. An earnest appeal is made to the Sir Knights not to forget the duties of hospitality at the coming Triennial. Fraternal dead receive tender mention, their own Grand Body mourning for Past Grand Commanders Charles W. Batchelor and Edmund H. Turner. Both the Grand Treasurer and Grand Recorder having resigned their offices he was called upon to appoint and install their successors.

Their funds have increased about one-fifth during the year and now amount to $3,283. according to the Grand Treasurer's report. We fancy that the demands for Triennial hospitalities will make quite a hole in them.

The Triennial Committee recommended that an appropriation of $5,000. be made to the local Triennial Committee at Pittsburg and one of the same amount for maintaining Grand Commandery headquarters; also that a per capita tax of ninety cents per member be levied on each Commandery. The several recommendations were adopted.

The Grand Commander announced the recent death of R. E. Sir Anthony E. Stocker, their Senior Past Grand Commander, and a beautiful memorial tribute appears in the proceedings.

The Representative to the Masonic Home presents a report detailing the workings of this noble charity. It is crippled for want of a permanent income and he makes an urgent plea to the Sir Knights to lend a helping hand that it may not be seriously hampered in its beneficent work. At the present time it has 37 inmates, but it has cared for 80 aged brethren since it was organized.

The Grand Officers were publicly installed at the Opera House in the presence of a large assemblage. An elaborate musical programme was a prominent feature of the occasion and Grand Commander Van Zandt delivered an eloquent address.

The proceedings contain the General Orders for Parade and

Review, which was scheduled for the opening day of the Conclave, but we fail to find any mention of its having taken place. Grand Commander Yohe's portrait engraved on steel adorns the volume.

The Report on Correspondence is the fourth effusion from the pen of Sir Lee S. Smith and he has filled 111 pages with an entertaining review of the doings of 43 Templar Grand Bodies. North Carolina for 1896 has courteous notice. Commenting on Grand Commander Liddell's reasons for granting all the dispensations asked for he has the following, and we are not going to quarrel with him about it :

"Well we think his reason broad enough to cover all emergencies, though we cannot agree with his conclusions, as nearly all of the dispensations were to ballot out of time. It does not work disastrously to refuse dispensations of this class, even with the smaller Commanderies. In point of fact we think it conducive to the life and efficiency of the Commanderies, as it is of the Order, to have fixed rules by which to be governed, and then to stand by them."

In his conclusion he has some vigorous language in relation to the various Turkish atrocities which fully establish his fitness to be the strong right bower of our Brother Hedges.

Seventy-four Commanderies, 11,491 Knights; gain 273.

Sir Harry M. Van Zandt, Harrisburg, Grand Commander.

Sir William W. Allen, Philadelphia, Grand Recorder.

Sir Lee S. Smith, Pittsburg, Chairman of Committee on Correspondence.

Next Conclave, Harrisburg, May 24th, 1898.

SOUTH DAKOTA.

FOURTEENTH ANNUAL CONCLAVE.   Mitchell, June 11th, 1897.

SIR JAMES J. CASSELMAN, R. E. Grand Commander.

Nine Grand Officers present, with the representatives of ten Commanderies and 16 Grand Representatives, Sir Martin G. Carlisle appearing for North Carolina.

The Grand Commander reports that the year has been marred by no grievance or discord and that their official circle has not been broken. He visited officially every Commandery but one, which failed to get a quorum at the appointed time. As another call upon them would involve a journey of *fourteen hundred* miles he felt that it would be paying too dearly for the whistle and conserved his energy for other purposes. While he found much to commend in his visits he is obliged to say that opening in full form "is more honored in the breach than the observance" and the by-laws in regard to procuring uniforms immediately after receiving the Orders are apparently not followed or enforced. He also has some well chosen words in relation to prompt payment of dues.

Decisions and dispensations are few in number and call for no comment, but he delivers himself of a sound chunk of wisdom on one topic, and we quote :

" I do not believe in granting such dispensations, unless it can be clearly shown that it is for the good of the Order, and not for the special benefit of the candidate, or at his request. When a man has lived a number of years within a few blocks of a Commandery without taking any steps to unite with the Order, and then, for some reason of his own, suddenly makes up his mind that he wants to get in immediately, I do not think that is imposing any hardship on him to let him wait the statutory time. I do not believe in letting down any of the safeguards to the entrance of our Asylums."

The absence of wine at the banquet tables wherever he has visited is approvingly noticed.

The Grand Treasurer reports that he has $1,395 on hand, more than double the amount he had at the beginning of the year.

A Committee on Triennial was appointed and $75 allowed them for " preliminary expenses."

After the closing of the Conclave the Sir Knights had the pleasure of attending a lawn reception, to which they were escorted by the wives and daughters of the Sir Knights of Mitchell.

"On arriving at the lawn, the ladies opened ranks, and the Officers and Sir Knights of the Grand Commandery passed through the lines uncovered, making a very nice effect. Upon reaching the lawn, we broke ranks, and after formal introduction, each lady selected a partner for the banquet which was spread on the lawn on a table formed in the shape of a Maltese cross, and loaded with all of the delicacies of the season. It was a unique and enjoyable affair, and every Sir Knight was loth to say, ' Hold, enough !' and when away congratulated himself that he was a Knight Templar and a favored guest."

It not being mentioned, we take it that there was no Eastern Star in this, although we believe that the Order exists in this jurisdiction.

The thoughtful countenance of Grand Commander Casselman appears as a frontispiece.

The Report on Correspondence is presented by Sir Samuel H. Jumper, and his second effort in this line reviews the proceedings of 40 Grand Jurisdictions in an entertaining manner, the result filling 79 pages.

His opening would be admirable reading for "dog-days," but in mid-winter is better fitted to give a chill to the denizen of the "Sunny South."

"Outside of our comfortable home the snow covers the prairies to a depth never before known. Drifts are larger and wider and deeper than a church. In many places houses are buried so deep, tunnels through the hard, white snow have been excavated from door and window for egress and light.

"In our snow-bound home, the drear monotony will be pleasantly broken as we receive the reports from New England seasoned with the salt spray of the dear old Atlantic; from the South, ladened with the perfume of the magnolia and the palm; from the West, with the sweet breath of the Pacific breezes; and for awhile we shall forget the cold and the snow and the angry blizzard."

North Carolina for 1896 has kindly notice and we quote a part of his comment on Sir Knight Liddell's address:

"We quote his remarks on the Christmas observance, as it is the first time we have found any objection to it. It seems to us that an hour from the family and home, spent as it should be, in the beautiful ceremony, is not out of place and harms no one. Possibly the 'Tar Heels' have not entered fully into the spirit of the occasion, as have their northern Brethren."

So far as the "spirit" is concerned, it generally goes the other way, and we reckon that the average Tar Heel can tote as much as his "northern Brethren."

With thanks for his kindly commendation of the Correspondent's work and hoping that Pittsburg will find him lining up with the Corps we pass to the next on the list.

Eleven Commanderies, 756 Knights; gain 10.

Sir Joseph T. Morrow, Mitchell, Grand Commander.

Sir George A. Pettigrew, Flandreau, Grand Recorder, (re-elected.)

Sir Samuel H. Jumper, Aberdeen, Committee on Correspondence.

Next Conclave, Sioux Falls, June 17th, 1898.

TENNESSEE.

THIRTY-FIFTH ANNUAL CONCLAVE.   Clarksville, May 12th, 1897.

SIR ROBERT W. HAYNES, R. E. Grand Commander.

The Grand Commandery in carriages were escorted by Clarksville Commandery with banners and music to the Court House where they listened to an eloquent address of welcome by Sir and Rev. Joseph B. Erwin, to which the Grand Commander made an equally eloquent response.

Every Grand Officer was at his post with 15 Commanderies represented. Seventeen Grand Representatives were introduced and welcomed, but we look in vain for the name of the Sir Knight who holds North Carolina's commission.

The Grand Commander's address is a high-toned production and recounts in an interesting manner his various official acts. He reports the death of Sir Joseph M. Anderson, who was Deputy Grand Cammander a quarter of a century ago.

In accordance with the action taken at the last Conclave, a committee prepared a set of rules and instructions for the Official Visitors and the Commanderies were visited by Inspectors appointed by the Grand Commander. While the results of this inspection may not have come up to expectations, the system was considered worthy of another trial.

Few dispensations and decisions were called for and his rulings were approved with one exception.

An appeal is made to uphold the Widows and Orphans' Home in its noble work and from his conclusion we quote :

"Charity is the purest attribute of virtuous minds. Its glory lies not in pretentious lavishings, in the pomp of power, or in the display of glittering magnificence: but chiefly in the succor it extends to the needy in times of sorrow and distress—like that, God's angels minister to those He loves; in the softest distillings of the dews of mercy, and in the practical demonstration of those divine truths which declare unmistakably the Fatherhood of God and the brotherhood of man.

"Finally, Brethren, let us, Knights of the Temple, look well to a healthier sentiment and a more systematic plan of dispensing Masonic charity, so as to avoid the arrogant imposter on the one hand, and to find out and relieve the worthy object of our brotherly love and care on the other."

The Grand Treasurer's balance shrunk a third during the year and is now only $158.

A Charter was granted to a Commandery which had been working under dispensation.

Resolutions were adopted protesting against the general use of the Maltese Cross by other orders and societies, it having "for centuries been the official insignia of our Order." The Grand Encampment is to be memorialized and other Grand Commanderies corresponded with on the subject :

"With the view of bringing about a moral influence that will stop other orders and societies from misleading the public by the use of our emblem."

We are of the opinion that our Tennessee Fratres are leading a "forlorn hope" and that the order is utterly powerless to prevent the misuse. Frater Hedges' proposed redemption of Palestine will be far easier of accomplishment.

In the evening Divine Service was attended at one of the city churches, which was profusely decorated with flowers and foliage and filled with a large and attentive audience. Impressive services were conducted by Rev. and Sir Knight William R. Grafton, Grand Prelate, who afterwards delivered a thoughtful and instructive discourse, which appears in the proceedings.

A Triennial Committee was provided for and $300 appropriated for headquarters. A committee was also appointed to formulate legislation on the question of Life Membership, and the question of buttons and gauntlets is to be wrestled with at the next Conclave.

Sir Wilbur F. Foster presents his third Report on Correspondence, which is fully up to the high standard of its predecessors. Forty-two Grand Jurisdictions have passed in review and 106 closely printed pages is the measure of his reportorial labors. North Carolina for 1896 has two pages of kindly notice. He writes us down as one who "thinks very poorly

of the Grand Representative system," which is putting it
rather stronger than the record will warrant, but we are not
going to quarrel with him on such a slight matter The courteous hospitality of Brother Foster when we visited his city last
summer was "as cool waters to a thirsty soul," and he may
criticise us with impunity.

He has little faith in any business being transacted by the
Grand Encampment and we quote one of his many expressions
on the subject, which we find in his review of Iowa.

" We enter our earnest protest against thrusting anything further in
the shape of *business* upon the attention of the Grand Encampment, to
startle her nerves and endanger her life. The attack of partial paralysis
with which she was prostrated in the midst of her work at Boston would
surely become total and fatal if unexpected and thoughtless demands of
this sort are to be permitted. Why is it that 'Smart Alecks' will be
continually startling the nerves of the dear old lady with unexpected and
unreasonable propositions to *do* something? Please let her 'rest in
peace,' so that she may serenely and smilingly enjoy her fine clothes, her
grand banquets, her carriage drives and the applause of the outside multi-
tude ; all of which, as everybody knows, constitute the great object of her
existence. We do hope people will be more careful or we may lose her."

There is much that we would like to "crib" for the delectation of our readers who are denied the pleasure of perusing
the complete report, but contenting ourself with a portion of
his conclusion we say good-night to Brother Foster and seek
our waiting couch :

" Well, we have reached the end of ' W.' No unknown 'X' demands
that its value shall be determined, and so, with the last of our 'copy'
gone to the printer, we close the door of our den with a s'am, and step
out into the glorious sunlight, the bounding life of the glad springtime.
We are off to the woods, the broad fields, the grand old hills, and the
merrily dancing streams, where the air is full of the music of singing
birds and fragrant with the perfume of a thousand flowers.

"O, what fun it is to *live!* Especially in the springtime of the year,
and in the springtime of life. The last has past forever with some of us,
but, thank God! the first comes back with ever-increasing beauty every
year. Ever fresh and fair ; ever brighter and more winsome as the years
go by. Surely we may gladly welcome its joyous advent, for is it not a
blessed premonition, a faint foretaste and type of that glorious Spring
that will some day dawn for each of us beyond the river, the wondrous
perfection of whose glory the heart of man can not conceive, and whose
brilliant, vigorous life will never fade into the season of the sere and yellow leaf."

Sixteen Commanderies, 1,091 Knights ; gain 1.

Sir William J. Ely, Clarksville, Grand Commander.

Sir Wilbur F. Foster, Nashville, Grand Recorder, (re-elected,) and Correspondent.

Next Conclave, Franklin, May, 1898. Date not fixed.

TEXAS.

FORTY-FOURTH ANNUAL CONCLAVE.   Houston, April 21st, 1897.

SIR J. F. BRINKERHOFF, R. E. Grand Commander.

The Grand Commandery was escorted to Christ Church and joined in the office of public devotion conducted by the Grand Prelate, Sir and Rev. J. C. Carpenter, who also delivered an elevating address. After returning to the Asylum they were welcomed by the Mayor and by Past Grand Commander Lubbock in behalf of Ruthven Commandery, and then got down to the business of the Conclave. Sir Knight Robert Brewster, Grand Recorder, was the only missing officer, he having been called to his reward since the last Conclave. Twenty-two Commanderies were represented and 26 Grand Representatives were in attendance, none appearing, however, for North Carolina.

The Grand Commander presents a full account of his official acts. A special Conclave was held for the purpose of attending the funeral of their veteran Grand Recorder, who was buried by the Grand Commandery with Knightly ceremonies :

" ' Dead on the Field of Battle,' was considered by the Spartan bands as the most glorious response which, on their return from their warlike expeditions, could be made in answer at roll call to the name of any missing from their ranks. Such a response might fittingly be made to the name of Sir Robert Brewster, Eminent Grand Recorder of the M. E. Grand Commandery Knights Templar of Texas, who, on July 25, 1896, from his home in Houston, where his face and form had been familiar for nearly three-score years, and in the full discharge of the trust which one-third of a century ago, amid the raging of civil strife, had been first confided to him by the Grand Commandery of Texas, laid aside the habiliments of warfare and entered into his final rest.

" His membership in the Grand Commandery was almost coincident with its existence, and in 1863 he was elected its Grand Recorder, which position by consecutive re-elections he retained until the close of his life. The days of man's age are three score years and ten, but unto Sir Knight Brewster, before he was gathered to his fathers, was allotted four score and four years more, and then, declining justly-earned relief, he fell at his post. A goodly record ; who shall surpass it ?''

The four decisions reported call for no especial comment and a large majority of the dispensations relate to the ballot and public appearance in uniform. The responses he received indicate that the Christmas Toast was generally observed.

He complains of the diversity of opinion about the interpretation of the Ritual and believes that the Grand Commandery should take some action towards securing uniformity in the work and a better understanding of their laws.

The Grand Treasurer reports his cash balance as being $1,024, a shrinkage of fully one-half, but we find that $1,000 has been placed in a Triennial fund, which accounts for the apparent loss.

An affecting letter was read from Mrs. Brewster, the widow of the deceased Grand Recorder, which was ordered printed in the proceedings, and we consider a brief extract well worthy of quotation.

" You may not know that I am the daughter of a Mason, and have all my life, as a daughter and a wife, regarded Masonry as an excellent Order, and one honored and loved by my family. My father was a Royal Arch Mason, at the time when they were afraid to meet, not like the bright and joyous time when my dear one went from the first to the thirty-second degree. How he loved it from the very first, we were young then, and although he was absent a good deal, still he enjoyed it so much I could not have the heart to lessen his pleasure by the slightest reproach of his absence."

The presence of Sir Henry B. Stoddard, Grand Generalissimo of the Grand Encampment, was announced and the distinguished Sir Knight returned his thanks for the courtesy shown him.

Commenting on the fact that no penalty is provided for failure to obey a certain law, the Committee on Jurisprudence say :

" We are of the opinion that this Grand Commandery may provide penalties for violations of the Constitution and Statutes of the Grand Encampment, when that body has failed to provide such penalty.

" We have also considered the resolution submitted to us amending the standing resolution in reference to public drills, and we respectfully

8

report it back with the recommendation that it be not adopted, for the reason that the Eminent Commander of a Subordinate Commandery already has the authority, and it is his duty to summon his Commandery whenever it may be necessary to carry out this or any of the resolutions of this Grand Commandery. And in addition to this, we are of the opinion that the multiplication of laws without penalties for their violation is not desirable. A few laws, properly enforced, is much preferable to a mass of legislation prescribing technical rules that are only observed on state occasions."

A Committee on Triennial Headquarters was appointed and with the funds at their disposal we shall expect our Texas Fratres to "cut a wide swath" at Pittsburg. We note that the collection taken up at the church was turned over to the Grand Commander to be distributed at his discretion and we reckon that there will be no difficulty in finding a willing recipient.

There appears to have been no election of Treasurer and Recorder but by some jugglery Sir Robert M. Elgin is installed as custodian of the sheckels, vice Sir J. C. Kidd, who in the same manner becomes Grand Recorder. May his tenure be as long as that of his lamented predecessor.

The Report on Correspondence is the usual able production sent out by Sir Robert M. Elgin, Chairman of the Committee, in which the doings of 37 Grand Jurisdictions have careful attention, the result filling seventy-eight pages.

North Carolina for 1896 has a fair share of space. Noting the dispensation permitting a Commandery "to assist in the rendition of the story of the reformation," he says :

"We do not know what that was, but wouldn't guess from the name that it was a Masonic occasion."

Our last proceedings will show him that that pitcher went to the fountain once too often.

Grand Commander Liddell's assumption that our Sir Knights are of mature years who prefer staying at home on Christmas brings out the following :

"We are of the opinion that the infusion of a good supply of young blood would make quite a change in this as in some other respects with our 'Old North State' Brothers. We old fellows are getting to be back numbers. We live in the past. It is the young men who have the ambition, the energy, enterprise and enthusiasm. We are good enough on a

Correspondence or Jurisprudence report and can lay down the law and the precedents. But when it comes to actual work and the exercise of executive ability the young are indispensable to a live, vigorous institution."

Replying to our inquiry as to the serial number of the reports he has prepared he says that he cannot give it from memory and has not the time and facilities to examine the Record :

"We have been long in the harness as a Correspondent and much longer as an active member of the Grand Commandery. To the best of our recollection we have missed attendance upon only a half dozen Annual Conclaves in forty years ; but there it is again. If we keep on some of these young fellows will imagine we are getting old."

We trust that his coming report will contain the desired information as a matter of justice to him and interest to the Corps. Lack of space prevents our drawing upon him at length and we must take our leave.

Thirty-one Commanderies, 2,115 Knights ; *loss* 14.

Sir L. T. Noyes, Houston, Grand Commander.

Sir J. C. Kidd, Houston, Grand Recorder.

Sir Robert M. Elgin, Houston, Chairman of Committee on Foreign Correspondence.

Next Conclave, Dallas, April 13th, 1898.

VERMONT.

FIFTY-FIFTH ANNUAL CONCLAVE.   Burlington, June 8th, 1897.
SIR ROBERT J. W..IGHT, R. E. Grand Commander.

Twelve Grand Officers present and every Commandery represented. North Carolina's representative was one of the 28 reported present.

The Grand Commander announces that they have had a peaceful and fairly prosperous year, and that their relations with sister jurisdictions have been most cordial. The death is reported of Sir Milton K. Paine, Past Deputy Grand Commander, and Sir Levi K. Fuller, who was widely known and had been Governor of the State.

Official visitation was apportioned among the "Line of

Knights.'' Regarding his own share, he reports a full attendance of Sir Knights in uniform and increased efficiency in the work. Courtesy and hospitality do not appear to have become "Lost Arts.'' The reports of his associates are very full and have practically nothing but commendation for what they saw and received. The use of the "short form" in opening and closing was found to be general and meets with unqualified disapproval.

The dispensations reported permit public appearance in uniform and the only decision called for was of such a trivial nature that it is merely mentioned.

The observance of either Easter or Christmas is noted as becoming more general and the hope is expressed that in time "every Commandery will consider the observance of one of these days as necessary and obligatory as a regular conclave.''

A dispensation was issued to form a new Commandery, which received a Charter at this Conclave.

The Grand Treasurer's Report shows a goodly increase in their funds, which now amount to $1,143.

The first four officers were made a Triennial Committee with power to act.

The Report on Correspondence comes from the cultured pen of Sir Kittredge Haskins, whose steel-engraved portrait adorns the proceedings and is made the text of an exceedingly well-written biographical sketch. This report is his fourth effort and 73 pages are filled with a courteous and entertaining review of the proceedings of 41 Grand Jurisdictions, all for 1896.

North Carolina has two pages of kindly notice and we quote his comment on Grand Commander Liddell's view of the Christmas Observance question:

"Every Sir Knight should love his family and do whatever he can to make them happy on Christmas day. But does that require him to ignore everything else? May he not become a little too domestic for his own good and that of his family? An hour spent in the Asylum on Christmas day, for the purpose contemplated in the Order, will not be lost upon the family at home. And, then, why not take the wife and children along with you? Appropriate and interesting services have been prepared for use on the occasion, at which any one may be present and participate therein, and on the return home, all will feel happier and

better for it   The day. and the observance, ought to be popular with
everyone, more especially with the members of our Christian Order of
Knighthood."

Replying to our conjecture that he had not outgrown the
"parading age," he says:

"When we wrote the matter referred to, we had passed the three-score
mile stone; but we never expect to live long enough to become so child-
ish as to think, even, that a semi-military organization wearing gold lace,
cocked hats, plumes and swords, and bearing banners, flags, etc., was
intended to be seen behind the tiled doors of an Asylum only."

And we take occasion to remark that "them's our sentiments."

We note that he is a firm believer in a permanent home for
the Grand Encampment and is emphatically in favor of Washington City, and also believes in divorcing the business meeting from parades, excursions and social entertainments.

Under Maryland, we find the following on the uniform
question:

"We have before said that a Sir Knight without a uniform, or the Sir
Knight who has one and habitually leaves it at home, is of little use to
his Commandery and might just as well never be seen at the Conclaves.
If they are fully uniformed, and wear it at the Conclaves, they are always
welcome and can be made of some use in the Asylum work."

Apparently he does not take any stock in making saloon-
keeping a bar against receiving the Orders, as witness the
following from Mississippi:

"We are taught that 'it is the internal qualifications of a man that
should recommend him to be made a Mason.' It is the *man* and not the
occupation that we should look to when a candidate presents himself at
our doors. Masonry, as we know it, is a *speculative* and not an *operative*
institution, and as such there can be no arbitrary line of demarcation
drawn upon the basis of occupation alone, without infringing well recognized landmarks of the Order."

We have great respect for his views as set forth above, at
the same time we firmly believe that those engaged in certain
occupations should never find an entrance to Templar Asylums.

Eleven Commanderies, 1,499 Knights; gain 41.

Sir Robert J. Wright, Newport, Grand Commander, (re-
elected.)

Sir Warren G. Reynolds, Burlington, Grand Recorder, (re-elected.)

Sir Kittredge Haskins, Brattleboro, Chairman of Committee on Correspondence.

Next Conclave, Burlington, June 14th, 1898.

———

VIRGINIA.

SEVENTY-FIFTH ANNUAL CONCLAVE.   Petersburg, December 6th, 1897.

SIR E. H. MILLER, R. E. Grand Commander.

Every Grand Officer was at his post and all of the Commanderies represented. Sixteen Grand Representatives were courteously welcomed by the Grand Commander, who "requested them to bear to their several Jurisdictions the fraternal greetings of the 'Old Dominion,' " but no one was on hand to "tote" the load for North Carolina.

The Grand Commander begins a well prepared address by saying that their meeting might with great propriety be called the "DIAMOND CONCLAVE" of the Grand Commandery. Peace and harmony have prevailed and his official duties have been light. Notwithstanding the year has been fraught with great financial peril their numbers show only a slight decrease. The fraternal dead of sister Jurisdictions are noted at length, their own body having been spared a visitation. Every Commandery was officially visited by the Grand Officers and other Sir Knights acting as inspectors, and their reports in detail show a generally satisfactory state of affairs.

Only four dispensations were issued, two relating to the ballot and the others permitting escort duty. He denied several requests for permission to appear in Templar dress at tableaus for charitable purposes, not deeming them Masonic occasions.

A few decisions called for were answered by quotations from the Code and offer no chance for criticism.

Their cash assets are only $39 according to the Grand Treasurers report, but they have a good number of shares in the Masonic Temple Association, so are not as hard up as it would appear by the report.

The report of the Committee on Education of the Masonic

Home is an interesting document and gives a good idea of the excellent and elevating work that is being accomplished at this institution.

The incoming "Line of Knights" were made a committee to secure headquarters and provide entertainment for the Grand Commandery at the coming Triennial.

By invitation the Grand Commandery united with Appomattox Commandery in public religious services at one of the city churches in the evening. The service was conducted by the Grand Prelate, who afterwards delivered an eloquent and instructive discourse. The balance of the evening was devoted to a banquet given in honor of the Grand Commandery by Appomattox Commandery which, with the concomitants of soul-stirring addresses and charming music made the occasion one long to be remembered.

No Report on Correspondence, and, as we find no mention of any committee, the same announcement will be in order another year.

Twenty Commanderies, 1,472 Knights ; *loss* 9.

Sir James H. Capers, Richmond, Grand Commander.

Sir James B. Blanks, Petersburg, Grand Recorder, (re-elected.)

Next Conclave, Richmond, November 10th, 1898.

WASHINGTON.

Tenth Annual Conclave.   Tacoma, June 2d, 1897.

Sir George E. Dickson, R. E. Grand Commander.

Only one Grand Officer failed to appear and every Commandery was represented. Twenty Grand Representatives were also in attendance but no one responded for North Carolina.

An address of welcome and the response with the opening ceremonies and the report of the Committee on Credentials brought the Grand Commandery to a fit condition to enjoy a fine lunch prepared for their delectation, with the accompaniments of music and toasts. We note that Sir Knight Blalock's task was to "Define the Similarity of the Ladies to the Walla

Walla Peach," but the proceedings are silent in regard to his course of reasoning.

The Grand Commander says that their growth has exceeded expectations the past year and that death has not invaded their ranks.

Four dispensations and two decisions are the sum of his labors in this line and we find nothing that calls for comment. The demands of his business prevented official visitation, much to his regret.

Seven Commanderies attended Divine Service on Easter Sunday, the average attendance being about forty Sir Knights, with a maximum of seventy-four.

The Grand Treasurer reports his cash balance as being $869, a falling off of about one-sixth during the year.

The business of the Conclave was light and not of general interest.

The Committee on Jurisprudence make the wise suggestion that dispensations should not be issued to receive and ballot on petitions and confer the Orders at the same Conclave, unless there is sufficient time to notify members of the date of the proposed action.

After the installation Grand Commander Weatherwax delivered a five-page metrical address, which was ordered printed in the proceedings. If this is a foretaste of his report next year the reviewer's task will not be an easy one. He says:

> "Sir Knights, once more before we shall call a halt,
> Look not too gravely on a brother's fault."

We hardly feel like characterizing his propensity for "dropping into verse" as a "fault," but trust that he will have a care that what is now only an acute attack, perhaps, may not become chronic.

The proceedings contain a portrait of Past Grand Commander Dickson.

Sir Knight Yancey C. Blalock, as chairman, presents his sixth Report on Correspondence, which fills 97 pages and reviews the proceedings of 28 Templar Grand Bodies. He intended to include all proceedings received, but the appropriation for printing being limited he had to lay some of them aside

for another year, and North Carolina appears to have been one
of the deferred ones.   As the Grand Commandery has, by resolution, limited the coming report to 60 pages, for financial
reasons, he will have to look sharp in order to "give them all
a show."   In the current report one jurisdiction is favored with
about one-fourth of the total number of pages.

He has a sound and forcible reply to Sir Knight Carson's
notice of his former strictures in regard to the paper on
"Androgynal Freemasonry," and we quote a portion with
hearty approval:

"We deny the assertion that the 'indiscriminate mingling of males and
females in a secret organization,' such as we refer to, will in any way
cause scandal, and still insist that the principles taught in the Order of
the Eastern Star, 'if sown in good ground,' will bring good results and
be elevating to the mind, but if planted among the wreck caused by
'tares' no effect *can* come from it."

Now that Brother Blalock is to have less space at his disposal we trust that he will give us more of his own ideas and
less of the "other feller's," as he has shown us that he is well
able to do it.

Nine Commanderies, 607 Knights; gain 15.

Sir Jacob Weatherwax, Aberdeen, Grand Commander.

Sir Yancey C. Blalock, Walla Walla, Grand Recorder, (re-
elected,) and Chairman of Committee on Correspondence.

Next Conclave, Tacoma,, June 8th, 1898.

WEST VIRGINIA.

TWENTY-THIRD ANNUAL CONCAVE.   Wheeling, May 12th, 1897.
        SIR JOHN C. RIHELDAFFER, R. E. Grand Commander.

All of the Grand Officers were present and every Commandery represented.   Fourteen Grand Representatives were introduced and welcomed, but North Carolina did not participate.

Growth and prosperity, peace and harmony, are the good
tidings that the Grand Commander reports.   Fraternal dead
are noted at length, their own circle mourning the death of Sir
and Rev. Hugh W. Torrance, formerly Grand Prelate.

A dispensation was issued to form a new Commandery and a

half-dozen others permitted public appearance and balloting on petitions without waiting the statutory time.

A Companion petitioned for the Orders and was rejected ; in due time he again petitioned but before the time for balloting he permanently removed to another Jurisdiction. The Grand Commander decides that he belongs in the Jurisdiction in which he now resides and that the Commandery which received his petition has no hold on him. Although the Committee on Jurisprudence approved this decision we are of the opinion that it is not correct. We do not believe that the Commandery can permit the withdrawal of the petition unless they waive Jurisdiction, which it would appear that they did not comtemplate doing.

The Grand Commander was able to officially visit nine Commanderies and found a generally creditable state of affairs, although he does not hesitate to criticise a lack of proficiency in drill and tactics, and irregularity in uniforms. He believes that an "Inspector General" would be an improvement on their present system of inspection.

Their funds have more than doubled during the year, being now $659 as reported by the Grand Treasurer.

The Committee on Triennial reported that they had secured headquarters at Pittsburgh and were authorized to make any further necessary arrangements.

The Commandery under dispensation continues in the same state for another year. The office of "Grand Inspector" was created and Sir Hugh Sterling elected for the term of five years.

A committee was appointed to procure a U. S. flag for the Grand Commandery, and it was further resolved :

"That each Commandery in this Jurisdiction, that has not already done so, do procure a regulation silk United States flag, which may be displayed in the Asylum or when on public parade."

The above looks a little like "crowding the mourners," but if they are all agreed, we suppose no one has a right to complain.

Phototypes of Past Grand Commander Riheldaffer and Grand Commander Tavenner embellish the proceedings.

The Report on Correspondence is submitted by Sir Walling W. Van Winkle, as Chairman of the Committee. It is a well

prepared review of 97 pages, 42 Grand Jurisdictions being noticed. North Carolina for 1896 has courteous attention with
no adverse comment. In fact, he has been exceedingly chary
about engaging in discussion, but we opine will get drawn into
it after he has been in the harness two or three years. His
line of action is laid down in his conclusion, as follows.

"In the preceding pages we have not attempted to criticise or take
part in any discussion, but simply attempt to present a review of the several reports received, noting such matters only that we thought might be
of interest to the fratres in this Jurisdiction. We trust our work will be
appreciated and criticism charitable. This is our first effort. We are
conscious of imperfections, emphasized by comparison with other reports
of former committees. We indulged the assumption this was an easy
task, and postponed work until ten days ago. We were wofully mistaken;
since we have been prodigal with the 'midnight oil' 'scaning upwards of
6,400 pages of printed proceedings, culling from addresses, committee reports, statistical tables, etc., the 'meat' in them. If we have extracted it
even partially to your satisfaction we will be contented. It is submitted
to you, such as it is, hoping that it may be worthy of your perusal. We
are not expecting to escape criticism.''

We are pleased to see that he continues on the Corps and
reckon that next time he will not procrastinate until the "ten
day" limit is reached.

For the the second time in the current year the "Mutuals" are called
upon to mourn the loss of one of their number. We have just learned
from the late Connecticut proceedings thatSir Odel S. Long, Past Grand
Commander, of West Virginia, died at his home in Charleston, after a
brief illness, on December 26th. Brother Long was Chairman of the Correspondence Committee for several years, but retired from the "Corps"
in 1895. He was an exceedingly genial and sparkling reviewer and personal intercourse at the Boston Triennial only served to strengthen the
fraternal feeling previously cultivated by correspondence alone. Peace
to his ashes.

Eleven Commanderies. 951 Knights ; gain 14.
Sir Lewis N. Tavenner, Parkersburg, Grand Commander.
Sir Robert C. Dunnington, Fairmont, Grand Recorder (re-
elected.)
Sir Walling W. Van Winkle, Parkersburg, Chairman of
Committee on Templar Correspondence.
Next Conclave, Parkersburg, May 11th, 1898.

WISCONSIN.

THIRTY-NINTH ANNUAL CONCLAVE   Milwaukee, October 12th, 1897.
SIR EDMOND C. DEANE, R. E. Grand Commander.

Every Grand Officer was at his post and all but one of the Commanderies represented. Twenty-one Grand Representatives were in attendance, North Carolina's not being included in the number.

The Grand Commander's address is a well-written production of moderate length. He announces the death of Sir Chandler P. Chapman, Past Grand Commander, Sir Lyell T. Mead, Past Grand Captain General, and Sir and Rev. S. S. Burleson, Past Grand Prelate.

Dispensations were issued to a limited extent, but they are not given in detail and no decisions are mentioned.

Official visitation received moderate attention. One visit was made noteworthy by a class of 21 being advanced to the Order of Red Cross and another occasion was honored by the presence of the respective heads of the several Grand Masonic Bodies in the State, the Grand Matron of the Order of the Eastern Star being classed as such, which will probably have the same effect as a red rag upon a bull when the account is read by an esteemed member of the Corps. It goes without saying that elaborate banquets and the presence of the ladies were prominent features of the occasions.

The usual inspections were made by the Grand Officers and we quote the severest strictures in his summing up:

"The weakest point shown by these reports seems to be a neglect of practice in the tactics of the asylum, thus marring the beauty and interest of the opening ceremony. This, with poor attendance and inattention to the matter of clothing worn at the Conclaves, are most subject to criticism, and should have special attention from officers of Commanderies."

We also consider the following worthy of a place:

"I am not of those who are of opinion that our Order is growing too fast. I cannot believe that the sublime truths, the divine teachings of our lectures, can be too often imparted to our worthy Companions. The field from which we draw recruits has been cultivated and improved by the ballot in Lodge and Chapter. Those who come to us are, as a rule, the best in intelligence, attainments, and all that goes to make applicants desirable.

"Then let us not be afraid to display our banners, to let our light shine before our Companions, that they may be attracted to us, and if found worthy, be admitted to a participation in our labors. Templar Masonry is no longer a subject of conjecture. Its merits are known, and its name familiar in almost every home in the land. As members of our Order we should be proud, though not boastful. The past has been grand, the present is assured, the future will be what we make it."

The Grand Treasurer reports his cash balance as being $3,670, an increase of nearly $800 during the year.

A Committee on Triennial was appointed and $750 appropriated for the expenses of the Grand Commandery on that occasion.

The question of inspection of the Commanderies was fully considered and, having abandoned the rendezvous system, they are going to have an Inspector General, to see if it will be any improvement over the work of the four principal officers, although a committee reported against trying the experiment until another year.

The Tennessee resolutions in regard to the use of the Maltese Cross by other orders were not endorsed, the committee to whom the matter was referred believing that,

"It is more in keeping with the dignity of the Order to quietly ignore the appropriating of any of the emblems of the Order, than to call the attention of the public thereto by protesting against such use, so long as it is impossible to enforce any set of resolutions upon this matter, the parties offending being beyond the jurisdiction of the Order."

Sir William C. Swain's fifteenth Report on Correspondence is well up to the high average of his former efforts and in its 93 pages he has paid his respects to 42 Grand Jurisdictions. We fancy that he still feels limited in regard to space, as under Texas we find the following:

"There are quite a number of other interesting points in this report, which we would be pleased to quote, but in deference to those who prefer to spend Grand Commandery money for Triennial Conclaves rather than good reading, we forbear."

"There are others," we are sure, who could complain of the pinching of the same shoe, but our advice to Brother Swain is to take in the next Triennial and have his share of the fun.

North Carolina for 1897 has brief but pleasant notice, but he has searched in vain for Sir Knight Martin's address on

Masonry in the Olden Time. Possibly those in authority preferred to have the money the printing would cost to spend for ''Triennial Conclaves,'' but we are inclined to think that lack of copy was the valid reason. Apparently he does not take much stock in Templar law as laid down by Grand Masters and approved by the Grand Encampment, as evidenced in the following, which refers to some of our expressions of opinion.

"He favors McCurdy's decision, that a Templar must apply for affiliation in the place of his residence, and considers it law, because it is so decided, and decision approved by the Grand Encampment. But let him wait a little. When the next Grand Master decides directly the opposite way, that decision will also be approved. Such is the way of that distinguished body. But, without disputing Chase's point that it might be better to affiliate at the place of residence, it interferes with personal liberty, and would prevent a man with a sentiment of love for his mother Commandery, from retaining his membership there when he had moved away. For the same argument which required him to apply for affiliation at the place of residence, would require him to dimit from his old Commandery when he moved from its jurisdiction."

Well, we suppose one decision is law until it is set aside by another that is fortunate enough to be affirmed, and as for his reasoning in the last sentence quoted, it strikes us as being a little too diaphanous for argument.

He is not in accord with Sir Knight Carson in his kicking against the Eastern Star and under Tennessee we find a sensible utterance on the liquor question.

"Let us be logical. In these days it is next to an impossibility for a man to be a politician and not indulge in methods which he would condemn in private life. Shall we, therefore, cease to go to the polls, or take an interest in the government of our country? Saloon-keepers are responsible for bringing their business into disrepute by disreputable practices. Therefore keep such saloon-keepers out of our Lodges, by means of the black ball, but not by legislation."

As usual, Brother Swain's report contains much that we would be more than pleased to quote for the delectation of our readers, but we must desist, and bid him good-night, with the hope that we may be able to join him in a draught of Monongahela—water, next October, if a Cuban draft does not get us in the meantime.

Twenty-seven Commanderies, 2,965 Knights; gain 139.
Sir Charles D. Rogers, Milwaukee, Grand Commander.

Sir John W. Laflin, Milwaukee, Grand Recorder,(re-elected.)
Sir William C. Swain, Milwaukee, Committee on Correspondence.

Next Conclave, Milwaukee, November 1st, 1898.

WYOMING.

TENTH ANNUAL CONCLAVE.   Green River, May 12th, 1897.
SIR ADRIAN J. PARSHALL, R. E. Grand Commander.

Eight Grand Officers present and five Commanderies represented.   It does not appear to have been a good day for Grand Representatives, as only eight were on hand to be "received with the honors befitting their station," and North Carolina did not participate.

The Grand Commander reports a harmonious and unusually prosperous year, with no break in their official circle.

Dispensations were issued to form two new Commanderies. No decisions were called for.   One of the three dispensations issued permitted public appearance in uniform and the others related to the ballot.

Permission was given the Commanderies to attend Divine service in uniform on Good Friday, Easter and Ascension Day' and the reports

"Indicate a general observance of the order, and justify the continuance of the custom which is the most popular of all Templar events observed in this State."

The Grand Treasurer's report shows a cash balance of $814 nearly a half more than he had at the beginning of the year.

The Commanderies working under dispensation were granted Charters.

A committee was appointed to recommend changes in the Jurisdictional lines, as the nearest Commandery to the petitioner is very often far from being the most accessible, owing to traveling facilities and impassable mountain ranges.   The report of the committee comes up as an amendment to the Code of Statutes at the next annual Conclave.

"Refreshments" notes that a public installation took place,

followed by an eloquent banquet, which the ladies graced by
their presence. Golden silence was not at a premium apparently, as the narrator says :

"Of course there were sentiments proposed and responded to. The inspiration of the occasion was sufficient to tip with *silver* the tongue of any
ordinary speaker."

The proceedings contain a portrait of Grand Commander
Parshall.

And now we come to the Report of the Committee on Correspondence, which has been conspicuous by its absence for
some years past. It is "submitted for the committee" by Sir
John C. Baird, but we doubt if the other members saw it before
it was in print. The proceedings of 43 Templar Grand Bodies
have had courteous attention and the exceedingly fine type
used make his XL pages equivalent to nearly double the number furnished by the average Correspondent.

North Carolina for 1896 is briefly noticed. He notes that
Grand Commander Liddell is "about the first to recommend the
restoration of the cuffs;" styles the Grand Recorder's report as
being thorough and business-like and credits the Correspondent with an excellent report. Thanks.

Noting the absence of the Alabama report after it was prepared, he says :

"Well, there are unsung songs, unkissed kisses, and in Alabama they
have unreported reports."

Under New Hampshire we find the following on the uniform
question :

"The eternal subject of uniform seems to disturb the sturdy Puritans of
New England just as much as it does the somewhat wild and woolly deni-
zens of the west. Evidently the bucolic farmer takes no more kindly to
a uniform and sword than does the festive cowboy of the plains."

Reviewing Virginia for 1896 he says :

"One dispensation will strike the Sir Knights of the North as being
somewhat peculiar. It was to permit St. Andrew Commandery to parade
in public as escort to the Grand Lodge at the laying of the corner-stone of
the Jefferson Davis monument. It is not clear how this event could be
construed as a strictly Masonic occasion. Mr. Davis was not a Mason,
and his peculiar claim to distinction was not based upon Masonic lines."

We are obliged to differ with him. We consider that it was

clearly in the province of the Grand Lodge to lay the corner-stone of such a memorial and that it was equally allowable for a Commandery to act as their escort. We commend the catho-licity of Brother Baird's views as further expressed on this subject :

"It is believed that the sentiment of toleration that exists will at least dull the keenness of sectional hate. Of this much we feel certain, that whenever foreign foes attack our shores, the men of the lost cause and their decendants will be in the van of the defenders of our common flag."

Barely a year has passed and current events show the correc-ness of this prediction.

Noting that some Grand Commanders would not permit Com-manderies to escort Grand Lodges, he says, under West Vir-ginia :

"There should be some uniformity on this subject. Whatever is in-consistent with Templarism in one State is none the less so in another State. It would relieve many a Grand Commander of an unpleasant duty. and place the responsibility where it properly belongs, in the Grand En-campment."

Seven Commanderies, 319 Knights ; gain 57.

Sir David H. Craig, Rawlins, Grand Commander.

Sir John C. Baird, Cheyenne, Grand Recorder, (re-elected.) Committee on Foreign Correspondence.

Next Conclave, Evanston, April 13th, 1898.

1898.

ELEVENTH ANNUAL CONCLAVE.   Evanston, April 13th.
SIR DAVID II. CRAIG, R. E. Grand Commander.

Nine Grand Officers present and six of their seven Com-manderies represented. Nine Grand Representatives "were formally presented and introduced with proper honors due their exalted station," but the name of North Carolina's is not on the list.

The Grand Commander announces a peaceful year with no decisions called for. The fraternal dead of sister jurisdictions are fully noted, their own official circle remaining unbroken.

He is gratified to report that the charming custom of the Christmas Observance was generally celebrated. He favors the idea of a National Masonic Temple at Washington, D. C., and recommends generous and immediate contributions toward the noble undertaking. One of their Commanderies has already contributed $100. to this object.

The Grand Treasurer's Report shows a ninety dollar shrinkage in their funds during the year, there now being $724. on the right side of the ledger.

The Committee on Doings of Grand Officers has the following to say in relation to the Grand Commander's views about the National Masonic Temple :

"We approve the suggestion of the erection of a Temple for Templar and Masonic purposes in the city of Washington. But in view of the claim that the establishment of the edifice is to be taken as an expression of the national desire for the city of Washington to be fixed as the permanent place of meeting of the Grand Encampment, we recommend that the subject of making the same be deferred until the next Annual Conclave. We believe that the salient moral effect of the meeting of the Grand Encampment in divers places not only promotes the welfare of the Order but is beneficient in the highest degree to the Christian religion "

One hundred dollars was appropriated towards paying the expenses of any of the Sir Knights who might attend the Triennial and the Commanderies are asked to contribute $1. per member to be added to the appropriation. The Grand Commander and several Eminent Commanders were made a Conclave Committee, with power to act.

They evidently "burned the wind" in issuing the volume of proceedings, as it appeared on the *third* day after the Conclave was held. It is embelished with a portrait of Past Grand Commander James G. Rankin and the flaming red covers may be a portent of war or an indication of the generation of intense heat due to the rapidity of the printer's movements.

The Report on Correspondence is from the pen of Sir John C. Baird. It is an interesting production of 52 pages, 42 Grand Jurisdictions receiving attention.

North Carolina for 1897 is courteously noticed and we quote a few lines:

"Neighbor Chase evidently has his share of the prevailing feeling that no printed Proceedings are complete without a report on Correspondence Especially is this view prominent during a period of discussion of some vital question. It occurs to us that one of the debatable points that ought to lie over for the Grand Encampment session of 1901, is the proposed permanent establishment of the Grand Encampment at Washington."

We have no idea that the question will be settled at the coming Triennial and have our doubts that the sentiment in regard to a permanent location will ever crystalize to the extent of settling upon a place.

Commenting on a California decision that a petitioner with "a useless right arm" was ineligible for the Orders, he instances a case where the *absence* of the right arm was not considered sufficient reason for rejection and says:

"No one questions his right to membership. The presence of brain and heart, and not the absence of an arm, determined that right. Such a Templar is Gen. Byron L. Carr, the present Attorney-General of Colorado. If it is a question of arms and legs, and not intelligence and worth, parades may well be dispensed with. The military simile is going too far. It reminds us of the resume once made of the qualities necessary to make a certain man a great statesman—"All he needs is brains and good morals; he has lungs.'"

We do not fully endorse his views as expressed in the foregoing, but do not see why a reasonable amount of discretion could not be exercised in deciding the extent of physical disability that would render a candidate ineligible.

His "Conclusion" would lead his readers to infer that it was something of an effort for him to be glad that he was through, but then the others have Wyoming on the list and he stops at Wisconsin.   See?

"We try to feel that 'sigh of relief' so frequently mentioned by the guild. But the end of the work is grateful, not so much because it is a task, as it is for the reason that our mind is at liberty to turn from the realm of addresses, reports, proceedings, statistics, Correspondence and Templar law, to those sadly neglected problems of abstruse municipal law that are involved in the papers that lie littered over our desk. We confess to a sort of love for the work, and the only 'fly in the ointment' is the necessity for economizing the use of pages in the Proceedings of a young and small Jurisdiction like ours."

Seven Commanderies, 326 Knights; gain 5.

Sir William A. Robins, Cheyenne, Grand Commander.

Sir John C. Baird, Cheyenne, Grand Recorder, (re-elected,) and Committee on Foreign Correspondence.

Next Conclave, Cheyenne, April, 12th, 1899.

CONCLUSION.

The long wished-for goal is reached at last and with relief we chronicle the end of another year's labor.

Forty-three Templar Grand Bodies have sat at our board, and although the fare may have been coarse, it was the best that our tent afforded.

Arizona is the only missing sister in the roster of 1897, but, with Indian Territory, reported for 1896. Connecticut, Louisiana and Wyoming for 1898 arrived in season for a double portion.

And now for closing words we know of nothing better than those Dickens puts into the mouth of Tiny Tim, ''God bless us, every one.'' Courteously submitted,

JOHN C. CHASE.

www.ingramcontent.com/pod-product-compliance
Lightning Source LLC
Chambersburg PA
CBHW021125270326
41929CB00009B/1048